ASL
at
Work

STUDENT TEXT

William (Bill) Newell
Cynthia Ann Sanders
Barbara Ray Holcomb
Samuel K. Holcomb
Frank Caccamise
Rico Peterson

DawnSignPress
San Diego, CA

The *ASL at Work* curriculum is a project of the
American Sign Language and Interpreting Education Department
National Technical Institute for the Deaf
Rochester Institute of Technology
Rochester, NY

Published by DawnSignPress

IBSN: 978-1-58121-081-1

Printed in the United States of America

10   9   8   7   6   5

ATTENTION

Table of Contents

Acknowledgments

There are many people to acknowledge for their contributions to producing *ASL at Work*. First and foremost is Keith M. Cagle, who served as an external consultant throughout the development of this curriculum. We express our deep appreciation to Keith for his expert feedback at each stage of the development process.

The curriculum would never have been produced without the tireless work of Katrina Evringham and Mary Jo Nixon Ingraham, our National Technical Institute for the Deaf (NTID) Word Processing Technicians, whose patience and expertise allowed us to produce a final manuscript through endless re-typings. In addition, we acknowledge the support of many other staff of NTID, who contributed in the early stages of development of this curriculum, including Carol Petote, Instructional Developer; Jorge Samper, Educational Resources Media Specialist; and Maria Buckley, Educational Resource Senior Artist/Designer.

During the development of this curriculum, teachers in the NTID American Sign Language and Interpreter Education Department, as well as teachers in the Rochester Institute of Technology College of Liberal Arts, in the NTID Masters on Science and Secondary Education Program, and in other upstate New York colleges and universities, field tested this curriculum in classes for interpreting students, liberal arts classes, classes for Deaf education majors, and other related service providers. We thank all the teachers who field tested this curriculum and provided us with feedback that assisted in its development.

We also acknowledge the work of the staff of DawnSignPress, who contributed to producing and publishing this curriculum. Special thanks to Joe Dannis, President of DawnSignPress, and Rebecca Ryan, Vice President of Marketing/Production, for their early encouragement and steady support of this work. Also special thanks to Marla Hatrak, Production Coordinator and to Alfredo Sierra, Production Artist.

We would also like to thank the following:
Actors: Antoinette Abbamonte, Deanna Bray, Lisa Chahayed, Matt Ellis, Rosa Lee Gallimore, CJ Jones, Don Lee Hanaumi, Danny Lucero, Mark Morales, Lauren Ridloff, Tim Scanlon
Illustrator: Robert Dorsey
Sign Illustrator: Linda Tom
Sign Models: Bibi Acosta, Ramy Busamante, Alvin Chege, Matt Ellis, Phung Ha-LeMaster, Marla Hatrak, Alfredo Sierra, Jenni Weiss

ASL at Work is primarily the product of the daily classroom activities and strategies of the authors. No curriculum in American Sign Language (ASL), however, stands alone as unique and independent of everything that has come before it. We "stand on the shoulders" of the authors of other ASL curriculums, past and present. Our teaching practices and strategies are influenced by the curricula we have used over the years. For example, you may note influences on our *ASL at Work* curriculum from the *Signing Naturally* and *Basic Sign Communication* curriculums. We acknowledge the groundbreaking contributions of the authors of these and other ASL curriculums that have significantly influenced our field of ASL teaching.

Foreword

Welcome to the study of American Sign Language (ASL).

ASL at Work is designed to help you learn the language of the Deaf community. The information that follows provides you with an overview of the curriculum. Before we get to that, there are a few things you should know about language learning in general and learning ASL in particular.

Learning a new language is sometimes described as learning a new way to see the world. The study of ASL will help you to learn about the perspectives of Deaf people. You may be surprised by the many differences and similarities between the Deaf and hearing communities. At the heart of all of this is communication. Unlike spoken languages, ASL, the language Deaf people use to communicate with each other, is visual. When you think about the many differences between how we use our eyes and how we use our ears, you begin to understand some of the fascinating opportunities that learning ASL offers. In ASL classes your eyes, hands, and body will learn to do what your ears and mouth do for you in English. *ASL at Work* will help you to make this important adjustment in the way you learn and the way you communicate—an adjustment that is both physical and mental.

Language is a social tool—it is the way we share with others the things that are important to us. We encourage you to communicate with Deaf people outside of the classroom as often as possible. After all, communicating comfortably with Deaf friends and colleagues is probably one of your reasons for taking this course. You have probably heard the expression "practice makes perfect." The more opportunities you take to use ASL with different people in a variety of situations, the more comfortable you will be. Another suggestion is to measure your progress with a calendar, not a stopwatch. Think about it this way: How long have you been using English? Are you still learning new things about English? Successful language learners tend to see language as a subject for lifelong learning, not one that can be mastered quickly and with little effort.

Why are you taking this class? How much ASL do you need to know? How much ASL do you want to know? It is important for you to consider these questions, maybe just by thinking about them or maybe by both thinking about them and writing them down. Thinking about what it is you want to learn can help you clarify your goals and organize your learning. *ASL at Work* provides clearly defined learning outcomes for each unit. Do they correspond with what you want to learn? Where they do, how well do they correspond? Where they don't, how are they different and what will you do to satisfy what you want to learn?

ASL at Work was designed primarily for adult learners. This design follows the principles of adult learning theory, particularly those aspects that encourage students to be independent learners. Of course, a curriculum is only as good as teachers and students make it. Working as hard outside the classroom as you do inside the classroom is one of the keys to success. We wish you the best success in your goal to learn ASL and to become one of the growing numbers of people in this country who use ASL to communicate with Deaf friends and colleagues.

Introduction to *ASL at Work*

ASL at Work is a comprehensive curriculum for learning conversational American Sign Language (ASL) and for learning about the language, culture, and community of ASL users. We call this curriculum *ASL at Work* because the title captures the multiple meanings we intend; that is, the title communicates the major thematic focus of the curriculum, which is teaching you to communicate with your Deaf co-workers with language that is focused on "communicating in the workplace." The title also means "using ASL to function, to communicate, to accomplish things." After all, this is what language is for. Human beings use language for many purposes and functions, and when they use a language effectively, "it works!" The cover design shows people communicating in ASL—ASL "at work."

Finally, *ASL at Work* communicates how you will learn ASL. From the first class period, your teacher and you will be "working together, interacting, and using ASL to learn ASL." ASL is the "language of instruction" as well as the "language being learned." ASL will be "at work" in the classroom.

Description of the *Student Text* and *Video Materials*

ASL at Work Student Text

This student text includes 16 instructional units (see the Table of Contents for unit titles). Each unit in this student text is organized into the following sections:

- Unit Overview

- Grammar

- Language, Culture, and Community

- Practice and Review Materials

- Unit Overview: This section provides an overview of what is included in each unit. It is intended to let you see at a glance what you will be learning in each unit. Unit Overview sections include the following parts:

- Grammar: This section provides explanations with illustrations for grammar principles introduced in each unit. English translations, which are provided below the illustrations, are shown in regular bold typeface.

- Language, Culture, and Community: This section provides information about Deaf people, their language and culture, and the community of Deaf and hearing people who use ASL. As appropriate, sign illustrations are provided, with English translations represented with regular bold typeface.

- Practice and Review Materials: This section includes (1) video exercises, including prompts for a Sample Expressive Dialogue, worksheets for comprehension practice, and Expressive Practice Prompts (EPPs); (2) grammar and language, culture, and community review questions; and (3) sign vocabulary illustrations for the signs taught in each unit.

Note: Unit 1 also includes a section that provides an introduction to fingerspelling.

Sign Illustrations

Illustrations can never take the place of learning signs from an instructor or from interacting with signers. The illustrations in this book are here to help you recall the signs taught.

Because ASL is a visually active language, the most difficult requirement of a sign illustration is to show movement. To facilitate the three-dimensional nature of signs, illustrations incorporate a number of helpful features.

Arrows show the direction, path, and repetition of the movement. Here are the arrows you will see.

Directional arrows point in the direction the sign is to be made.

Bi-directional arrows indicate a back and forth motion.

Path arrows show you the path of the sign's movement.

Repetitive arrows indicate that the sign's movement repeats twice or more.

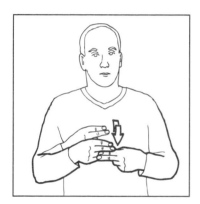

A touch is when part of the sign touches the chest, shoulder, or other part of the body. Touches are shown with touch marks.

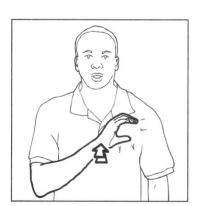

When a sign is supposed to be "wiggled" or moved back and forth slightly, there will be wiggle marks indicating this. Here are examples of wiggle marks.

Some signs change location from beginning to end. In this book, line thickness is used to distinguish the beginning of the sign's motion from that at the end of the sign's motion. If the lines of the arms and hands are thin, they indicate the placement of the arms and hands at the beginning of the sign. If at a different place on the drawing the lines of the arms and hands are thick, they indicate the placement of the arms and hands at the end of the movement. Here are some examples of signs with movement indicated by line thickness.

  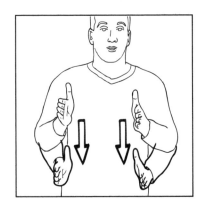

English Translation

The primary English translations of signs are represented by bold, italicized type; for example, ***school.*** If other English translations of signs are listed, these are separated from the primary translations with commas (,) and they are represented by regular, italicized type; for example, ***school,*** *academic.*

If the English translations of signs require two or more English words, these signs are represented by bold italicized type with hyphens between each English word; for example, ***the-two-of-them*** and ***don't-understand.***

When verb signs may be confused with other meanings, we add **to**; for example, **to-show.** When the meanings of verb signs are clear, we represent these as words or phrases without using **to;** for example, **learn** and **close-the-door.**

When the English translations for signs may not be clear, we use parentheses with another English word to clarify the meaning of each sign; for example, **spring** (season). "Season" clarifies the meaning of the sign and is not a translation of the meaning.

When English words can be considered equivalent translations, we use a slash (/) to separate the equivalent English translations; for example, **he/she/it.** When context requires the masculine or feminine pronoun for this sign, we use **he** and **she** by themselves as the English translation for the sign.

Other Sections of This Student Text

In addition to the 16 instructional units, other sections of this student text include the following:

1. Index of Grammar Principles

2. Index of Language, Culture, and Community Information

3. Index of Sign Vocabulary Illustrations

These sections help you to locate grammar principles, language, culture, and community information, and illustrations of signs that you are learning and may wish to review.

ASL at Work Video Materials

The purposes for the *ASL at Work Video Materials* are: (1) to provide practice in the use of conversational skills learned in class, (2) to develop expressive and receptive ASL skills, and (3) to practice grammar and conversational strategies within the context of dialogues and narratives.

Intended for your practice and review outside of class time, each unit of the video materials on the DVD includes the following:

1. Demonstration of a Sample Expressive Dialogue

2. Comprehension Practice Dialogues and/or Narratives

3. Demonstration of Expressive Practice Prompts

ASL at Work DVD Navigation

The Main Menu lists 16 Units on two pages.

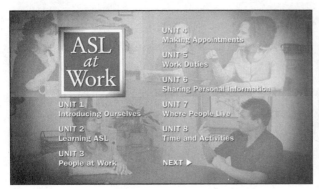 

You click on which unit you would like to work with. The next page will show the following exercises for the Unit:

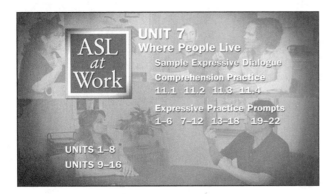

Next, you select which exercise you want to work with: Sample Expressive Dialogue, Comprehension Practice, or Expressive Practice Prompts. If you click on Expressive Practice Prompts, you can click the number of the prompt you want to practice.

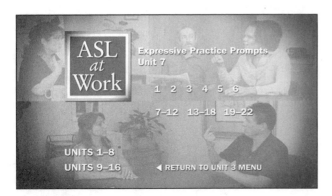

All of the video exercises will automatically jump back to the menu page where you selected the exercise. You can play the video for the exercise previously seen by clicking on the exercise or you can choose a different exercise.

Preparing Yourself for the Instructional Units:

For the 16 instructional units, the following strategies may be helpful as you begin your exciting journey to learn ASL and to learn about the culture and community of ASL users.

1. At the beginning of your learning for each unit, review the Unit Overview section to familiarize yourself with what you will be learning.

2. Read the brief description on the cover page of each unit and carefully read the learning outcomes. Think about the kind of things people say when they talk about the topic covered in the unit. For example, Unit 1 introduces language associated with introducing ourselves. You will learn how to ask for someone's name and state your own name. You will learn to greet someone. Is there any thing unique to how Deaf people introduce themselves? As stated earlier, the learning outcomes identify what you should expect to learn in each unit.

3. Look over the vocabulary listed in the Unit Overview. Maybe you know some of these signs from interactions with Deaf people you associate with. If you don't, don't worry. This is why you are in an ASL class and why you have a teacher to guide your learning. You certainly may look at the sign vocabulary illustrations in the back section of each unit. Hey, you probably can't resist! But don't try to learn signs from these illustrations. The sign vocabulary illustrations are two-dimensional representations of a three-dimensional phenomenon. They can often be misleading. It is always better to learn signs in class through interactions with your teacher and classmates, with the sign vocabulary illustrations used for review or when you have forgotten how to produce a sign.

4. You may wish to briefly read through the Grammar and the Language, Culture, and Community sections, but do not worry about whether you understand or do not understand everything in these sections. Again, you will be learning this information as your teacher guides your learning of this material. The purposes for these sections are to provide you with explanations and examples of grammar principles and with language, culture, and community information. It will be helpful for you to refer to these sections when reviewing and studying. Your teacher will probably ask you to read these sections as part of your homework.

Outside-of-Class Practice and Review

Following the above strategies in preparation for learning the content in each unit should be helpful to you. In addition, it is important to practice signing outside of class and to practice signing with others. Forming a practice group and scheduling a regular time to meet outside of class provides many benefits. In addition, you should set aside regular times outside of your class time to practice and review what you are learning on your own. For every hour of class time, you should expect to spend a minimum of 1 hour outside of class practicing and reviewing what you are learning. And, by all means, practice what you learn in the classroom by using your developing ASL skills with your Deaf friends and colleagues.

The *ASL at Work Video Materials* are one very important outside of class practice activity you should do. Practicing the Sample Expressive Dialogues and Expressive Practice Prompts with your classmates can be especially helpful to developing your ASL skills.

For practice and review of sign vocabulary it is helpful to write the vocabulary on 3x5 inch cards and to periodically flip through the cards and mentally and/or physically perform the signs. Use the Sign Vocabulary Illustrations section of each unit in your student text to look up signs you may not recall.

Your teacher will provide many opportunities in class to practice fingerspelling skills. In addition to this practice, you should practice your fingerspelling outside of class by yourself, with your partner, and with your outside-of-class group. Also, your teacher may recommend Web sites and software programs for practicing receptive fingerspelling skills.

A Note of Encouragement

We are happy that you are interested in learning to communicate in ASL with Deaf people, and we wish you great success as you progress both in your development of ASL skills and in your learning about the language, culture, and community of ASL users.

Introducing Ourselves

In this unit you learn to introduce yourself, to converse about your work or college major, and to open a conversation politely. Also, you learn to express the numbers 0 to 10, you learn basic fingerspelling principles, and you are introduced to the cultural practice of "name signs."

Unit 1 Overview

Learning Outcomes

1. Introduce yourself
2. Ask about and state your work or college major
3. Open and close a conversation politely
4. Count to 10
5. Fingerspell the first names of classmates
6. Learn the meanings of the terms Deaf culture and Deaf community
7. Learn about name signs for people and places

Vocabulary

0 to *10*	*nice*
hello, hi	*to-meet*
name	*who*
me/I	*work,* job
you	*major,* career, profession
he/she/it	*teacher,* instructor, professor
what	*student,* learner

Grammar

1. Spatial Referencing for People, Places, and Things Present
2. Expressing Wh-Questions
3. Conversational Regulators: Conversational Openers and Correcting Information

Language, Culture, and Community

1. Which Hand Do I Use?
2. Name Signs for People and Places
3. Deaf Culture and the Deaf Community

Unit 1 Overview

Practice and Review Materials

1. Video Exercises

   – Sample Expressive Dialogue

   – Comprehension Practice

   – Expressive Practice Prompts

2. Grammar and Language, Culture, and Community Review Questions

3. Sign Vocabulary Illustrations

Fingerspelling

1. The ASL Alphabet

2. Fingerspelling Principles and Practice

3. Fingerspelling Drills

1. Spatial Referencing for People, Places, and Things Present

2. Expressing Wh-Questions

3. Conversational Regulators: Conversational Openers and Correcting Information

1. Spatial Referencing for People, Places, and Things Present

Pointing the index finger at persons, places, and things that are present within the communication area is a form of the ASL grammatical feature spatial referencing. The index finger handshape is used for the pronouns *me/I, you, he/she/it, we/us, you-all,* and *they/them/those;* see Figures 1.1-1.6.

me/I
Fig. 1.1

you
Fig. 1.2

he/she/it
Fig. 1.3

we/us
Fig. 1.4

you-all
Fig. 1.5

they/them/those
Fig. 1.6

2. Expressing Wh-Questions

Wh-questions ask for specific information. Questions that ask who, what, when, where, why, how, how many, how much, and how long are Wh-questions. In ASL, there are a set of facial and body signals that indicate Wh-questions. These signals, which are called non-manual signals, include the following:

- Squinting the eyebrows together

- Tilting the head slightly forward

- Looking directly at the addressee

- Maintaining eye contact while holding the end position of the last sign

The two sentences illustrated in Figures 1.7 and 1.8 show how Wh-questions are expressed in ASL.

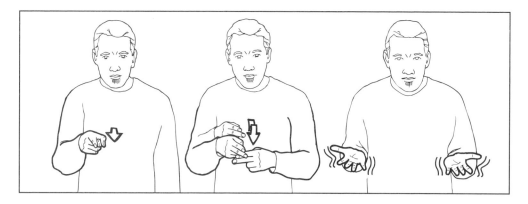

What is your name?
Fig. 1.7

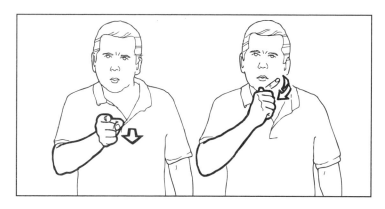

Who are you?
Fig. 1.8

3. Conversational Regulators: Conversational Openers and Correcting Information

A. Conversational Openers: In ASL, there are several ways to indicate that you want to begin a conversation with someone. Waving your hand slightly with fingers spread, palm facing down, and arm extended toward the person is one way. This signal is used to gain attention. When the person looks at you, you may begin a conversation. You may start by saying "Hello" or you may ask a direct question; for example, asking someone his/her name. Figure 1.9 shows this conversational opener.

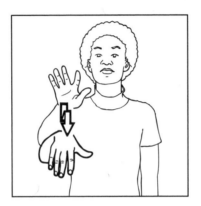

"wave hand: gaining attention"
Fig. 1.9

B. Correcting Information: Another important aspect of conversing with people is correcting information when something has been stated that is not true or not accurate. ASL uses the gesture "wave no," which indicates that something that has just been stated is not true or not accurate and that you wish to correct this information. Figure 1.10 shows this conversational regulator.

"wave no"
Fig. 1.10

Unit 1 Language, Culture, and Community

1. Which Hand Do I Use?

Signs may be produced with one or two hands. For one-handed signs and for fingerspelling, you should use the hand you write with and feel most comfortable using for manual tasks (see Figure 1.11). This is called your dominant hand. The other hand is called your non-dominant or passive hand. For two-handed signs, if one hand moves and one hand does not, your dominant hand should be the moving hand (see Figure 1.12). If both hands move, they will perform the same or reciprocal movements and have the same handshapes (see Figure 1.13).

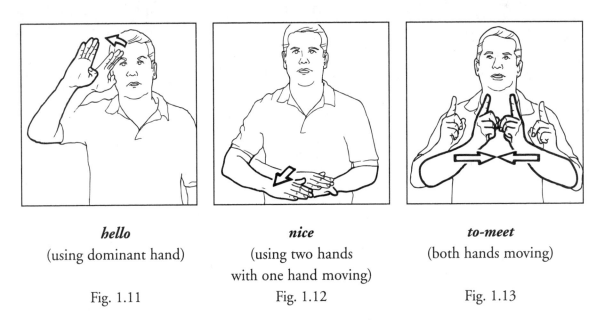

hello	*nice*	*to-meet*
(using dominant hand)	(using two hands with one hand moving)	(both hands moving)
Fig. 1.11	Fig. 1.12	Fig. 1.13

2. Name Signs for People and Places

Deaf people often develop "name signs" for people and places. These name signs are used to refer to members of the Deaf community or to stores, restaurants, and other places members of the Deaf community frequently refer to. Name signs are rule governed; that is, there are appropriate and inappropriate ways to produce name signs. For example, the locations where name signs may occur and the appropriate handshapes that name signs may take are restricted. Dr. Sam Supalla (1992) identified two basic types of name signs, Descriptive Name Signs (DNSs), and Arbitrary Name Signs (ANSs). DNSs are based on distinctive features of individuals' appearances. For example, Laurent Clerc, the first Deaf teacher in the United States, had a prominent scar on the right side of his face due to a fall into a fire when he was an infant. His name sign, which uses the index and middle fingers (U-handshape) to touch the side of the cheek, makes reference to this scar. ANSs usually incorporate the first letter of a person's first name or the first letters of a person's first and last names and are located in neutral space or on the body in a location commonly used for name signs (for example, chest or wrist).

Name signs are not universal or standard. Not everyone named Barbara, for example, has the same name sign. Also, people may have more than one name sign in a lifetime, especially if they move to new localities and their name signs are already in use for other people in their new localities. It is important to be aware that a name sign is not something you create for yourself. Name signs are generally given to you by Deaf people with whom you interact. Generally, name signs are given to acquaintances, friends, co-workers, and others when they have a close association with members of the Deaf community. You should not expect to have a name sign immediately. Ask your teacher to show you some name signs used by Deaf people to refer to people and places in your locality. If you have a name sign, when you introduce yourself, you should generally fingerspell your first and last names and then give your name sign.

Reference and Readings

Kelly-Jones, N., & Hamilton, H. (1981). *Signs Everywhere.* Los Alamitos, CA: Modern Signs Press.

Meadow, K. (1977). Name signs as identity symbols in the deaf community. *Sign Language Studies, 16,* 237–246.

Supalla, S. J. (1992). *The Book of Name Signs.* San Diego, CA: DawnSignPress.

3. Deaf Culture and the Deaf Community

Throughout *ASL at Work,* we use a common convention when discussing people who are deaf and hard of hearing. We use a capital "D" for the word "Deaf" when we are referring to Deaf culture or the people who identify themselves as members of Deaf culture. We use lower case "d" for the word "deaf" when we are referring to the condition of hearing loss or to a person or people who do not identify with Deaf culture. Because Deaf culture is at the core of the larger Deaf community, we also use a capital "D" when referring to the Deaf community.

As a student of ASL, it is important that you begin to understand the terms Deaf culture and Deaf community. However, trying to define in a few paragraphs how individuals or groups identify themselves is fraught with the real danger of oversimplification. Books and articles have been written that define these terms. Even with these scholarly efforts, people will disagree about who is and who is not a member of Deaf culture and on specific qualities of people who are members of Deaf culture.

By Deaf culture we mean the visually based culture of people who are deaf and who form a linguistic minority that uses ASL as their primary language for interacting with other members of their group. Deaf culture includes art forms, traditions, values, beliefs, behaviors, and cultural practices of Deaf people who primarily socialize with and marry other Deaf people. The culture is formed and finds cohesiveness through sharing a common language, ASL, and common living experiences as a minority group within the larger mainstream culture.

Compared to Deaf culture group members, the Deaf community is a larger and more heterogeneous group of people. The Deaf community includes D/deaf people and their hearing friends and supporters. It includes the people, institutions, and structures that support deaf and hard-of-hearing people. At the core of the Deaf community is Deaf culture, but not all members of the Deaf community are members of Deaf culture. Many members of the Deaf community are connected with deaf and hard-of-hearing people through their professional work or because they share common interests in civil rights or consumer issues affecting deaf and hard-of-hearing people.

As a hearing person learning ASL, you are at the threshold of the Deaf community. If your newly acquired ASL skills progress to the point where you will have a lasting connection to Deaf people through friendships or work and if your learning includes beginning to understand and support the values, beliefs, goals, behaviors and cultural practices of Deaf people, then you will become a member of the Deaf community.

Throughout this course of study, you will be introduced to aspects of Deaf culture and the Deaf community. Hopefully you will come to appreciate and celebrate Deaf culture and become a welcomed new member of the Deaf community.

For more in-depth information about Deaf culture and the Deaf community, we suggest the following readings.

Padden, C. (1980). The Deaf community and the culture of Deaf people. In C. Baker & R. Battison (Eds.), *Sign language and the Deaf community: Essays in honor of William C. Stokoe* (pp. 89–103). Silver Spring, MD: National Association of the Deaf.

Padden, C., & Humphries, T. (1988). *Deaf in America: Voices from a culture.* Cambridge: Harvard University Press.

Deaf culture. Retrieved February 16, 2004, from NETAC TipSheets, NETAC: Northeast Technical Assistance Center at the National Technical Institute for the Deaf: http://netac.rit.edu/downloads/TPSHT_Deaf_Culture.pdf

Unit 1 Practice and Review Materials

1. Video Exercises

    – Sample Expressive Dialogue

    – Comprehension Practice

    – Expressive Practice Prompts

2. Grammar and Language, Culture, and Community Review Questions

3. Sign Vocabulary Illustrations

Sample Expressive Dialogue

Read the dialogue prompts below and then watch how each signer expresses these prompts on the video. Sign along with both Signer A and Signer B or with either Signer A or Signer B on the video. You may wish to practice this dialogue with a classmate outside of class time, and your teacher may review this dialogue in class and ask you to sign this dialogue with a classmate.

Introducing Yourself

Signer A: Ask for name of Signer B

Signer B: Give name

Signer A: Ask for work or major

Signer B: Give work or major

Signer A: Polite close

Signer B: Polite close

For the signing you observe, please write below any helpful notes and questions that you may have for your teacher.

Comprehension Practice 1.1

Watch the dialogue all the way through and then answer as many of the questions below as you can. If necessary, view the dialogue a second time to see whether you are able to understand more and answer any additional questions.

Meeting Each Other

1. How do these two people open the conversation?

2. What is the woman's name?

3. What is the man's name?

4. What are their jobs?

5. How do these two people close the conversation?

For the signing you observe, please write any helpful notes and questions that you may have for your teacher.

Comprehension Practice 1.2

Watch the dialogue all the way through and then answer as many of the questions below as you can. If necessary, view the dialogue a second time to see whether you are able to understand more and answer any additional questions.

Discussing Majors

1. What question does the first student ask the second student?

2. What are the names of these students?

3. At one point in the conversation, the student in the light colored dress doesn't understand something. Describe what she does.

4. The student in the blue blouse is an art major. True or false?

5. Both students have the same major. True or false?

6. How do these two students close the conversation?

For the signing you observe, please write any helpful notes and questions that you may have for your teacher.

Expressive Practice Prompts

These Expressive Practice Prompts show you the types of questions and statements you should be able to express in ASL by the end of Unit 1. Your teacher may use these Expressive Practice Prompts in class. You should practice these with your practice partner and group outside of class as well.

1. Introduce yourself and ask another person for his/her name.

2A. Introduce yourself and tell the class your work.

2B. Introduce yourself and tell the class your major.

3. Ask a classmate for his/her work or major.

4. Count to 10.

5. Ask a classmate who he/she is.

6. Ask a classmate who someone else in class is.

7. Ask a classmate what another classmate's work or major is.

8. Express that you are pleased to meet a classmate.

9. Greet a classmate; ask his/her name.

10. Express that you are a student.

Grammar and Language, Culture, and Community Review Questions

These questions will assist you as you read the Grammar and the Language, Culture, and Community sections in this unit.

1. When people you wish to talk about are in your presence, how do you indicate who you are talking about?

2. When you want to express a Wh-question (for example, who, what, when, why, how, and how many), what do your head and eyebrows do to let people know you are asking them a question?

3. What are two conversational regulators you learned in Unit 1?

4. Explain the convention of using capital "D" or lower case "d" when referring to people who are deaf.

5. What are two very important factors influencing the formation of Deaf culture?

6. How does the Deaf community differ from Deaf culture?

7. Which hand should you use to fingerspell and to make movements for signs produced with one hand?

8. What are the two types of "name signs" and how do they differ?

Sign Vocabulary Illustrations

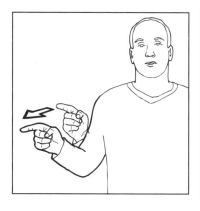

he/she/it

hello, *hi*

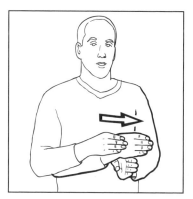

major, *career, profession*

me/I

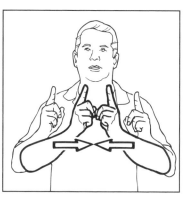

to-meet

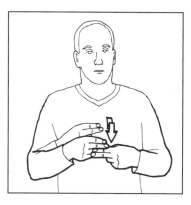

name

nice

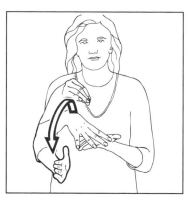

student, *learner*

 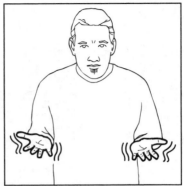

teacher, instructor, professor   *what*

who   *work,* job   *you*

Numbers

0   *1*   *2*

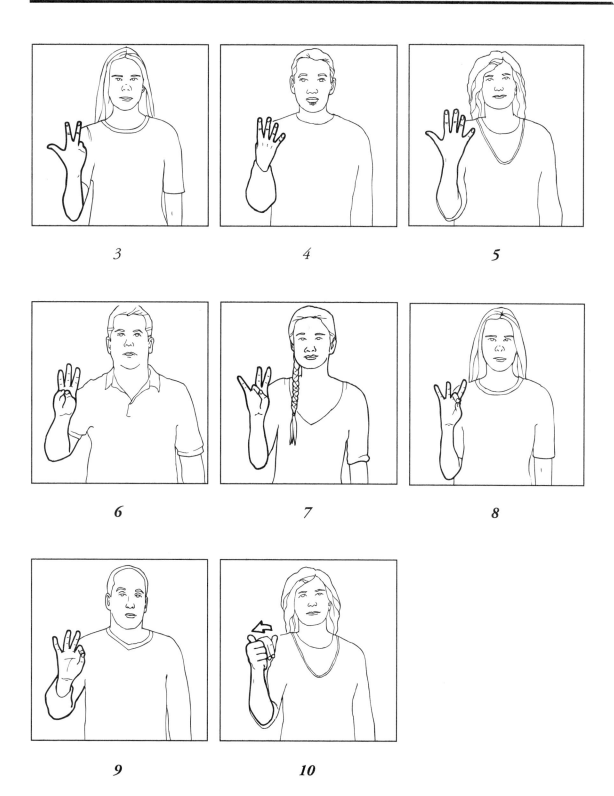

3

4

5

6

7

8

9

10

Unit 1 Fingerspelling

1. The ASL Alphabet

2. Fingerspelling Principles and Practice

3. Fingerspelling Drills

The ASL Alphabet

Fingerspelling Principles and Practice

1. Your goal is to fingerspell clearly at a normal rate. Practice maintaining clarity as your skills allow you to increase fingerspelling to a more near-normal to normal rate. Clarity is more important than speed.

2. Fingerspell with your dominant signing hand positioned in the neutral signing space in front of your shoulder.

3. The palm of your hand generally faces forward/outward, with the exception of letters *g* and *h* (palm to side) and *p* and *q* (palm down).

4. Letters should be clearly and completely formed, with a smooth transition between letters. Do not bounce or jerk your hand.

5. As each letter is formed, the hand is held steady or may move slightly to the side in space from left to right for right-handed dominant signers and from right to left for left-handed dominant signers.

6. When executing double "open" letters (e.g., a double *l*), the hand moves slightly to the side (i.e., left to right for right-handed dominant signers and right to left for left-handed dominant signers). For "closed" letters (e.g., *e, s, t*), the fingers open and close slightly to indicate a double letter and the hand may move slightly to the side.

7. Fingerspell in syllables and hold for a moment at the end of a word.

8. Between words, in addition to a pause, the hand may move slightly to the side to indicate the start of a new word.

9. Fingerspelling is primarily used to spell proper nouns (names of people, places, and things). Therefore, focus your expressive fingerspelling practice on spelling these proper nouns. A good place to start is learning to spell the names of all your classmates and your teacher.

10. Fingerspell words you read in newspaper articles, words from television dialogue shows and commercials, letters and numbers you see on license plates (keep your eyes on the road, of course!), names from the telephone book, and words you see on billboards, other signs, doors, and buildings.

11. When practicing fingerspelling with a partner and your outside-of-class group, use controlled contexts. This helps you to develop correct habits for reading fingerspelled words as whole words rather than letter by letter. An example of controlling the context is to practice by using categories, for example, bath soap brands, makes of cars, breeds of dogs, and baseball teams. Using a context helps you to narrow the range of possible words and, therefore, more easily predict and see the whole word being fingerspelled.

References

Groode, J. L. (1992). *Fingerspelling: Expressive and Receptive* (Video). San Diego, CA: DawnSignPress.

Guillory, L. M. (1973). *Expressive and Receptive Fingerspelling for Hearing People.* Baton Rouge, LA: Claitor's Publishing Division. Library of Congress Catalog Card Number: 66-17803.

Fingerspelling Drills Worksheet

These are examples of the types of drill exercises you can build for practicing letter combinations. Expand on these and create additional exercises using real letter combinations.

Three-Letter Drills

AB	AD	AG	AM	AN	AY	AP	AR
CAB	DAD	BAG	BAM	BAN	BAY	CAP	BAR
DAB	FAD	JAG	CAM	CAN	DAY	GAP	CAR
FAB	HAD	LAG	DAM	DAN	FAY	LAP	FAR
GAB	LAD	NAG	HAM	FAN	HAY	MAP	JAR
JAB	MAD	RAG	JAM	MAN	JAY	NAP	PAR
LAB	PAD	SAG	PAM	PAN	MAY	RAP	TAR
NAB	SAD	TAG	RAM	RAN	NAY	SAP	
TAB	TAD	WAG	SAM	TAN	RAY	TAP	
			YAM	VAN	SAY	YAP	

AS	AX	AT	ED	EE	EG	EM	EN
GAS	FAX	BAT	BED	BEE	BEG	BEM	BEN
HAS	JAX	CAT	FED	FEE	KEG	DEM	DEN
LAS	LAX	FAT	JED	GEE	LEG	FEM	FEN
PAS	MAX	HAT	KED	LEE	MEG	GEM	GEN
TAS	PAX	MAT	LED	SEE	PEG	HEM	HEN
VAS	SAX	PAT	MED	TEE	REG	JEM	PEN
	VAX	RAT	PED	VEE		LEM	TEN
	TAX	SAT	TED	WEE		REM	YEN
	WAX					TEM	

ER	ET	EW	IB	ID	IE	IG	IM
DER	BET	DEW	BIB	BID	BIE	BIG	BIM
FER	GET	FEW	DIB	DID	DIE	DIG	DIM
HER	JET	HEW	FIB	HID	FIE	FIG	HIM
PER	LET	MEW	GIB	KID	HIE	HIG	JIM
SER	NET	NEW	JIB	LID	LIE	JIG	KIM
VER	PET	PEW	LIB	MID	PIE	PIG	RIM
WER	WET	SEW	NIB	RID	TIE	RIG	TIM
	YET		RIB		VIE	WIG	VIM

Adapted from: Guillory, L. M. (1973). *Expressive and Receptive Fingerspelling for Hearing Adults*. Baton Rouge, LA: Claitor's Publishing Division.

Fingerspelling Drills

Four-Letter Drills

EAT	EAP	EAR	EAN	ARE	EEN	EET	OWN
BEAT	HEAP	BEAR	BEAN	BARE	BEEN	BEET	DOWN
DEAT	LEAP	DEAR	DEAN	CARE	SEEN	DEET	GOWN
FEAT	REAP	FEAR	LEAN	DARE	TEEN	FEET	SOWN
HEAT		GEAR	MEAN	FARE		HEET	TOWN
MEAT		LEAR	WEAN	MARE		MEET	
NEAT		NEAR		PARE		PEET	
SEAT		SEAR		RARE			
		TEAR		WARE			
		WEAR					

OPE	AKE	ALK	INK	OCK	ING	ITE	OME
COPE	BAKE	BALK	BINK	BOCK	BING	BITE	COME
DOPE	CAKE	FALK	DINK	DOCK	DING	CITE	DOME
HOPE	FAKE	TALK	LINK	LOCK	KING	KITE	HOME
LOPE	LAKE	WALK	MINK	MOCK	PING	LITE	SOME
MOPE	MAKE		PINK	ROCK	SING	MITE	TOME
ROPE	RAKE		RINK	TOCK	WING	RITE	
	SAKE		SINK	SOCK	ZING		
	TAKE		WINK				

ILL	ELT	ALL	ANG	ENT	EAK	EAM	EEP
FILL	BELT	BALL	BANG	BENT	BEAK	BEAM	BEEP
GILL	FELT	FALL	FANG	CENT	LEAK	REAM	CEEP
HILL	MELT	HALL	GANG	DENT	PEAK	SEAM	DEEP
KILL	PELT	MALL	HANG	GENT	REAK	TEAM	KEEP
MILL	WELT	PALL	PANG	LENT	TEAK	WEAM	PEEP
PILL		TALL	RANG	PENT	WEAK		SEEP
SILL		WALL	SANG	RENT			
WILL				TENT			

ONE	ASH	ATE	ORE	UST	INE	AST	ANE
BONE	BASH	DATE	BORE	BUST	DINE	CAST	BANE
GONE	CASH	FATE	CORE	DUST	FINE	FAST	CANE
HONE	DASH	GATE	FORE	GUST	LINE	LAST	LANE
NONE	LASH	HATE	LORE	JUST	MINE	MAST	MANE
TONE	MASH	LATE	PORE	MUST	PINE	PAST	PANE
ZONE	RASH	MATE	SORE	RUST	VINE	VAST	SANE
	SASH	RATE	TORE		WINE		VANE

Adapted from: Guillory, L. M. (1973). *Expressive and Receptive Fingerspelling for Hearing Adults*. Baton Rouge, LA: Claitor's Publishing Division.

Learning ASL

In this unit you learn to talk about learning American Sign Language (ASL). Also, you learn to identify people who are present, to indicate you understand and don't understand, and to communicate more than one (plural). Also, you begin to learn to use conversational regulators.

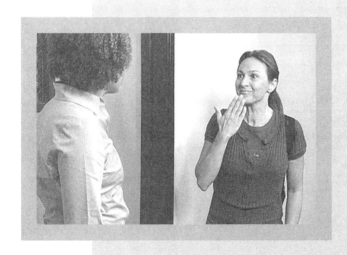

Unit 2 Overview

Learning Outcomes

1. Identify people who are present
2. Indicate understanding and not understanding
3. Make affirmative and negative statements
4. Express yes/no questions
5. Show how many using number incorporation
6. Show more than one using horizontal and vertical sweep
7. Begin learning about and how to use conversational regulators

---

Vocabulary

we/us	*this/it*
the-two-of-us	*yes*
the-three-of-us	*no*
you-all	*don't-understand*
the-two-of-you	*understand,* comprehend
the-three-of-you	*deaf*
they/them	*hearing person*
the-two-of-them	*hard-of-hearing*
the-three-of-them	*again,* repeat
class	*oh-I-see*
teach	*slow*
learn	*ask-a-question-to*
A-S-L	*thank-you/you're-welcome*
to-sign	*how-many*
to-spell/fingerspell	

Grammar

1. Expressing Yes/No Questions
2. Affirmative Head Nod and Negative Headshake
3. Use of Number Incorporation with Pronouns for Plural
4. Horizontal and Vertical Sweep for Plural
5. What Makes a Sign?

Unit 2 Overview

Language, Culture, and Community

1. Getting Attention

2. Indicating Understanding with *"oh-I-see"*

3. Requesting Clarification

Practice and Review Materials

1. Video Exercises

   – Sample Expressive Dialogue

   – Comprehension Practice

   – Expressive Practice Prompts

2. Grammar and Language, Culture, and Community Review Questions

3. Sign Vocabulary Illustrations

Unit 2 Grammar

1. Expressing Yes/No Questions

2. Affirmative Head Nod and Negative Headshake

3. Use of Number Incorporation with Pronouns for Plural

4. Horizontal and Vertical Sweep for Plural

5. What Makes a Sign?

1. Expressing Yes/No Questions

Similar to Wh-questions in ASL (see Unit 1, Introducing Ourselves, Grammar section, #2), there are a set of non-manual signals (facial and body signals) that indicate a yes or no question is being asked. These non-manual signals include the following:

- Raising the eyebrows

- Moving the head and shoulders slightly forward

- Looking directly at the addressee

- Maintaining eye contact while holding the end position of the last sign

Figure 2.1 shows this grammatical feature.

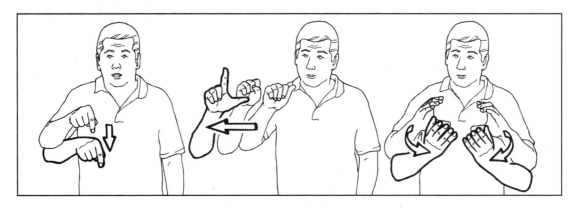

Is this the ASL class?
Fig. 2.1

2. Affirmative Head Nod and Negative Headshake

Affirmative head nod is an up-down head movement that indicates the signer is making a statement that is true or factual. Affirmative head nod, therefore, is an ASL non-manual grammatical signal that functions like the verb "to be" in English to make true or factual statements. Figures 2.2 and 2.3 show use of the affirmative head nod.

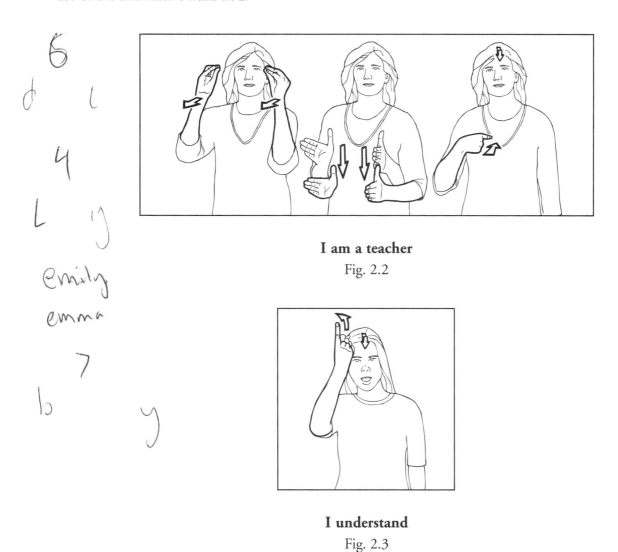

I am a teacher

Fig. 2.2

I understand

Fig. 2.3

Negative headshake is a side-to-side head movement negating a statement. This non-manual signal means that what is being stated is not true or factual. Negative headshake is also used with negative signs; for example, ***not*** and ***don't-understand.*** Figures 2.4 and 2.5 show use of the negative headshake. Compare Figures 2.2 and 2.4. Notice that the signs in these two sentences are exactly the same. The different meanings are being created through the use of the affirmative head nod and negative headshake.

I am not a teacher.

Fig. 2.4

I don't understand.

Fig. 2.5

3. Use of Number Incorporation with Pronouns for Plural

Number handshapes may be incorporated into pronoun signs to communicate how many. For example, using the inflected number handshape two and moving back and forth between another person and you is translated as "the two of us," and using this same handshape and moving back and forth between two other persons may be translated as "the two of you." See Figures 2.6 and 2.7.

the-two-of-us.
Fig. 2.6

the-two-of-you
Fig. 2.7

Pronouns that incorporate number include the following:

the-two-of-us	*those-two, they*	*the-two-of-you*
the-three-of-us	*those-three, they*	*the-three-of-you*
the-four-of-us	*those-four, they*	*the-four-of-you*

The number of people referred to is incorporated or included in the production of the sign by using the appropriate "number" handshape. Later in this course, you will learn other signs that can be modified in this way.

4. Horizontal and Vertical Sweep for Plural

A sweeping motion of the hand and arm on the horizontal or vertical plane may be used to indicate plurality. For example, a horizontal sweep with the index finger handshape may be used when signing *we, you all, they, these,* and *those.* A vertical sweep would be used if names are listed on a chalkboard and the signer is referring to these names; that is, the signer points at the top name and sweeps down (vertically) to indicate *these, those*, or *they.* Figures 2.8 and 2.9 show the horizontal and vertical sweep for plural.

these
(horizontal sweep)
Fig. 2.8

these
(vertical sweep)
Fig. 2.9

5. What Makes a Sign?

Signs have four basic manual parts or parameters: handshape, location, movement, and orientation (primarily the direction the palm faces). In addition, for some signs certain facial expressions (non-manual signals) are important to conveying their meaning. For the purposes of this discussion, we will focus on the four basic manual parameters that make up signs.

The four manual parts of signs are analogous to spoken language sounds or phonemes (vowels and consonants); that is, the phonemes of spoken language and the four basic manual parts of signs are the "building blocks" by which the vocabulary of languages are created and expressed. Just as changing one phoneme in a spoken word may change the meaning, changing one of the four basic manual sign parts may change the meaning as well.

For example, two signs that differ only in the sign parameter of handshape are ***please*** and ***sorry.*** As shown in Figures 2.10 and 2.11, these two signs have the same location (center of chest), orientation (palm toward signer), and movement (circular). What distinguishes these two signs is that ***please*** has a palm flat handshape and ***sorry*** has an A-handshape.

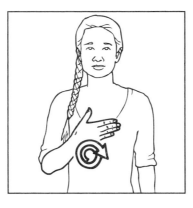

please
Fig. 2.10

sorry
Fig. 2.11

An example of two signs that differ only in the sign parameter of location is **mother** and **father.** As shown in Figures 2.12 and 2.13, these two signs have the same handshape (5-handshape), orientation (palm facing to side), and movement (thumb of 5-handshape taps or touches the face of the signer). What distinguishes these two signs is that **mother** is produced in the chin area location and **father** is produced in the forehead area location.

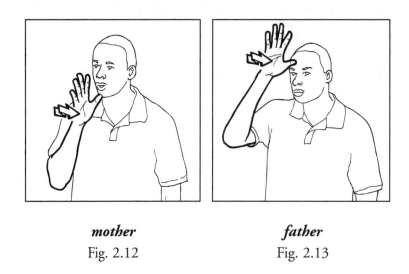

| **mother** | **father** |
| Fig. 2.12 | Fig. 2.13 |

An example of two signs that differ only in the sign parameter of movement is **he/she/it** and **they.** These two signs have the same handshape (index), location (neutral space), and orientation (palm facing to side). What distinguishes these two signs is movement; that is, forward/away movement from the signer for **he/she/it** and side movement sweep from the signer for **they.**

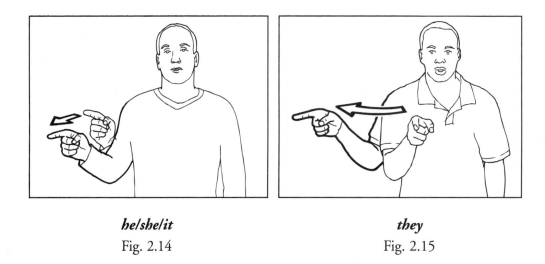

| **he/she/it** | **they** |
| Fig. 2.14 | Fig. 2.15 |

An example of two signs that differ only in the sign parameter of orientation is ***children*** and ***things.*** As shown in Figures 2.16 and 2.17, these two signs have the same handshape (palm flat, fingers together), location (neutral space to the dominant side of the signer's signing space), and movement (horizontally in space with a slight bouncing motion). What distinguishes these two signs is that ***children*** has the palm facing downward and ***things*** has the palm facing upward.

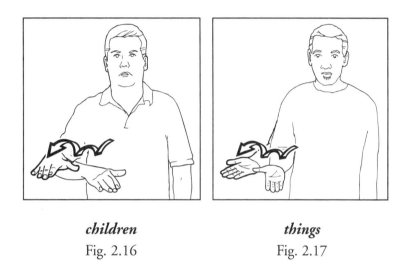

children

Fig. 2.16

things

Fig. 2.17

With the four basic manual parts of sign vocabulary (handshape, location, movement, and palm orientation [primarily the direction the palm faces]), signers have the building blocks needed to naturally develop an infinite number of signs.

1. Getting Attention

2. Indicating Understanding with *"oh-I-see"*

3. Requesting Clarification

1. Getting Attention

In ASL conversations, there are several ways to gain the attention of individuals you wish to talk with. As stated in Unit 1, Introducing Ourselves, Grammar section, #3A, waving your hand slightly with fingers spread, palm facing down, and arm extended toward the person is one way. Signing **you** repeatedly is another way of gaining attention and opening a conversation.

If the person you wish to talk with is not looking at you, you may physically touch the person lightly on the shoulder or elbow, or you may ask someone standing near the person to get his/her attention for you. Physically touching others to gain their attention is acceptable within the Deaf community. In this and subsequent course units, your teacher will demonstrate how to use various techniques for gaining attention and opening conversations.

2. Indicating Understanding with *"oh-I-see"*

Manual and non-manual signals are used to indicate understanding in ASL conversations. The simplest form of this feedback is a nodding of the head, indicating that the person is following or understanding what is being signed. It does not necessarily indicate agreement with what is being signed. If a person does not understand, you might see a Wh-question expression appear. This would signal the other person to repeat or clarify what had just been stated. Other forms of feedback include the sign **oh-I-see** (see Figure 2.18). This sign is often used to provide feedback, which is comparable to saying "That's interesting." As you develop your ASL skills, you will learn to recognize conversational regulators such as head nodding, headshaking, question expression, and other signals that indicate understanding, misunderstanding, requesting clarification, and other feedback signals between ASL communicators.

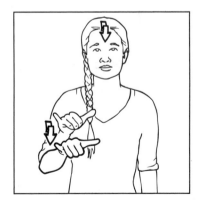

oh-I-see
Fig. 2.18

3. Requesting Clarification

As stated in #2 of this Language, Culture, and Community section, a Wh-question expression may be used to indicate that something just stated was not understood and should be repeated. In addition, as you will learn in this unit, you may sign *again, don't-understand,* or *fingerspell again slow* when you don't understand and want a signer to repeat something that was just signed or fingerspelled. Figures 2.19 and 2.20 show examples of these requests for clarification. There are additional ways that requests for clarification are made in ASL. You will learn these in subsequent course units.

I don't understand. Repeat that.
Fig. 2.19

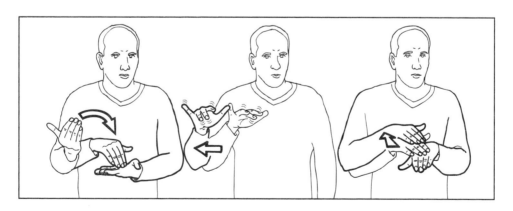

Please repeat what you just fingerspelled slowly.
Fig. 2.20

Unit 2 Practice and Review Materials

1. Video Exercises

    – Sample Expressive Dialogue

    – Comprehension Practice

    – Expressive Practice Prompts

2. Grammar and Language, Culture, and Community Review Questions

3. Sign Vocabulary Illustrations

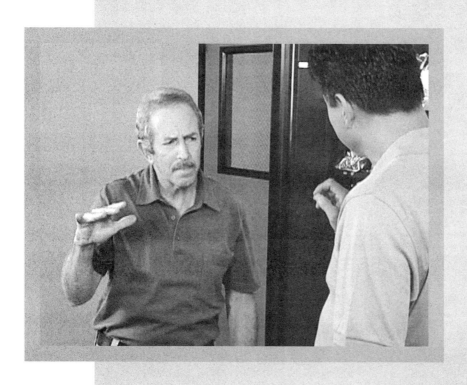

Sample Expressive Dialogue

Read the dialogue prompts below and then watch how each signer expresses these prompts on the video. Sign along with both Signer A and Signer B or with either Signer A or Signer B on the video. You may wish to practice this dialogue with a classmate outside of class time and your teacher may review this dialogue in class and ask you to sign this dialogue with a classmate.

Talking about a Teacher

Signer A: Greet Signer B and ask if this is an ASL class

Signer B: Confirm that this is an ASL class

Signer A: Ask who the teacher is

Signer B: Give the teacher's name

Signer A: Close the conversation with "Thank you"

For the signing you observe, please write below any helpful notes and questions that you may have for your teacher.

Comprehension Practice 2.1

Watch the dialogue all the way through and then answer as many of the questions below as you can. If necessary, view the dialogue a second time to see whether you are able to understand more and answer any additional questions

Discussing ASL Class

1. How does the man in the green shirt open the conversation?

2. What is the first question asked?

    One you learing asl

3. What is the teacher's name?

4. How do these two signers use signing space to consistently refer to "the ASL teacher"?

5. The ASL teacher is hearing. True or false?

    False

6. What sign does the man in the green shirt use at the end of this conversation?
    Explain what this sign means.

For the signing you observe, please write any helpful notes and questions that you may have for your teacher.

Comprehension Practice 2.2

Watch the dialogue all the way through and then answer as many of the questions below as you can. If necessary, view the dialogue a second time to see whether you are able to understand more and answer any additional questions.

Talking about Learning ASL

1. What does the man in the blue shirt ask the other man?

2. Which of the two men is a student?

    blue

3. The man in the green shirt is a _____.
    (line of work)

4. Describe how the man in the green shirt uses the sign *to-learn.* What does this sign mean?

5. How does the man in the blue shirt request clarification of the other man's fingerspelling?

6. These two people talk about another person. What is this person's name?

7. How well does the man in the blue shirt understand his teacher?

For the signing you observe, please write any helpful notes and questions that you may have for your teacher.

Expressive Practice Prompts

These Expressive Practice Prompts show you the types of questions and statements you should be able to express in ASL by the end of Unit 2. Your teacher may also use these Expressive Practice prompts in class. You should practice these with your practice partner and group outside of class as well.

1. Ask for something to be fingerspelled again.

2. Indicate yourself and one other person.

3. Express that you are learning ASL.

4. Identify and name your teacher.

5. Express that you understand.

6. Express that you don't understand.

7. Ask a classmate if this is an ASL class.

8. Ask a classmate what he/she is learning.

9. Indicate yourself and two other people.

10. Express that you are a student learning ASL.

11. You are asked what you are learning. Provide a response.

12. You are asked if you understand your ASL teacher. Provide a response.

13. Ask a classmate to fingerspell his/her name again.

14. Ask a classmate whether he/she is deaf or hearing.

15. A classmate offers you something that you don't want to accept. Decline this offer politely.

16. Ask a classmate if he/she understands ASL.

Grammar and Language, Culture, and Community Review Questions

These questions will assist you as you read the Grammar and the Language, Culture, and Community sections in this unit.

1. What non-manual signals are used to indicate yes/no questions?

2. Compare Figures 2.3 and 2.5. What non-manual signals are being used to communicate the affirmative statement and the negative statement?

3. When using pronouns, how may the number of people being referred to be indicated?

4. How is the concept of "more than one" being communicated in Figures 2.8 and 2.9?

5. What are the four basic parts or parameters of signs?

6. If someone is not looking at you, how can you gain his/her attention to begin an ASL conversation?

7. One conversational regulator used to indicate that you are understanding or following what is being stated is to nod your head. Describe a conversational regulator that indicates that you did not understand and wish something to be clarified.

8. When someone fingerspells something and you do not understand, how can you request clarification?

Sign Vocabulary Illustrations

again, *repeat*

ask-a-question-to

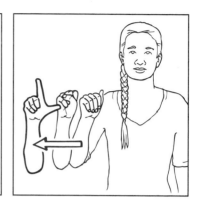

A-S-L

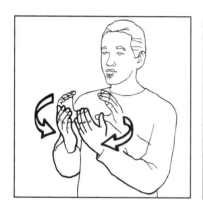

class

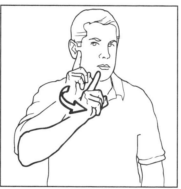

deaf

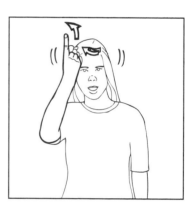

don't-understand

hard-of-hearing

hearing-person

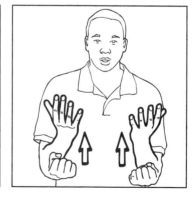

how-many

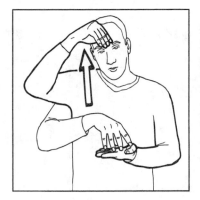

learn

no

oh-I-see

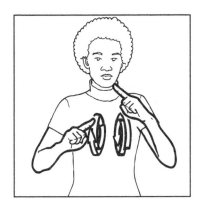

to-sign

slow

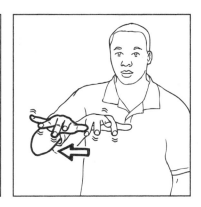

to-spell/fingerspell

teach

thank-you/you're-welcome

they/them

the-three-of-them

the-three-of-us

the-three-of-you

the-two-of-them

the-two-of-us

the-two-of-you

this/it

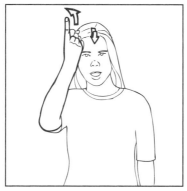

understand, comprehend

we/us

yes   *you-all*

People at Work

In this unit you learn to communicate about people in the workplace and you learn how to request and give directions to nearby locations. You also learn about an important historic event in the lives of Deaf people.

Unit 3 Overview

Learning Outcomes

1. Ask about co-workers

2. Request and give directions to nearby locations

3. Sign numbers from *11* to *20*

4. Express negative statements using *"none"* and *"not"*

5. Ask and tell about people who are not present

6. Contrast and compare two people, places, or things

7. Learn about an important historic event in the lives of Deaf people

Vocabulary

11 to *20*	*custodian,* janitor	*bathroom,* restroom, toilet
girl, female	*my*	*room,* office
boy, male	*your*	*office* (work space)
woman	*his/her/its*	*door*
man	*our/ours*	*elevator*
person	*their*	*classroom*
people	*school*	*l-a-b*
president	*company* (business)	*basement*
vice-president	*police*	*stairway,* stairs
faculty	*college,* university	*upstairs,* up
staff	*university*	*downstairs,* down
boss, coach, chair	*hallway*	*floor,* story, level
secretary	*department*	*where*
assistant, aide	*organization/office*	*number*
dean	*right-side*	*none,* no (amount)
counselor, advisor	*left-side*	*not*
supervisor	*water fountain*	

Unit 3 Overview

Grammar

1. Possessive Pronouns

2. Spatial Referencing for People, Places, and Things Not Present

3. Use of Space for Contrasting and Comparing

4. Person Affix for Changing Verbs to Nouns

5. Use of Numbers and Quantifiers for Plural

6. Use of *"No," "Not,"* and *"None"* for Negating Responses

7. Use of Space for Signer's Perspective

8. Real-World Orientation

Language, Culture, and Community

1. Deaf President Now (DPN)!

2. Sign Variation

Practice and Review Materials

1. Video Exercises

    – Sample Expressive Dialogue

    – Comprehension Practice

    – Expressive Practice Prompts

2. Grammar and Language, Culture, and Community Review Questions

3. Sign Vocabulary Illustrations

1. Possessive Pronouns

2. Spatial Referencing for People, Places, and Things Not Present

3. Use of Space for Contrasting and Comparing

4. Person Affix for Changing Verbs to Nouns

5. Use of Numbers and Quantifiers for Plural

6. Use of *"No,"* *"Not,"* and *"None"* for Negating Responses

7. Use of Space for Signer's Perspective

8. Real-World Orientation

1. Possessive Pronouns

ASL uses the palm-flat handshape to indicate possessive. Figure 3.1 shows how the possessive pronoun *his/her/its* is used in an ASL sentence.

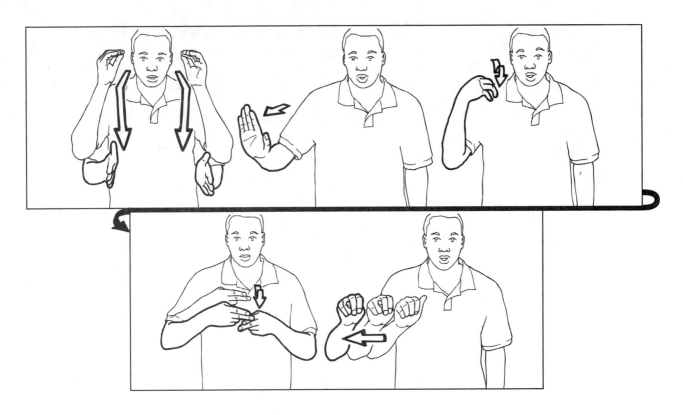

That teacher's boss is Ann.

Fig. 3.1

Other possessive pronoun signs using the palm-flat handshape include the following:

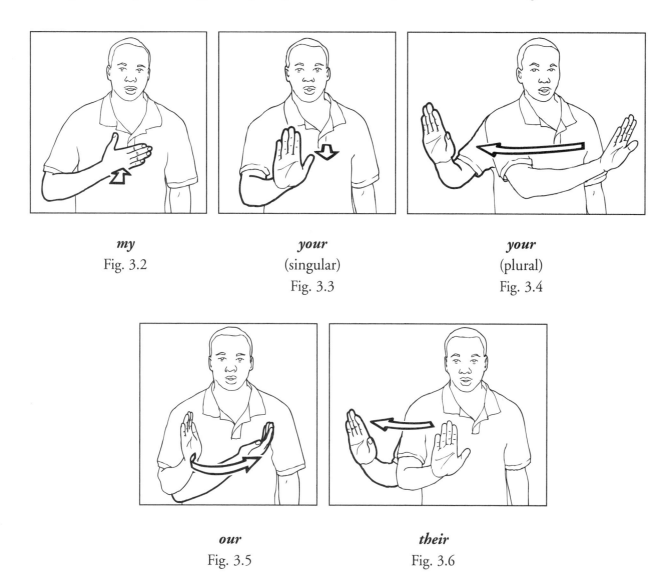

my
Fig. 3.2

your
(singular)
Fig. 3.3

your
(plural)
Fig. 3.4

our
Fig. 3.5

their
Fig. 3.6

2. Spatial Referencing for People, Places, and Things Not Present

In Unit 1, Grammar section, #1, spatial referencing for people, places and things that are present was explained. In ASL, persons, places, and things that are not present can be discussed without confusion by establishing points in space to the right or left side of the signer as locations for these absent persons, places, or things. These reference points remain constant during any single conversation unless moved as dictated by the conversation. All persons in the conversation use the same points, as established, to refer to the same persons, places, and things. One way of establishing these reference points is by pointing to a location immediately after the person, place, or thing being referenced has been mentioned.

Figure 3.7 shows how the referent to "the teacher" is being established in space and then referred to.

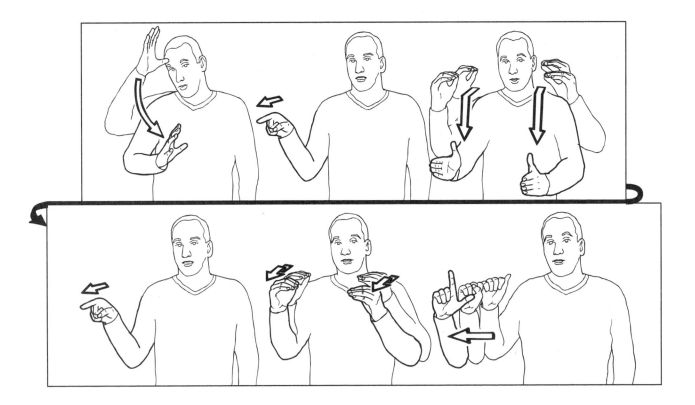

That man is the teacher. He teaches ASL.

Fig. 3.7

3. Use of Space for Contrasting and Comparing

To contrast or compare, signers establish absent referents (persons, places, and things) to the sides of the signing space. When making a comparison:

- The first referent is established to the non-dominant hand side of the signer.

- The second referent is established to the dominant hand side of the signer.

- When pointing or referring to each referent, the signer shifts his/her body and head slightly in the direction of the referent established on each side of the signing space.

An example of this is shown in Figure 3.8.

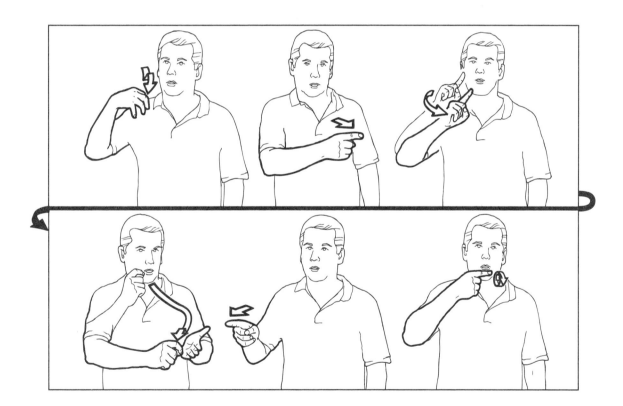

The boss is deaf and the secretary is hearing
Fig. 3.8

4. Person Affix for Changing Verbs to Nouns

In ASL, a person's occupation or profession can be indicated by adding the person affix to a verb. For example, *teach* can become *teacher* by adding the person affix. Other nouns you have learned that use the person affix include student (learn + person affix), *counselor (counsel* + person affix), and *supervisor (supervise* + person affix). As you can see from signs in this unit, not all nouns for professions or occupations use the person affix; for example, *boss, secretary, assistant, president,* and *policeman* do not use the person affix.

The person affix is most often used in formal signing; for example, in making a formal presentation or lecture. In informal, conversational use of ASL, this affix is often omitted because the person being referenced is clear and ASL tends to use verbs rather than nouns when referring to work or professions. For example, in answer to the question, "What do you do?", ASL signers tend to state, "I teach," rather than "I am a teacher." In addition, rather than use the person affix, some occupations are described. For example, a banker would be explained as "She works in a bank." A receptionist would be explained as "He works at the front desk."

Use of the person affix (formal) is shown in Figure 3.9 and use of the verb (informal) is shown in Figure 3.10.

I am a teacher. (formal)

Fig. 3.9

I teach. (informal)

Fig. 3.10

5. Use of Numbers and Quantifiers for Plural

In ASL, plurality may be expressed through the use of numbers and quantifiers such as *few, many, several, some,* and *none.* For example, if you wish to communicate "Three secretaries have many assistants," *"secretaries"* is pluralized by signing *"three,"* and *"assistants"* is made plural using the quantifier *"many."* This is shown in Figure 3.11 below.

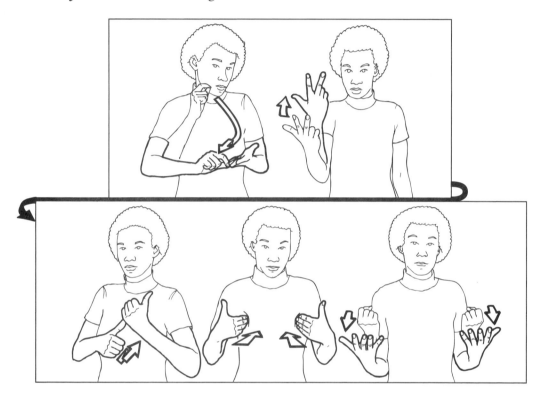

Three secretaries have many assistants.

Fig. 3.11

6. Use of *"No," "Not,"* and *"None"* for Negating Responses

Statements in ASL may be negated by using the signs meaning *no, not,* and *none.* These signs are always accompanied by a negative headshake and facial expression. As explained in Unit 2, Grammar section, #2, negative headshake and facial expression can also be used without the signs meaning *no, not,* and *none* to make negative statements. Examples are shown in Figures 3.12–3.14.

My office is not upstairs.

Fig. 3.12

No, this is not the ASL class.

Fig. 3.13

There are no female students in my ASL class.

Fig. 3.14

7. Use of Space for Signer's Perspective

When giving directions, signers use their own perspective to indicate right side or left side. The directions to the right side of a hallway, for example, would be signed by waving the hand toward the right side of the signer's signing space. Indicating the left side of a hallway would be signed by waving toward the left side of the signer's signing space.

Because signers give directions from their own perspective, when receiving sign language you must visualize from the signer's perspective. For example, you see your teacher signing something that looks like it is to your right side, but, from your teacher's perspective, it is actually on the left side. This is a challenging aspect of learning to receive and understand ASL directions. Because of this, before explaining directions, signers will sometimes turn their bodies to stand next to you so that you are both (signer and receiver) facing in the same direction. Your teacher will demonstrate and give you practice with using signer's perspective.

Figure 3.15 shows the sign indicating something is on the right side and 3.16 shows the sign indicating that something is on the left side from the signer's perspective

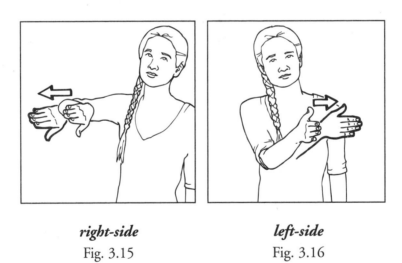

right-side
Fig. 3.15

left-side
Fig. 3.16

8. Real-World Orientation

Signers use real-world orientation when referring to locations. For example, suppose two signers are talking with each other. One asks, "Where do you work?" The other signer works in a school that is actually behind him. As illustrated in Figure 3.17, the person would answer, "My school is back over there."

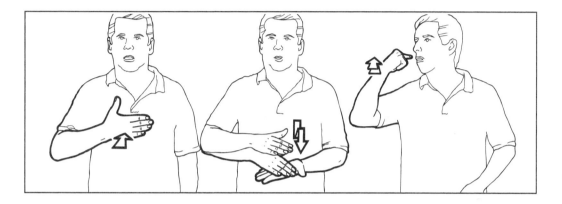

My school is back over there.
Fig. 3.17

1. Deaf President Now (DPN)!

2. Sign Variation

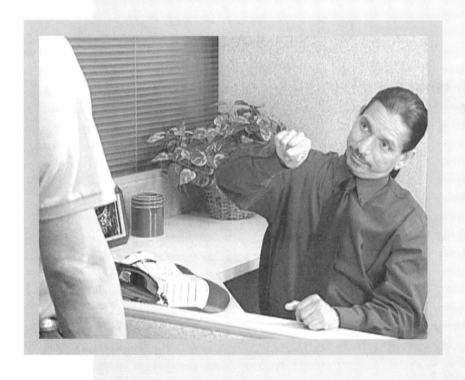

1. Deaf President Now (DPN)!

March 7–13, 1988 marks a historic week in the history of Deaf people. It is *The Week the World Heard Gallaudet* (Gannon, 1989). On March 13, 1988, after a week of protest and the closing down of the Gallaudet University campus in Washington, D.C., Elizabeth Zinser resigned as the seventh president of the university.

What was so significant about this university president's resignation? She was a hearing person who could not sign. She had no background or experience with deaf and hard-of-hearing people. She had been selected as the seventh hearing president of Gallaudet University, the first and only university in the world for deaf and hard-of-hearing students. She had been selected by the Gallaudet University Board of Trustees, which was composed predominantly of hearing persons, most of whom had little or no signing skills. She had been president of Gallaudet for only 7 days when she was forced to resign because Deaf students, with the support of some university faculty, finally said in ASL, *"Finish, Deaf president now!,"* which translates, "It's been long enough; Gallaudet University must have a Deaf president!"

This protest by students and faculty that forced the resignation of the seventh appointed president of Gallaudet was significant for the university, but it was profoundly more significant for deaf and hard-of-hearing students at all levels of education. Newell (1991) noted:

> The events of March, 1988, whereby students of Gallaudet University demanded that
> a deaf president and a majority deaf board of trustees be selected to run the college
> was the symbolic and real beginning of a new era . . . an era when we may finally see
> the full acceptance and use of ASL in the educational, social, and vocational lives of
> deaf people.

The Deaf President Now! protest signaled a new phase in the struggle of Deaf people to have a voice in the programs and institutions that affect their lives and the lives of deaf and hard-of-hearing people. At Gallaudet University, the impact of this protest was realized by the appointment of a Board of Trustees with a majority deaf membership and the appointment of the first deaf Gallaudet University President, Dr. I. King Jordan.

The Deaf President Now! protest caused profound changes in how institutions, agencies, and programs serving deaf and hard-of-hearing students view the role of deaf persons in setting the agenda. Since that historic month in the spring of 1988, the majority of superintendents hired at schools for the deaf have been deaf or hard-of-hearing. Since March 1988, agencies serving deaf and hard-of-hearing persons have included deaf and hard-of-hearing persons on advisory boards and in key administrative positions. Deaf people have a stronger voice in the decision making for programs that affect their lives. Deaf and hard-of-hearing administrators are leading programs and shaping the curriculum for educational programs and ASL is now more widely accepted as a viable part of educational and service programs.

But what actually happened from March 7–13, 1988? The effects are described above; for an in-depth description of the events, read *The Week the World Heard Gallaudet* by Jack Gannon (1989).

References

Gannon, J. (1989). *The Week the World Heard Gallaudet*. Washington, D.C.:Gallaudet University Press.

Newell, W. J. (1991). ASL is not a four-letter word: Deaf education can dance with the boogieman. In S. Polowe-Aldersley, et al. (Eds.), *CAID/CEASD Proceedings: Professions on Parade* (pp. 48–52). Washington, D.C.: CAID/CEASD.

2. Sign Variation

Signs shown in isolation in ASL dictionaries are referred to as citation form signs and they are similar to word entries in dictionaries for spoken languages. In using ASL for communication, however, the exact production of a sign, similar to the exact pronunciation of a spoken word, is influenced by several factors. For signs, these factors include the signs preceding and following a sign, the setting (for example, formal versus informal and small versus large group communication), individual signing styles, and dialectical sign variants.

As a beginning signer, these sign variants may lead to some confusions and frustration for you. For example, you may ask, "Why can't everyone produce a sign exactly as it is shown in my book or how my teacher produces it? and "Why can't there be just one sign for a concept or meaning?" It is important to appreciate that sign variants enrich ASL, providing options for how to best express your ideas and feelings. Just as people learn to understand the acceptable variations in the pronunciation of a spoken word and dialectical spoken word variants, with practice and experience you will begin to understand, recognize, and use the acceptable variants of a sign.

Figures 3.18 and 3.19 show citation and conversational forms for *man* and Figures 3.20 and 3.21 show two dialectical variations for *birthday.*

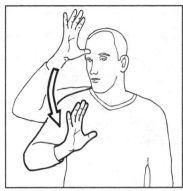

man (citation form)
Fig. 3.18

man (conversational form)
Fig. 3.19

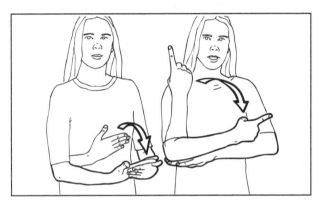
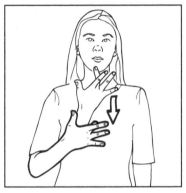

birthday
(widely used across US)
Fig. 3.20

birthday
(California)
Fig. 3.21

Readings

Kelly-Jones, N., & Hamilton, H. (1981). *Signs Everywhere.* Los Alamitos, CA: Modern Signs Press.

Baker, C., & Cokely, D. (1980). *American Sign Language: A teacher's resource text on grammar and culture.* Silver Spring, MD: T. J. Publishers.

Unit 3 Practice and Review Materials

1. Video Exercises

    – Sample Expressive Dialogue

    – Comprehension Practice

    – Expressive Practice Prompts

2. Grammar and Language, Culture, and Community Review Questions

3. Sign Vocabulary Illustrations

Sample Expressive Dialogue

Read the dialogue prompts below and then watch how each signer expresses these prompts on the video. Sign along with both Signer A and Signer B or with either Signer A or Signer B on the video. You may wish to practice this dialogue with a classmate outside of class time and your teacher may review this dialogue in class and ask you to sign this dialogue with a classmate.

Giving Directions

Signer A: Gain the attention of Signer B

Signer A: Ask where the bathroom is located

Signer B: Give directions (The bathroom is located on the left side of the hallway.)

Signer A: Confirm with the question "Is it on the right side?"

Signer B: Correct with "wave no" and give corrected information

Signer A: Say "thank you"

For the signing you observe, please write below any helpful notes and questions that you may have for your teacher.

Comprehension Practice 3.1

Watch the dialogue all the way through and then answer as many of the questions below as you can. If necessary, view the dialogue a second time to see whether you are able to understand more and answer any additional questions.

Asking for Directions

1. How does the man in the green shirt get the attention of the man in the blue shirt seated at the desk?

2. How does the man in the green shirt open the conversation?

3. What does the man in the green shirt ask about?

4. How does the man in the blue shirt indicate that the office is on a different floor?

5. What specific information about the location of the office does the man in the blue shirt give?

6. How does the man in the green shirt check to be sure that he has understood the directions?

7. How does the man in the blue shirt confirm that the man in the green shirt has understood correctly?

For the signing you observe, please write any helpful notes and questions that you may have for your teacher.

Comprehension Practice 3.2

Watch the dialogue all the way through and then answer as many of the questions below as you can. If necessary, view the dialogue a second time to see whether you are able to understand more and answer any additional questions.

Trying to Locate a Co-Worker

1. What question does the man ask to open the conversation?

2. What is the secretary's response?

3. How does the secretary distinguish between the two different people?

4. Whose office is upstairs and what is this person's job?

5. Who is the counselor and where is this person's office?

6. The man asks a clarifying question regarding the specific location of the office located downstairs. What does he try to clarify?

7. Describe how these two signers consistently use space to identify and talk about the two people that they are discussing.

For the signing you observe, please write any helpful notes and questions that you may have for your teacher.

Comprehension Practice 3.3

Watch the dialogue all the way through and then answer as many of the questions below as you can. If necessary, view the dialogue a second time to see whether you are able to understand more and answer any additional questions.

Finding a Classroom

1. How does the man open the conversation?

2. What does the man ask?

3. What is the answer to his question?

4. What sign does the woman use to indicate she needs to correct the man's understanding of the class location?

5. Where is the classroom located?

6. What is the classroom number?

7. How does the man confirm the information given to him?

For the signing you observe, please write any helpful notes and questions that you may have for your teacher.

Expressive Practice Prompts

These Expressive Practice Prompts show you the types of questions and statements you should be able to express in ASL by the end of Unit 3. Your teacher may use these Expressive Practice prompts in class. You should practice these with your practice partner and group outside of class as well.

1. Tell the class the name of your boss/department chairperson.

2. Count from 11 to 20.

3. Ask a classmate for the name of the secretary in his/her department.

4. Ask a classmate for the ASL classroom number.

5. Ask a classmate whether the president of this college is a man or a woman.

6. Express how many male and female students are in the class.

7. Ask a classmate how many secretaries work in the vice-president's office.

8. Express that the water fountain is on the right side of the hallway.

9. Express that the counselor's office is downstairs.

10. Express that the ASL lab is in the basement.

11. Express that your department has no secretary but it has two staff assistants.

12. Tell a classmate that there is no elevator. Tell him/her to use the stairs to go to the basement.

13. Ask a classmate whether he/she is faculty or staff.

14. Express that the ASL classroom is upstairs on the left side of the hallway.

15. Ask a classmate what his/her ASL teacher's name is.

16. Ask a classmate if his/her department has a student assistant. Ask what the student assistant's name is.

17. Ask a classmate if he/she has a school counselor.

18. Ask a classmate where the police department is.

Grammar and Language, Culture, and Community Review Questions

These questions will assist you as you read the Grammar and the Language, Culture, and Community sections in this unit.

1. What is the primary production difference between the personal pronoun signs *I/me, you, he/she/it* and the possessive pronoun signs *my/mine, your, his/her?*

2. When people or things are not present in the immediate area where you are signing, how can you make yourself clear about the person or thing you are referring to?

3. How do signers make use of space to contrast and compare things?

4. How does the verb sign **teach** become the noun sign **teacher?**

5. In what context or setting are you most likely to see the person affix sign used?

6. What are two ways that plurals may be expressed in ASL?

7. What are two ways that statements may be negated in ASL?

8. When giving directions, how does a signer communicate something is on the right side or the left side?

9. Provide an example of use of real-world orientation by a signer.

10. What was the main goal of the Deaf President Now! student protest at Gallaudet University in March 1988?

11. Explain two factors that influence how signs may vary in their production.

Sign Vocabulary Illustrations

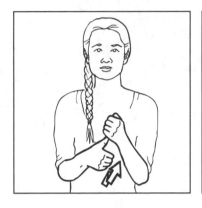

assistant, *aide*

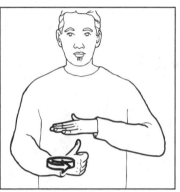

basement

bathroom, *restroom, toilet*

boss, *coach, chair*

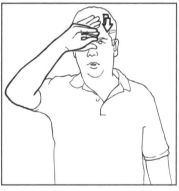

boy, *male*

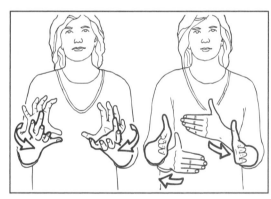

classroom

college, *university*

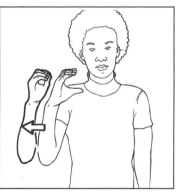

company (business)

counselor, *advisor*

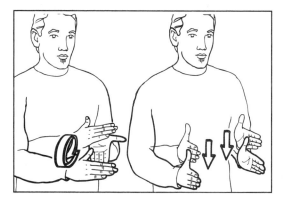

custodian, *janitor* (1)

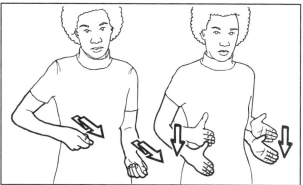

custodian, *janitor* (2)

dean

department

door

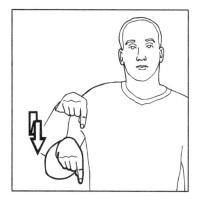

downstairs, *down*

elevator

faculty

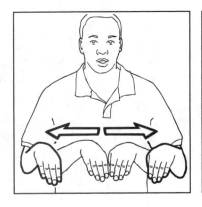

floor, *story, level*

girl, *female*

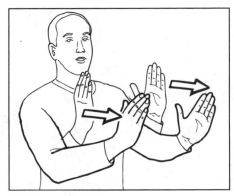

hallway

his/her/its

l-a-b

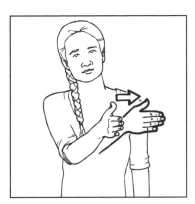

left-side

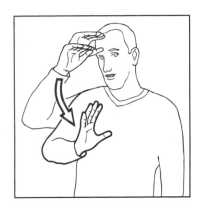

man

my

none, *no* (amount)

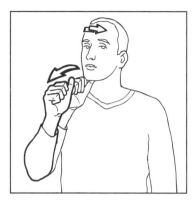

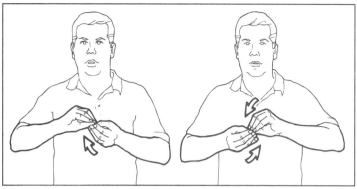

not

number

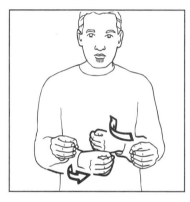

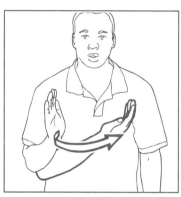

office (work space)

organization/office

our/ours

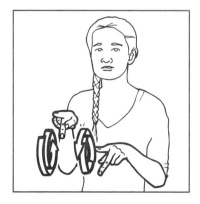

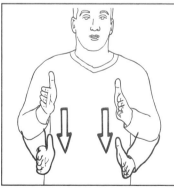

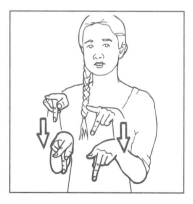

people

person (1)

person (2)

police

president

right-side

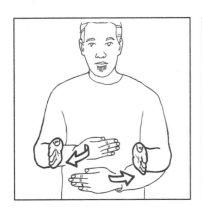

room, *office*

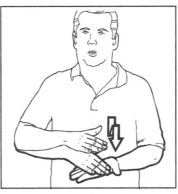

school

secretary

staff

stairway, *stairs*

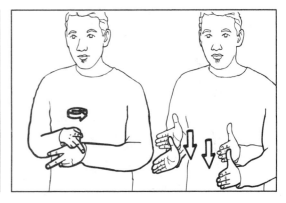

supervisor

their

university

upstairs, up

vice-president

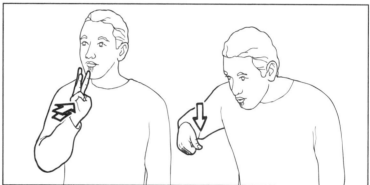

water fountain

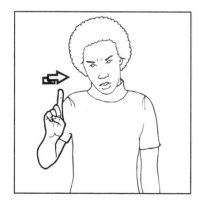

where

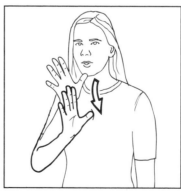

woman

your

Numbers

11

12

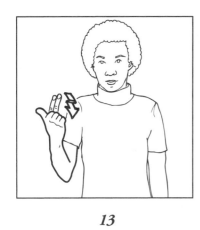

13

14

15

16

17

18

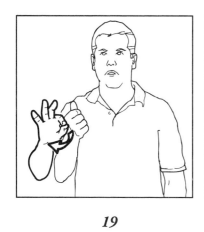 

19   *20*

Making Appointments

In this unit you learn to count from 21 to 30 and you learn time-related vocabulary and grammar for talking about scheduling appointments. Also, you learn the importance of maintaining eye contact when communicating in ASL and how writing may be used to facilitate communication between Deaf and hearing co-workers. In addition, you learn about classifiers and more about conversational regulators.

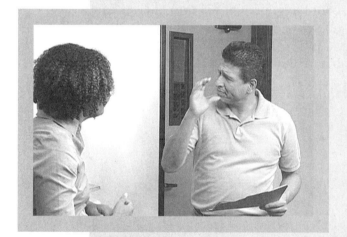

Unit 4 Overview

Learning Outcomes

1. Sign numbers from *21* to *30*

2. Ask where someone is

3. Give simple directions

4. Use *"excuse-me"* and *"wait"* to open a conversation

5. Use *"wait-a-minute"* to interrupt a conversation

6. Use number incorporation with time

7. Include the wh-question sign at the beginning and end of a question for emphasis

8. Learn about classifiers

9. Learn about the importance of eye contact and how to confirm information

10. Learn about telling time in ASL

11. Learn more about conversational regulators

Unit 4 Overview

Vocabulary

Sunday	*here*	*depart,* leave
Monday	*want*	*now*
Tuesday	*don't-want*	*write*
Wednesday	*see*	*leave-something*
Thursday	*right,* correct	*when*
Friday	*meeting,* conference	*make-record-of* (document)
Saturday	*sit*	*forget*
today	*stand*	*remember*
tomorrow	*wait*	*can*
yesterday	*appointment*	*can't*
morning, a.m.	*need to*	*sick*
noon	*talk-with,* converse	*know*
afternoon, p.m.	*to-change*	*don't-know*
evening, p.m.	*look-for*	*wait-a-minute*
night	*late*	*later*
day	*early*	*first*
21 to *30*	*come-to*	*last,* final
time	*go-to*	*full* (no room left)
hour	*#back*	*telephone,* phone
minute	*breakfast*	*f-a-x*
schedule, calendar, graph	*lunch*	*pager*
to-excuse, forgive	*dinner*	*e-m-a-i-l*
sorry, regret	*busy*	*to-email*
to-help, assist, aid	*maybe*	*address*

Grammar

1. Number Incorporation with Time Signs

2. Wh-Question Signs at the Beginning and End of Questions

3. Whole Entity Classifiers

Language, Culture, and Community

1. Classifiers

2. Importance of Eye Contact

3. Telling Time in ASL

4. Confirming Information

5. Opening Conversations with *"excuse-me"* and *"busy"*

6. Interrupting a Conversation with *"wait-a-minute"*

7. Use of Written Communication between Deaf and Non-Signing Hearing People

---

Practice and Review Materials

1. Video Exercises

   – Sample Expressive Dialogue

   – Comprehension Practice

   – Expressive Practice Prompts

2. Grammar and Language, Culture, and Community Review Questions

3. Sign Vocabulary Illustrations

1. Number Incorporation with Time Signs

2. Wh-Question Signs at the Beginning and End of Questions

3. Whole Entity Classifiers

1. Number Incorporation with Time Signs

In Unit 2, Learning ASL, you learned that number sign handshapes up to 5 may be incorporated into pronouns signs to communicate how many. Number sign handshapes (1 to 9) may also be incorporated into other signs to show how many. For example, the number sign handshapes *two,* *three,* and *five* combined with the movement for the sign *minute* produce the meanings *two-minutes, three-minutes,* and *five-minutes.* Numbers may also be incorporated to show *two-hours, three-hours,* and so forth. When telling time, number handshapes combine with the location parameter for *time* to produce *one-o'clock, two-o'clock, three-o'clock,* and so forth. When combining number signs with the sign *time,* palm orientation for numbers is always forward. See Figures 4.1–4.3 for examples of number incorporation with time adverbials.

five-minutes

Fig. 4.1

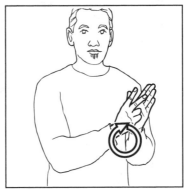

two-hours

Fig. 4.2

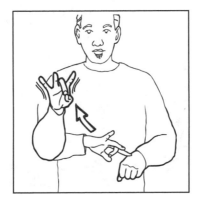

eight-o'clock

Fig. 4.3

2. Wh-Question Signs at the Beginning and End of Questions

Generally, Wh-question signs occur at the end of questions. However, if a signer wishes to emphasize that a question is being asked and an answer is being requested, Wh-question signs may occur at both the beginning and the end of questions. In Figures 4.4 and 4.5, the same Wh-question is expressed with the wh-question sign at the end of the question position (Figure 4.4) and with the wh-question sign at both the beginning and the end of the question for emphasis (Figure 4.5).

Where do you work now?

Fig. 4.4

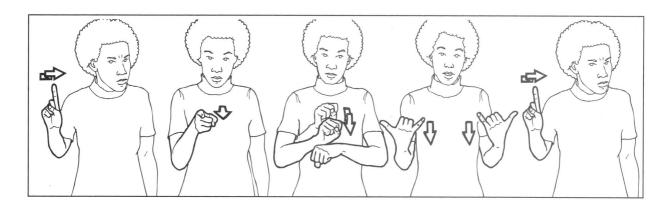

Where do you work now?

Fig. 4.5

3. Whole Entity Classifiers

A general explanation of classifiers is provided in #1 of the Language, Culture, and Community section of this unit. Whole entity classifiers, one type of classifier, are classifiers in which a handshape represents a whole person, animal, or inanimate object. Whole entity classifier handshapes include index finger, A, B, and bent V.

<u>Classifier Handshape</u>   <u>Used to Represent</u>

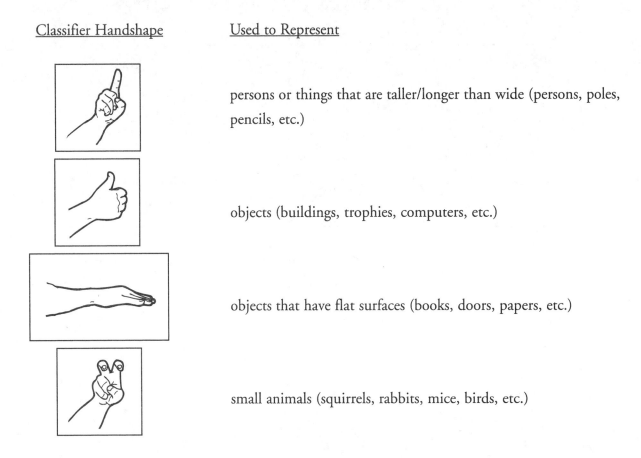

persons or things that are taller/longer than wide (persons, poles, pencils, etc.)

objects (buildings, trophies, computers, etc.)

objects that have flat surfaces (books, doors, papers, etc.)

small animals (squirrels, rabbits, mice, birds, etc.)

The Language, Culture, and Community Classifier information #1 (pp. 106–107) in this unit includes an example of a whole entity classifier handshape "index finger" used within the predicate or verb phrase in a sentence. In this example, the index finger handshape represents "a man."

In Unit 3, People at Work, the sign *door* was introduced. The "B handshape" occurs in this sign, but this is not an example of a whole entity classifier. The sign *door* is a noun just like the sign *man* is a noun. However, suppose a signer wishes to express that there are three doors located along one side of a hallway. In this expression, the noun *door* is signed and then the classifier handshape B is placed in three separate locations to indicate the three doors along the hallway. The classifier B handshape is being used to represent the door and is used within the predicate phrase in the statement, "There are three doors along that hallway." This expression is shown in Figure 4.6. The noun represented by a whole entity classifier must first be signed prior to using the whole entity classifier.

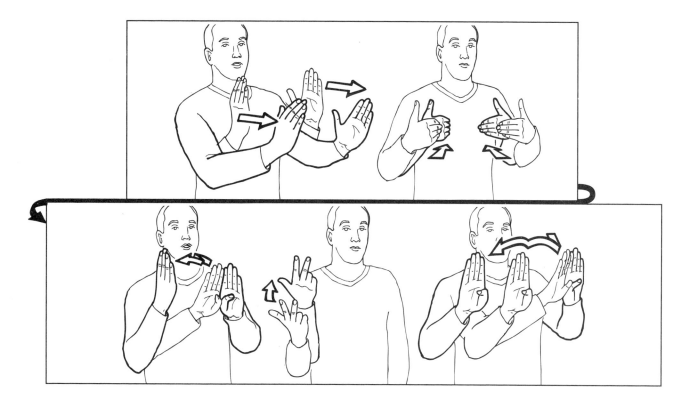

There are three doors along the hallway.

Fig. 4.6

Unit 4 Language, Culture, and Community

1. Classifiers

2. Importance of Eye Contact

3. Telling Time in ASL

4. Confirming Information

5. Opening Conversations with *"excuse-me"* and *"busy"*

6. Interrupting a Conversation with *"wait-a-minute"*

7. Use of Written Communication between Deaf and Non-Signing Hearing People

1. Classifiers

One remarkable aspect of ASL is the use of classifiers. Learning how and when they are used is important to becoming an effective ASL communicator.

There are several different types of classifiers. ASL uses classifiers to represent whole objects or people, to show how things are handled or used, to describe the parts of animate and inanimate things, and to specify the size, shape, and texture of objects and elements. Each classifier type uses a specific set of handshapes. These different types of classifiers, the handshapes used with them, and how they are used are introduced as they are relevant to the topics included in this curriculum. In this unit, whole entity classifiers are introduced (see #3 in the Grammar section of this unit).

What Are ASL Classifiers?

Classifiers are handshapes that are used to represent nouns in predicate phrases. Similar to pronouns in English, the referent or noun (what is being represented by the classifier) must be signed or clearly understood from context prior to using a classifier. For example, the index finger handshape, when used as a whole entity classifier, represents things that have the characteristic of "taller/longer than wide." Women, men, girls, boys, telephone poles, trees, and pencils are examples of entities that have the characteristic "taller/longer than wide" and, therefore, signers may use the index finger handshape to represent this "class" of nouns. The name classifier comes from the idea that there is a class of things represented by each particular classifier handshape.

Classifier handshapes with movements are used to express predicate phrases. A predicate is the "action" or "verb" part of a sentence. For example, if you say, "The man came up to me," "the man" is the subject, "came up to" is the verb, "me" is the object, and the verb and object together "came up to me" is called a predicate phrase. ASL uses classifiers to express the whole predicate phrase, "(he) came up to me," with one classifier sign. In this case, the sign *man* is produced and then the index finger classifier handshape moves from neutral signing space in front and to the side of the signer toward the signer, indicating "the man approaching the signer." This is shown in Figure 4.7 on the next page.

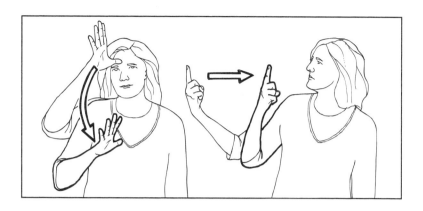

The man came up to me.
Fig. 4.7

2. Importance of Eye Contact

Because ASL is received through sight (a gestural–visual language), Deaf people maintain eye contact with each other when engaged in conversation. It is considered rude to break eye contact when communicating with a Deaf person. If eye contact is broken, a person cannot be "listening" and the Deaf person will stop signing.

For example, if two hearing people are meeting and the telephone rings, both will hear the phone ringing and they can choose to acknowledge and answer the phone call or ignore it. Sometimes one of the hearing persons may gesture with his/her finger to interrupt the conversation and say something like, "Let me get this call."

However, because eye contact is important in ASL conversations, if a hearing person is meeting with a Deaf person, a ringing telephone should be ignored until the conversation can be interrupted. If the hearing person decides to interrupt his/her conversation with a Deaf person, the hearing person should inform the Deaf person that the telephone is ringing and he/she (the hearing person) wishes to answer it. In this case, the hearing person should use a gesture with his/her index finger to indicate "wait a moment" and then communicate that the telephone is ringing and he/she wishes to answer it. Of course, alternatively the hearing person may ignore the telephone, allowing the answering machine to answer the call, and continue communicating with the Deaf person. In fact, if the meeting is a scheduled meeting, it may be considered appropriate etiquette to allow an answering machine to respond to telephone calls whether one is meeting with a Deaf or a hearing person.

3. Telling Time in ASL

In English when people are asked "What time is it?," they will often respond, "Ten to two" or "Twenty after three." In ASL the appropriate way to respond is by signing **Time one fifty**. Figures 4.8 and 4.9 show two examples of how clock time is expressed in ASL.

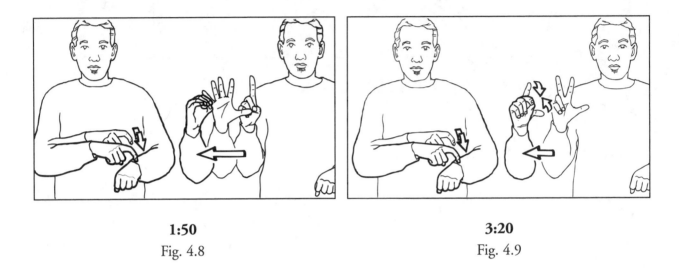

1:50

Fig. 4.8

3:20

Fig. 4.9

4. Confirming Information

In Unit 1, Introducing Ourselves, "wave no" was introduced as a conversational regulator signers use to communicate something that is not correct or to state that they do not wish to accept something that is offered. Another conversational behavior is the use of *right/correct* as either a question or a statement to confirm that something stated by another signer was understood correctly or is correct. Figures 4.10 and 4.11 show these uses.

Your name is Bob. Correct?

Fig. 4.10

That's right.
Fig. 4.11

5. Opening Conversations with *"excuse-me"* and *"busy"*

In Unit 1, Introducing Ourselves, **hello** and the "wave hand" gesture were introduced as ways in which signers open conversations. When signers wish to ask permission before beginning a conversation (for example, in the case of approaching someone in an office to make an appointment), they may use the phrase **excuse-me** or **busy** with yes/no-question expression to ask "Are you busy?" These conversational openers are requests for permission to interrupt the person addressed. Figures 4.12 and 4.13 show these conversational openers.

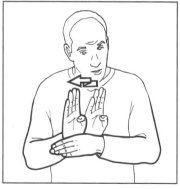

Excuse me?   **Are you busy?**
(May I interrupt you to ask a question?)
Fig. 4.12   Fig. 4.13

6. Interrupting a Conversation with *"wait-a-minute"*

In Unit 2, Learning ASL, the concept of conversational regulators was introduced with the examples of head nodding and ***oh-I-see.*** In this unit, another conversational regulator, ***wait-a-minute,*** is introduced. This sign is used to interrupt a signer when the receiver needs to attend to something else and cannot maintain eye contact with the signer. The importance of eye contact during signed conversations is explained in #2 of the Language, Culture, and Community section of this unit. Figure 4.14 shows an example of the use of ***wait-a-minute.***

Wait a moment. The phone is ringing.
Fig. 4.14

7. Use of Written Communication between Deaf and Non-Signing Hearing People

To make communication accessible and reduce anxiety with non-signing hearing people, Deaf people often use paper and pencil to write brief conversational messages. This method of communication is traditional among Deaf people as a strategy for communicating with non-signers.

Unit 4 Practice and Review Materials

1. Video Exercises

   – Sample Expressive Dialogue

   – Comprehension Practice

   – Expressive Practice Prompts

2. Grammar and Language, Culture, and Community Review Questions

3. Sign Vocabulary Illustrations

Sample Expressive Dialogue

Read the dialogue prompts below and then watch how each signer expresses these prompts on the video. Sign along with both Signer A and Signer B or with either Signer A or Signer B on the video. You may wish to practice this dialogue with a classmate outside of class time and your teacher may review this dialogue in class and ask you to sign this dialogue with a classmate.

Making an Appointment

Signer A: Open the conversation with an attention-getting behavior

Signer B: (You are on the phone) Express "Wait one minute"

Signer A: Express that you need to see the chairperson

Signer B: Explain that the chairperson is not here

Signer A: Ask what time the chairperson will be here

Signer B: Express that he/she will be back at 3:00

Signer A: Express that you will come back at 3:00

Signer B: Get Signer A's attention and ask for his/her name

Signer A: Give your first and last name

Signer B: Fingerspell the last name to confirm

Signer A: Confirm the name

Signer B: Close conversation with "Thank you"

Signer A: Close the conversation with "Ok, Fine"

For the signing you observe, please write any helpful notes and questions that you may have for your teacher.

Comprehension Practice 4.1

Watch the dialogue all the way through and then answer as many of the questions below as you can. If necessary, please view the dialogue a second time to see whether you are able to understand more and answer any additional questions.

A Problem Finding an Office

1. Whose office is the man looking for?

2. The office is down the hall on the left side. True or false?

3. What is the problem with the directions?

4. How does the man know there is a problem?

5. What alternative does the man ask about?

6. What non-manual signals does the woman use to help clarify the directions?

For the signing you observe, please write any helpful notes and questions that you may have for your teacher.

Comprehension Practice 4.2

Watch the dialogue all the way through and then answer as many of the questions below as you can. If necessary, view the dialogue a second time to see whether you are able to understand more and can answer any additional questions.

Scheduling an Appointment

1. What is the man's name?

2. Who does the man want to see?

3. Why can't the man see the person he has an appointment with? What option does the secretary offer?

4. How does the man respond? What does he want to do?

5. What does the secretary learn on the phone?

6. When the man re-enters the office, how does the secretary let him know that she needs to tell him additional information?

7. What alternative does the secretary offer?

8. Explain the directions the secretary provides so that the man can locate the office he needs to go to.

For the signing you observe, please write any helpful notes and questions that you may have for your teacher.

Comprehension Practice 4.3

Watch the dialogue all the way through and then answer as many of the questions below as you can. If necessary, view the dialogue a second time to see whether you are able to understand more and answer any additional questions.

Rescheduling an Appointment

1. How does the woman open the conversation?

2. How does the man respond?

3. How long is the woman asked to wait?

4. The woman explains that she has been waiting for a long time. How does she modify the sign *to-wait* to indicate this?

5. The man offers an appointment at what time and day?

6. How does the woman respond?

7. What is the woman's name?

For the signing you observe, please write any helpful notes and questions that you may have for your teacher.

12/1

Expressive Practice Prompts

These Expressive Practice Prompts show you the types of questions and statements you should be able to express in ASL by the end of Unit 4. Your teacher may use these Expressive Practice Prompts in class. You should practice these with your practice partner and group outside of class as well.

1. Express that you need to see a teacher. Express this in three different ways.

2. Express that you have an appointment with Dr. Jones.

3. Tell a classmate to please sit and wait 5 minutes.

4. Express that your boss is in a meeting.

5. Express that you have an appointment this Tuesday at 10:00 a.m.

6. Express that the office is not on this floor. Express that it is upstairs on the third floor.

7. Sign the days of the week.

8. Ask a classmate what time he/she can come tomorrow for an appointment.

9. Express that your boss is not here.

10. Express that you are busy today. Ask if the appointment can be changed to tomorrow.

11. Tell your classmate your work phone number.

12. Express that the teacher is not here. Tell the person to write a note and leave it with you.

13. A classmate asks to see a counselor. The counselor is not here. Apologize and express that the counselor is not here.

14. Express that your schedule is full today. Ask if the person can come back tomorrow.

15. Fingerspell your first and last names.

16. Ask a classmate what time he/she comes to work.

17. Ask a classmate if his/her schedule is full this afternoon.

18. Tell a classmate to send you a fax this afternoon.

19. Express that you are looking for the counselor and that you need an appointment today.

20. Count from 21 to 30.

Grammar and Language, Culture, and Community Review Questions

These questions will assist you as you read the Grammar and Language, Culture, and Community sections in this unit.

1. How are the questions being expressed in Figures 4.4 and 4.5 different and why?

2. Name two whole entity classifier handshapes and tell what they may be used to represent.

3. What rule about using classifiers is demonstrated in Figure 4.6?

4. How are classifier handshapes used in ASL sentences?

5. Why is eye contact important when communicating in ASL?

6. Provide an example of the appropriate way in ASL to respond to the question "What time is it?"

7. Identify an ASL conversational regulator that may be used to communicate something stated by another signer was understood correctly or is correct.

8. Identify two ASL conversational regulators that may be used as conversational openers to request permission to interrupt the people addressed.

9. How is the ASL conversational regulator *wait-a-minute* used?

10. Why do Deaf people often write brief conversational messages?

Sign Vocabulary Illustrations

address

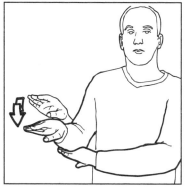

afternoon, p.m.

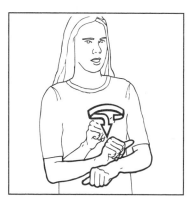

appointment

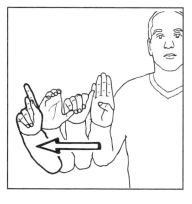

#back

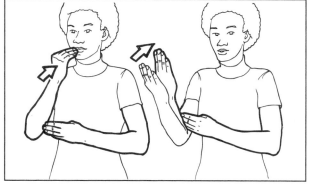

breakfast (1)

breakfast (2)

busy

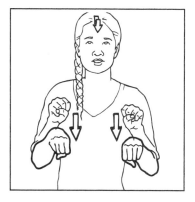

can

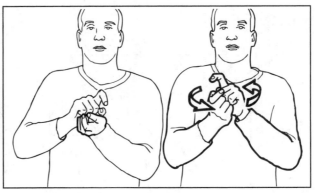

can't   *to-change*

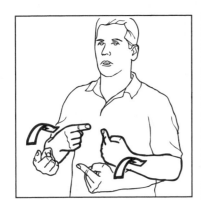

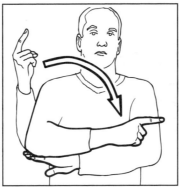

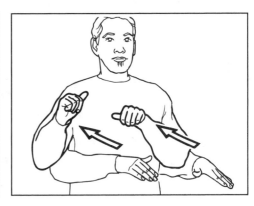

come-to   *day*   *depart,* leave

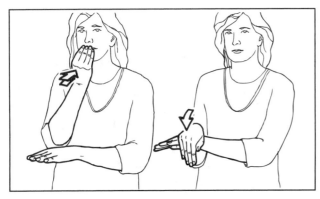

dinner (1)   *dinner* (2)

don't-know

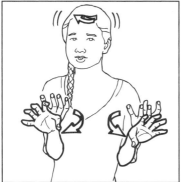

don't-want

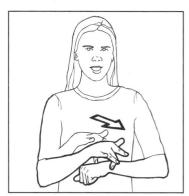

early

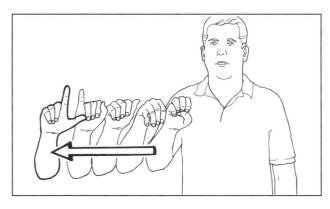

e-m-a-i-l

to-email

evening, p.m.

to-excuse, forgive

f-a-x

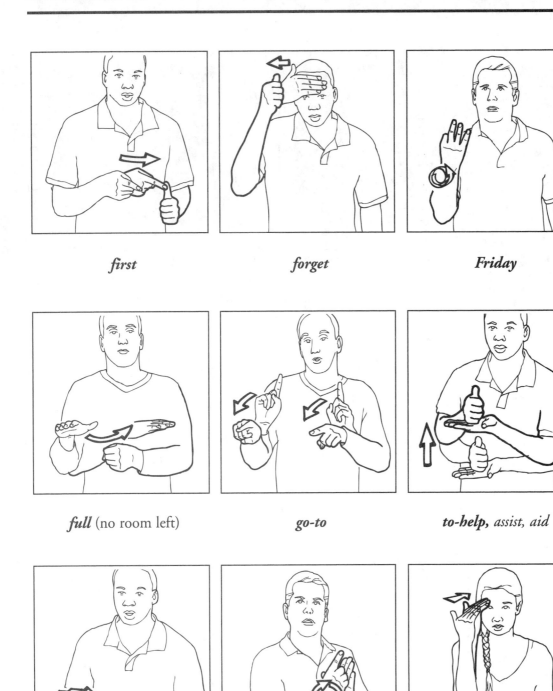

first   *forget*   **Friday**

full (no room left)   **go-to**   **to-help,** *assist, aid*

here   *hour*   *know*

last, final

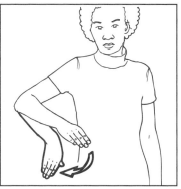

late

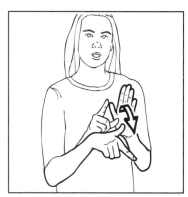

later

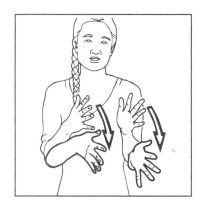

leave-something

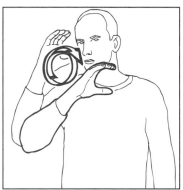

look-for

lunch (1)

lunch (2)

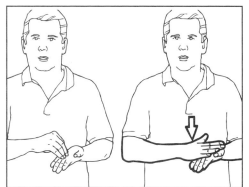

make-record-of (document)

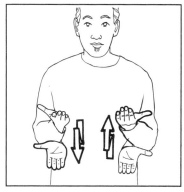

maybe

meeting, *conference*

minute

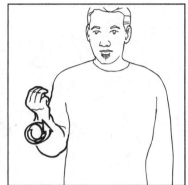

Monday

morning, *a.m.*

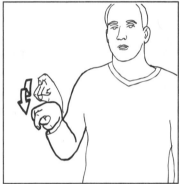

need-to

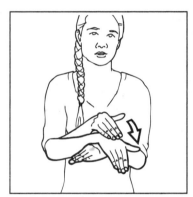

night

noon

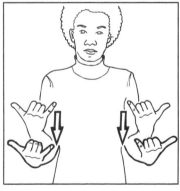

now

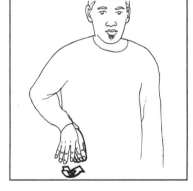

pager

remember

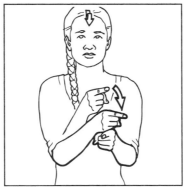

right, *correct*

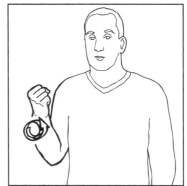

Saturday

schedule, *calendar, graph*

see

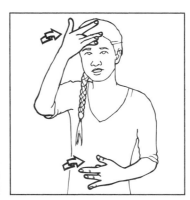

sick

sit

sorry, *regret*

stand

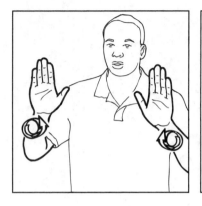

Sunday

talk-with, *converse*

telephone, *phone*

Thursday

time

today

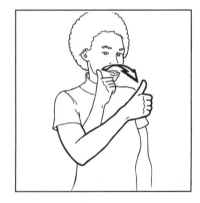

tomorrow

Tuesday

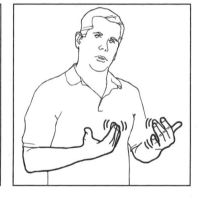

wait

wait-a-minute

want

Wednesday

when

write

yesterday

Numbers

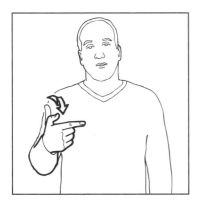

21

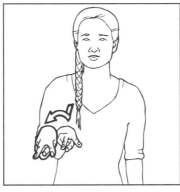

22

23 (1)

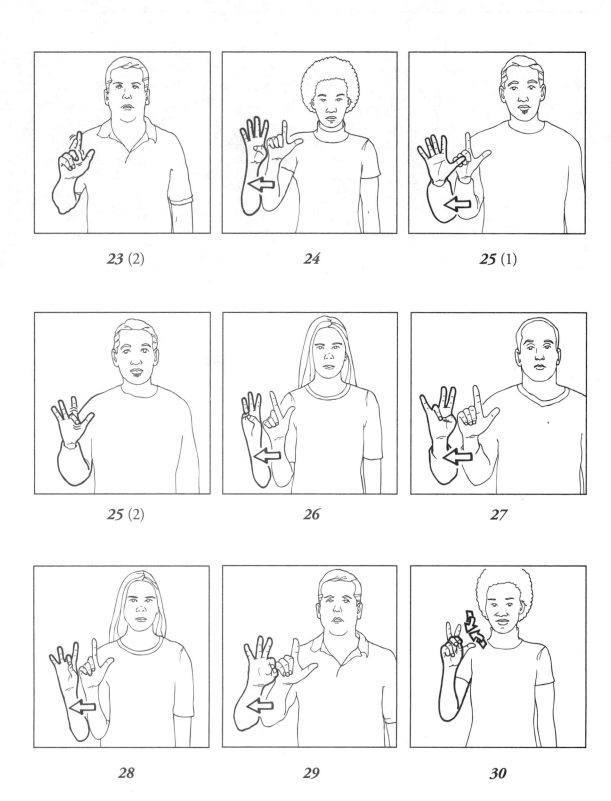

23 (2)   **24**   **25** (1)

25 (2)   **26**   **27**

28   **29**   **30**

In this unit you learn vocabulary and grammatical structures that relate to discussing your work. You also learn about technology that Deaf people use in their daily lives and how Deaf people communicate with co-workers.

Unit 5 Overview

Learning Outcomes

1. Learn sign vocabulary for office supplies and colors

2. Talk about work duties

3. Express likes and dislikes about work responsibilities

4. Express that something happens habitually

5. Express statements and questions using topic/comment structure

6. Discuss related people, places, and things using listing on the non-dominant hand

7. Learn about technology that helps Deaf people in their daily lives

8. Learn how Deaf people communicate with co-workers

Vocabulary

typing, keyboarding	*orange*	*why*
filing	*brown*	*paper*
copying	*black*	*pencil*
answer, respond	*white*	*p-e-n*
answering machine	*gray*	*eraser*
duty	*make*	*paper-clip*
responsibility	*read*	*stapler*
what-to-do	*clean-up*	*ruler*
every day, daily	*love-it*	*computer*
routine	*to-like*	*printer* (machine)
color	*enjoy, pleasure*	*television*
blue	*so-so*	*book*
green	*o-k*	*desk/table*
yellow	*don't-like*	*chair, seat*
purple	*bored-with*	*tape* (adhesive)
red	*hate*	*rubber-band*
pink	*detest-it*	*things*

Unit 5 Overview

Grammar

1. Sign Verb Movement for Repeated Action

2. Sign Movement Modifications and Non-Manual Signals for Degree

3. Topic/Comment Sentence Structure

4. Reversal of Orientation and Movement for Negation

5. Listing on the Non-Dominant Hand for Related Items

Language, Culture, and Community

1. Closing a Conversation with *"o-k"*

2. Technology in the Lives of Deaf People

3. How Do Deaf People Communicate with Co-Workers?

Practice and Review Materials

1. Video Exercises

   – Sample Expressive Dialogue

   – Comprehension Practice

   – Expressive Practice Prompts

2. Grammar and Language, Culture, and Community Review Questions

3. Sign Vocabulary Illustrations

1. Sign Verb Movement for Repeated Action

2. Sign Movement Modifications and Non-Manual Signals for Degree

3. Topic/Comment Sentence Structure

4. Reversal of Orientation and Movement for Negation

5. Listing on the Non-Dominant Hand for Related Items

1. Sign Verb Movement for Repeated Action

When regular or habitual action is being stressed, this is communicated by repetition of sign verb movement. For example, see the signs for ***writing*** and ***cleaning*** in Figures 5.1 and 5.2.

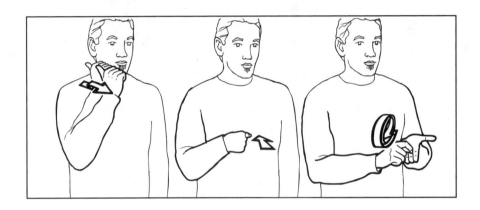

I write everyday.
(repeat movement of ***write***)
Fig. 5.1

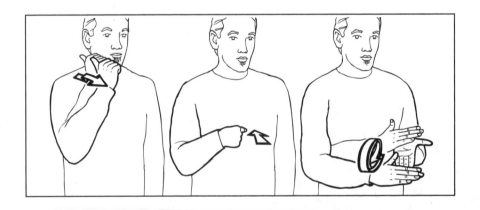

I clean up everyday.
(repeat movement of ***clean-up***)
Fig. 5.2

2. Sign Movement Modifications and Non-Manual Signals for Degree

In English, words such as "very," "a little bit," really," "quite," and "too" are used to convey degree. In ASL, the meaning of these modifiers may be communicated by sign movement modifications with non-manual signals (primarily facial expressions). For example, the sign *blue* may be modified, with appropriate facial expression and changes to the movement parameter, to mean "deep blue." This and one other example with similar sign movement modifications and non-manual signals for degree are shown in Figures 5.3–5.6 below.

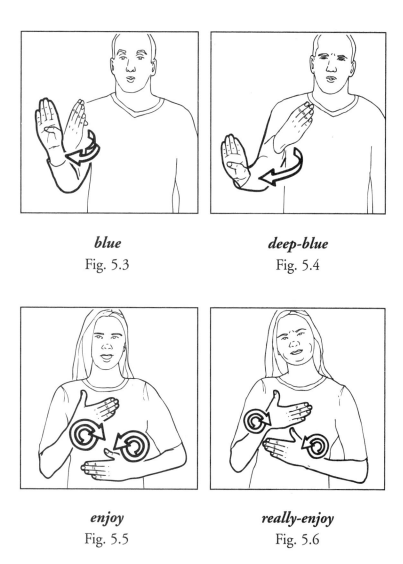

blue

Fig. 5.3

deep-blue

Fig. 5.4

enjoy

Fig. 5.5

really-enjoy

Fig. 5.6

3. Topic/Comment Sentence Structure

One common ASL sentence structure is "topic/comment" structure. With topic/comment structure, a signer first communicates the "topic" or "focus" of the sentence and then offers a comment. This structure is accompanied by non-manual signals, which indicate that a topic and a comment are being expressed. The topic portion of the sentence is marked by raised eyebrows and the comment portion of the sentence is marked with the non-manual signals that are appropriate to the type of sentence being expressed. For example, if the comment portion of the sentence is a statement, then it will be accompanied by an affirmative head nod. If the comment portion of the sentence is a yes/no question, then it will be accompanied by a yes/no question facial expression. There is a slight pause between the topic and the comment portions of the sentence. Figure 5.7 shows a topic/comment sentence structure example with the topic being "typing" and the comment being a statement, "I like it." Figure 5.8 shows a topic/comment sentence structure example with the topic being "typing" and the comment being a question, "Do you like it?"

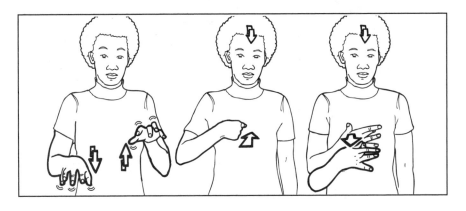

I like typing.
Fig. 5.7

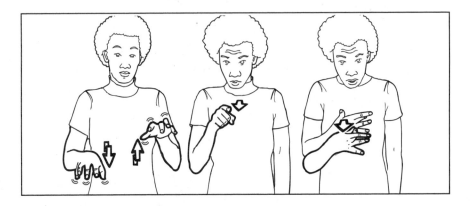

Do you like typing?
Fig. 5.8

4. Reversal of Orientation and Movement for Negation

Three unique verbs in ASL incorporate the concept of negation by reversing sign orientations and movements. Three verb signs that demonstrate this ASL grammatical feature are shown in Figures 5.9–5.14.

to-like

Fig. 5.9

don't-like

Fig. 5.10

know

Fig. 5.11

don't-know

Fig. 5.12

want

Fig. 5.13

don't-want

Fig. 5.14

5. Listing on the Non-Dominant Hand for Related Items

Signers use the non-dominant hand to "list" and discuss several people (names, ages, etc.), places, or things, to discuss sequencing of events, and to discuss steps in processes or procedures. For example, suppose someone asks you about your job duties or responsibilities. If you have two primary duties, you would use your index finger and middle finger on your non-dominant hand to indicate these two duties. First you would point to your index finger and "name" your first duty, and then point to your middle finger and name your second duty. If you have three duties, you will use the number handshape **three** and point to your thumb for the first duty, your forefinger for the second duty, and your middle finger for the third duty. If you have four main duties, then you would use the number handshape **four**. Figures 5.15 and 5.16 show examples of listing on the non-dominant hand for two and three duties, respectively.

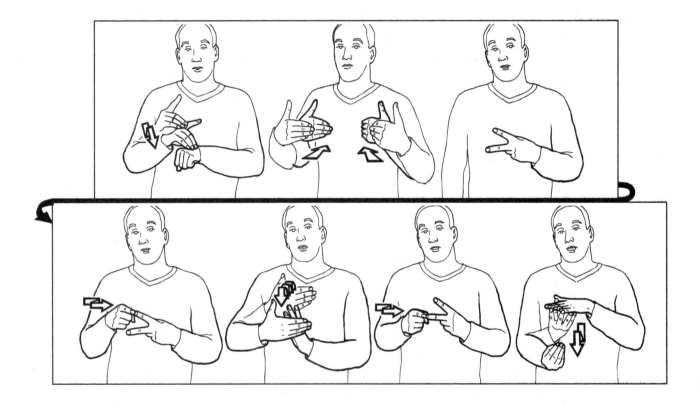

I have two duties, filing and copying.

Fig. 5.15

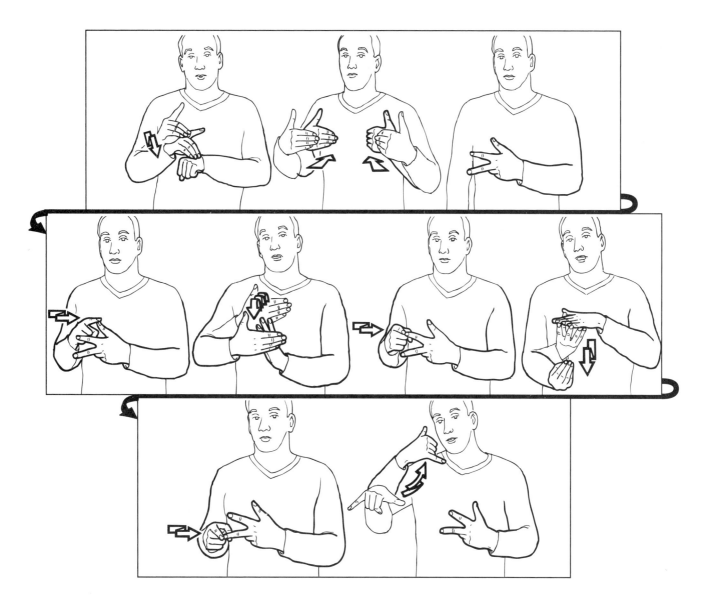

I have three duties, filing, copying, and answering the phone.

Fig. 5.16

Unit 5 Language, Culture, and Community

1. Closing a Conversation with **"o-k"**

2. Technology in the Lives of Deaf People

3. How Do Deaf People Communicate with Co-Workers?

1. Closing a Conversation with *"o-k"*

In Unit 2, Learning ASL, you learned the sign ***thank-you/you're-welcome.*** In ASL this sign may be used by both parties to close a conversation politely. Usually it is used by persons who do not know each other well and where formality is required. In this unit, the sign ***o-k*** is introduced. This sign may be used to close a conversation when signers are indicating acceptance or acquiescence. Figures 5.17 and 5.18 show ***o-k*** and ***thank-you/you're-welcome.***

o-k
(I agree with you.)
Fig. 5.17

thank-you/you're-welcome
Fig. 5.18

2. Technology in the Lives of Deaf People

Deaf people face the challenge of living in a world where sight must be substituted for sound. When the newborn infant cries in the middle of the night, how do Deaf parents know? When the telephone rings or the doorbell chimes or the smoke detector goes off, how do Deaf people recognize and respond to these "signals"? How do Deaf people know what the characters on their favorite sitcom say? How do Deaf people contact their friends and make appointments with doctors? Many daily aspects of life seem to depend on sound and hearing, yet Deaf people routinely go about their daily lives with little difficulty. Why? Because they use technological innovations, many of which they have invented or helped to invent, that turn the world of sound into a world of vision.

Deaf people's homes are equipped with a combination of wiring and infrared, wireless, and digital signaling devices to respond with flashing lights when specific sounds occur. The baby cries in the next room. A light begins to flicker mimicking the coos or cries of the infant. The Deaf parents know that there is a need to respond or that they can ignore the light. The doorbell, telephone, and smoke detector trigger other lights and have their own distinctive patterns. When a Deaf family sits down to watch television, closed captions (required on all TVs 13 inches or larger made in the United States since 1993) display what the characters are saying. To make appointments, Deaf people can pick up the telephone and, using telecommunication devices, their computers, or video phones, they can call directly to make appointments with others using relay services.

Technology is always changing. Today Deaf people use Video Relay Service, or VRS. There are a number of VRS providers located in cities across the United States. Deaf people use specially equipped television monitors connected to the Internet to contact a video relay interpreter, who serves as an intermediary between deaf/hard-of-hearing and hearing callers. VRS allows Deaf people to communicate freely in sign language.

In addition to the above traditional technologies that help Deaf people substitute sight for sound, the advent of the Internet, email, and cell phone towers now allows Deaf people to easily contact others with e-mail addresses using instant messaging, pagers, and other personal data assistant devices. Who knows what the future holds? "Beam me up Scotty!"

Note: As technology changes, through natural sign development processes, signs evolve and new signs are coined to reflect these changes in technology. Your instructor may include in your instruction signs in use for "current" technology. (In Unit 6, Sharing Personal Information, #2 of the Language, Culture, and Community section discusses mechanisms for developing ASL signs.)

3. How Do Deaf People Communicate with Co-Workers?

Deaf people use many strategies to communicate with co-workers, including ASL, speech, speechreading, simultaneous communication (sign language and spoken language together), natural gestures, interpreting, and writing. Often, Deaf people use a combination of these strategies. Some Deaf people can speak and speechread well. However, speaking and speechreading are not always reliable, and it is important to be aware that a Deaf person may have understandable speech, but she/he may not be able to understand fully when someone speaks. Sometimes the choice of communication strategies to use is dependent on the seriousness of the communication situation. Many Deaf people prefer to use ASL or some form of sign language as a first choice for communication with co-workers, and writing as a second choice. In addition, Deaf people often use writing for short, clarifying notes or to highlight their main ideas. Writing is often the most reliable form of communication when a co-worker does not know basic ASL. Also, Deaf workers may use gestural communication to facilitate routine and repetitive tasks, and if their co-workers show an interest, they may teach co-workers some basic ASL.

With the passage of the Americans with Disabilities Act (ADA) in 1990, Deaf workers have greater communication access in work environments. Employers are required to provide reasonable accommodations for Deaf and hard-of-hearing workers. These accommodations include interpreters, adapted telephones with volume control, telecommunication devices and other adaptive communication technologies and techniques.

1. Video Exercises

    – Sample Expressive Dialogue

    – Comprehension Practice

    – Expressive Practice Prompts

2. Grammar and Language, Culture, and Community Review Questions

3. Sign Vocabulary Illustrations

Sample Expressive Dialogue

Read the dialogue prompts below and then watch how each signer expresses these prompts on the video. Sign along with both Signer A and Signer B or with either Signer A or Signer B on the video. You may wish to practice this dialogue with a classmate outside of class time and your teacher may review this dialogue in class and ask you to sign this dialogue with a classmate.

Discussing Job Responsibilities

Signer A: Get attention by waving hand in line of sight for Signer B

Signer B: Acknowledge Signer A

Signer A: Ask Signer B what job responsibilities/duties he/she has

Signer B: Respond with three responsibilities/duties

Signer A: Pick one responsibility/duty and ask Signer B if he/she likes it

Signer B: Express that you dislike it strongly

Signer A: Ask Signer B which of the other two responsibilities/duties he/she likes

Signer B: Express opinion about one or both of the remaining responsibilities/duties

For the signing you observe, please write any helpful notes and questions that you may have for your teacher.

Comprehension Practice 5.1

Watch the dialogue all the way through and then answer as many of the questions below as you can. If necessary, view the dialogue a second time to see whether you are able to understand more and answer any additional questions.

Giving Directions for a Task

1. How does the conversation open?

2. What instructions is the student given?

3. What detail does the student misunderstand?

4. How does the secretary correct the misunderstanding?

5. After the first task is completed, what does the secretary want the student to do?

6. What does the student ask?

7. Which file cabinet does the secretary want the copies put in?

For the signing you observe, please write any helpful notes and questions that you may have for your teacher.

Comprehension Practice 5.2

Watch the dialogue all the way through and then answer as many of the questions below as you can. If necessary, view the dialogue a second time to see whether you are able to understand more and answer any additional questions.

Describing Work Responsibilities

1. What is the woman's occupation?

2. What are the five duties she mentions?

    a. _____

    b. _____

    c. _____

    d. _____

    e. _____

3. When the woman expresses her duties, how does she indicate that most of her duties involve very repetitive activities?

4. What does the man ask next?

5. Which duty does the woman like the best and what sign does she use to express this?

6. Which duty does she like the least?

7. How does the woman introduce and make reference to her five work duties?

For the signing you observe, please write any helpful notes and questions that you may have for your teacher.

Comprehension Practice 5.3

Watch the dialogue all the way through and then answer as many of the questions below as you can. If necessary, view the dialogue a second time to see whether you are able to understand more and answer any additional questions.

Discussing Work

1. What does the first man ask?

2. What does the second man answer?

3. Does the man in the green shirt have a favorable impression of the person in question?

4. What does the first man ask next?

5. What do the men agree about?

6. What two different signs do the men use to express their dislike?

For the signing you observe, please write any helpful notes and questions that you may have for your teacher.

Comprehension Practice 5.4

Watch the dialogue all the way through and then answer as many of the questions below as you can. If necessary, view the dialogue a second time to see whether you are able to understand more and answer any additional questions.

Talking about Departments

1. What is the first question the woman asks the man?

2. What are the names of these two people?

3. What is the general topic the two people talk about in this dialogue?

4. Which person has a female boss? What is the boss' name?

5. How many secretaries work in the woman's department? What are their names?

6. How does the man contrast the number of secretaries versus the number of student assistants working in his department?

7. How many teachers are in each of their departments?

8. What type of worker does the man have in his department that the woman does not have in her department?

9. What sign does the woman use for negation when discussing a type of worker that her department does not have?

10. How many people are in the woman's department?

11. The woman tells us about the groups of people that work in her department. Describe how she uses her body and space to separate each of these groups.

For the signing you observe, please write any helpful notes and questions that you may have for your teacher.

Expressive Practice Prompts

These Expressive Practice Prompts show you the types of questions and statements you should be able to express in ASL by the end of Unit 5. Your teacher may use these Expressive Practice Prompts in class. You should practice these with your practice partner and group outside of class as well.

1. Ask a classmate if he/she likes work.

2. Express three things you do on your job.

3. Express that you hate filing and copying.

4. Ask a classmate what his/her job duties are.

5. Express one thing you like/enjoy doing on your job and one thing you dislike/hate doing.

6. Express two job duties/responsibilities and indicate which one you like best.

7. Express something you do every day. (Include the sign *everyday* in your response).

8. Express that you hate cleaning up your desk.

9. Name three objects that you may find in a desk.

10. Ask a classmate whether his/her TV is black and white or color.

11. Express that you want a classmate to make 20 copies on green paper and 10 copies on yellow paper.

12. Ask a classmate where the blue book is.

13. Express colors you like and dislike.

14. Sign five different colors.

Grammar and Language, Culture, and Community Review Questions

These questions will assist you as you read the Grammar and Language, Culture, and Community sections in this unit.

1. What sign movement is being used to communicate that something is done regularly or habitually?

2. Look at Figures 5.3–5.6. How are the signs **blue** and **enjoy** being modified to show intensity?

3. Look at Figures 5.7 and 5.8. What is this type of ASL structure called and what non-manual signals accompany this structure?

4. Look at Figures 5.9–5.14. How is the concept of negation being expressed in the examples shown?

5. Describe how signers discuss two or more people, places, or things for example, work duties.

6. Name two technologies that help Deaf people respond to important sounds in the environment and name one technology that helps Deaf people communicate easily with one another over distances.

7. Describe the variety of ways that Deaf people communicate with co-workers.

8. What law protects the rights of deaf workers to reasonable accommodations in the workplace?

9. Explain when it is appropriate to use the sign **"o-k"** to close a conversation.

Sign Vocabulary Illustrations

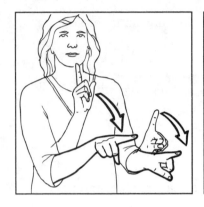
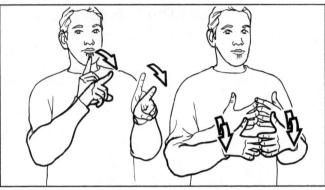

answer, *respond*   **answering machine**

black   **blue**   **book**

bored-with   **brown**   **chair,** *seat*

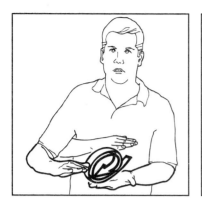

clean-up

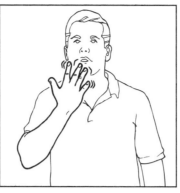

color

computer

copying

desk/table (1)

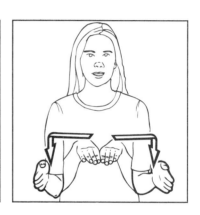

desk/table (2)

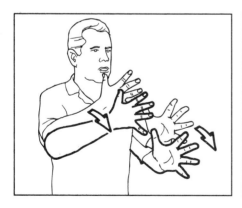

detest-it

don't-like

duty

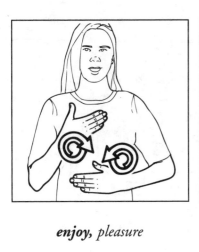

enjoy, *pleasure*

eraser

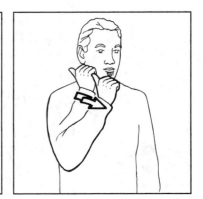

everyday, *daily*

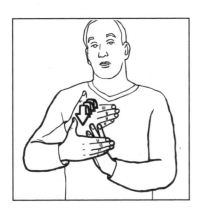

filing

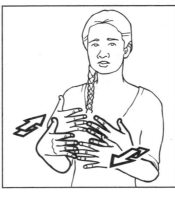

gray

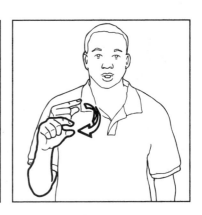

green

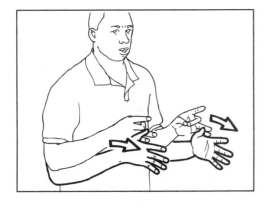

hate

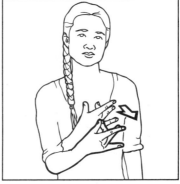

to-like

love-it

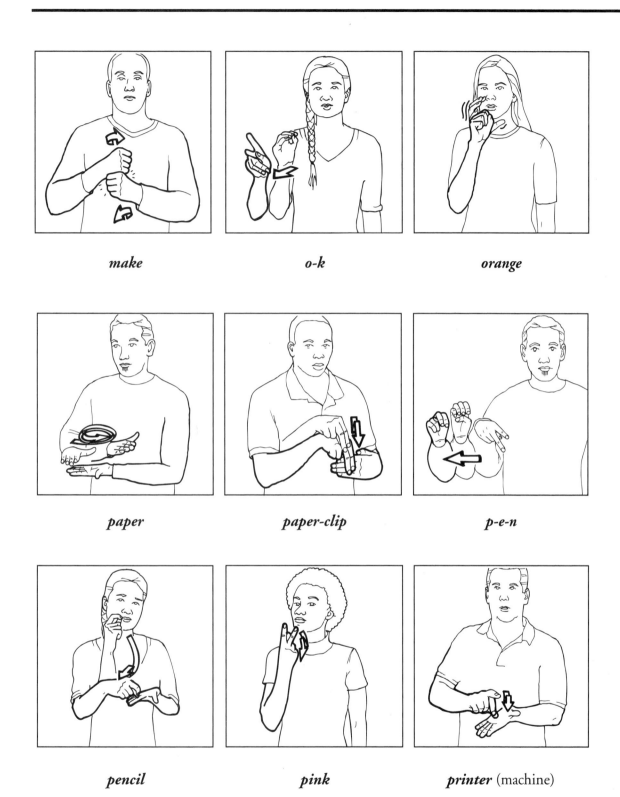

make   *o-k*   *orange*

paper   *paper-clip*   *p-e-n*

pencil   *pink*   *printer* (machine)

purple

read

red

responsibility

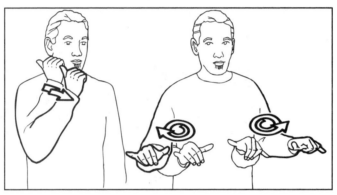

routine

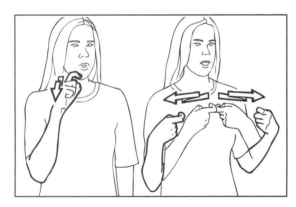

rubber-band

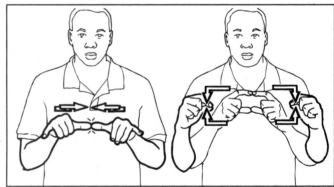

ruler

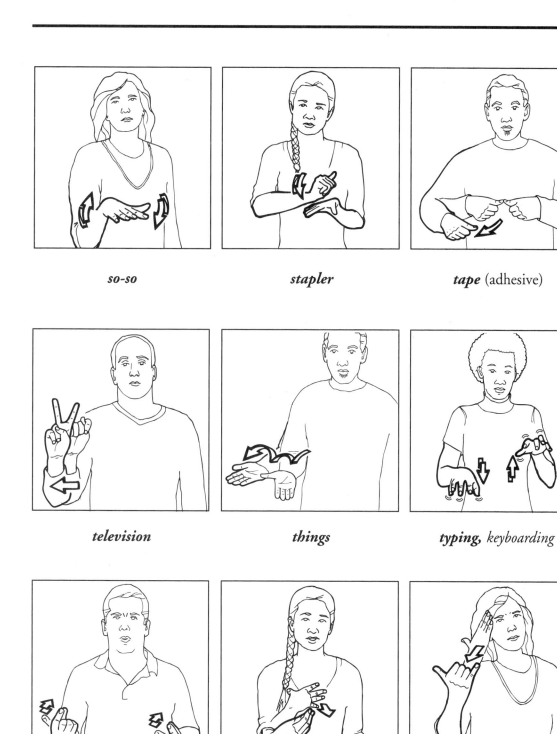

so-so

stapler

tape (adhesive)

television

things

typing, keyboarding

what-to-do

white

why

yellow

Sharing Personal Information

In this unit you learn to talk about your family and you learn that signs sharing a common element of meaning often share a common production parameter. You also learn the special place that Deaf children of Deaf parents hold in Deaf culture and the high value placed on personal and social relationships with other Deaf people.

Unit 6 Overview

Learning Outcomes

1. Ask about and tell others about family

2. Show the birth order of children and/or brothers and sisters

3. Learn that signs sharing a common element of meaning often share a common production parameter

4. Learn about the special place Deaf children of Deaf parents hold in the Deaf culture and community

Vocabulary

married	*separated*	*daughter*
husband	*divorced*	*brother*
wife	*remarry*	*sister*
single	*family*	*children*
friend	*father*	*child*
boyfriend	*mother*	*have* (possessive)
girlfriend	*parents*	*age, old*
sweetheart	*pregnant*	*how-old*
go-steady	*baby*	*31* to *60* *
engaged	*son*	

*Signs for *31* to *60* are not included in the Unit 6 Sign Vocabulary Illustrations section of this unit.

Grammar

1. Compound Signs

2. Listing on the Non-Dominant Hand for Rank Order

3. Number Incorporation with Age

4. Using Numbers for Quantity, Time, and Age

5. Numbers from *26* to *66*

Unit 6 Overview

Language, Culture, and Community

1. Female–Male Signs

2. How Are Signs Created?

3. Deaf Children of Deaf Parents

4. Asking Personal Questions

Practice and Review Materials

1. Video Exercises

   – Sample Expressive Dialogue

   – Comprehension Practice

   – Expressive Practice Prompts

2. Grammar and Language, Culture, and Community Review Questions

3. Sign Vocabulary Illustrations

1. Compound Signs

2. Listing on the Non-Dominant Hand for Rank Order

3. Number Incorporation with Age

4. Using Numbers for Quantity, Time, and Age

5. Numbers from *26* to *66*

1. Compound Signs

Husband and *wife* are examples of compound signs. Compound signs are made up of two or more signs combined to make a sign that has a distinct meaning from its parts. In a compound sign, the handshapes and movements of the two signs combined are modified. The individual signs that make up the compound show changes in handshape so that the individual sign parts lose their individual identities in the compound sign. Figures 6.1 and 6.2 show the two signs, *female* and *married,* which, when combined, form the compound sign *wife* (Figure 6.3). For wife, notice how the handshape for *married* is assimilated into the sign *female*.

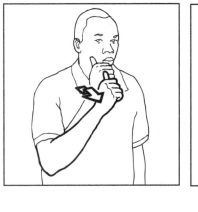

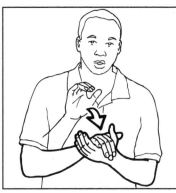

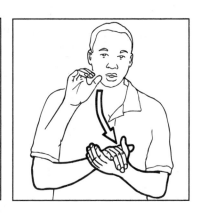

female
Fig. 6.1

married
Fig. 6.2

wife
Fig. 6.3

2. Listing on the Non-Dominant Hand for Rank Order

As you learned in Unit 5, Work Duties, one way that ASL makes reference to people and things not present is to use the fingers of the non-dominant hand to "list" them. For example, if a signer has two brothers and two sisters, with the dominant hand index finger the signer first points to the non-dominant hand thumb for his/her oldest sibling, to the non-dominant hand index finger for the second oldest sibling, and then each successive finger, continuing the order from oldest to youngest and spelling the name of each sibling. When doing this, the signer includes himself/herself in the rank order he/she holds among the siblings. If the signer wishes to give more information about one sibling, he/she points to or touches his/her non-dominant hand thumb or finger that has become the referent for that sibling and then provides information about that sibling. Similarly, when using listing to discuss children, depending on the number of children, signers first point to the thumb or index finger and then each successive finger of their non-dominant hand to indicate each child and the birth order from oldest to youngest. After pointing to and touching the thumb or index finger, a signer will spell the name of the oldest child. Next, the signer will point to his/her index finger or middle finger and spell the name of the second oldest child, and so forth in order. All signers in a conversation will use their own non-dominant hand to make reference to the children who have been referenced in this way by another signer. See Figure 6.4. (Note: In discussions of one's family it is not generally customary to include parents when using listing on the non-dominant hand because there is an implied rank order and, of course, parents do not fit the schema of rank order.)

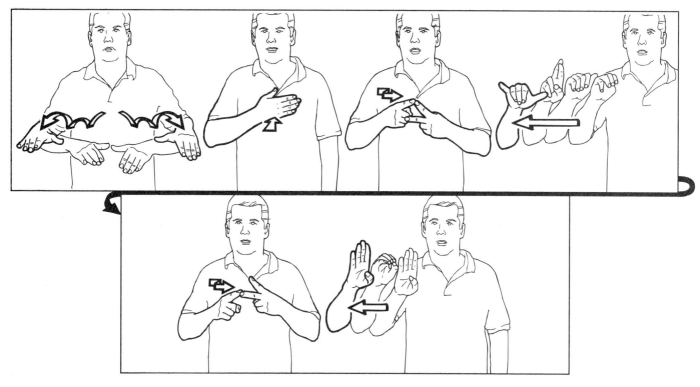

My children are Mary and Bob.

Fig. 6.4

3. Number Incorporation with Age

Number incorporation with time adverbials was discussed in Unit 4, Making Appointments. Number sign handshapes (up to 9) may be incorporated with the sign *age* to indicate the age of a child. For these signs, the number handshape is placed at the chin in the location for the sign *age* and the sign moves out and downward (see Figures 6.5 and 6.6). For ages above 9, a compound sign is used with initial handshape, location, and palm orientation for the sign *age* and a final handshape formed during the movement of the sign out and downward, which indicates the age of the individual (see Figures 6.7 and 6.8).

three-years-old
Fig. 6.5

seven-years-old
Fig. 6.6

thirty-five-years-old
Fig. 6.7

forty-three-years-old
Fig. 6.8

4. Using Numbers for Quantity, Time, and Age

When communicating a number quantity in ASL (for example, number of children in a family and number of people working in a department), the numbers 1 to 5 have the palm of the hand oriented toward the signer (see Figure 6.9). The numbers 6 to 9 have the palm oriented away from the signer. When numbers are used to tell time and to provide a person's age, the numbers 1 to 5 are produced with the palm orientation facing away from the signer (see Figures 6.10–6.15). Number signs beyond 9 have varying palm orientations, which usually take a bit of practice for beginning signers to recognize and produce. The rules for using numbers in ASL are complex and you will be introduced to these rules gradually as you continue learning and practicing ASL.

Counting and Telling How Many

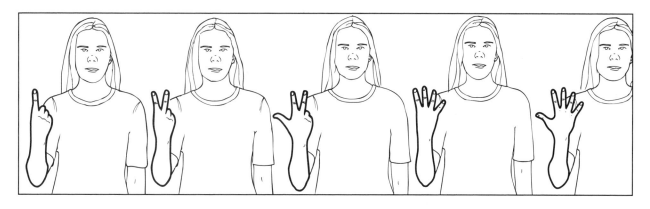

one, two, three, four, five
Fig. 6.9

Telling Time

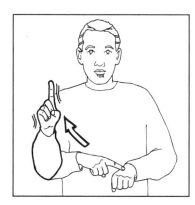  

| *1-o'clock* | *3-o'clock* | *5-o'clock* |
| Fig. 6.10 | Fig. 6.11 | Fig. 6.12 |

Telling Age

1 year old
Fig. 6.13

2 years old
Fig. 6.14

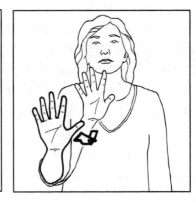

5 years old
Fig. 6.15

5. Numbers from *26* to *66*

The numbers *26* to *66* follow a regular pattern in their production, combining handshapes of the single-digit numbers *0* to *6.* All of the double-digit numbers, *33, 44,* etc., have palm orientation facing down while producing the number. Figure 6.16 illustrates the number *33* with this palm orientation. Other numbers from *26* to *66* combine two digits with the palm facing forward. Figures 6.17 and 6.18 illustrate the numbers *45* and *57* as examples of the production of numbers produced with palm facing forward. Numbers *67* to *99* have special movement patterns that you will learn about in Unit 10.

33
Fig. 6.16

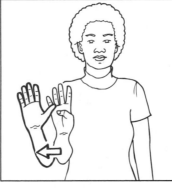

45
Fig. 6.17

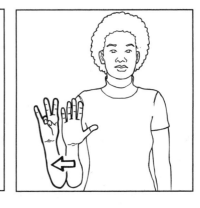

57
Fig. 6.18

Unit 6 Language, Culture, and Community

1. Female–Male Signs

Often ASL signs that share a common element of meaning also share a common parameter of production. For example, signs referencing the female gender share the lower part of the face (generally the cheek area). For example, the signs *girl, wife, sister*, and *daughter* are produced in the cheek area. Signs that relate to male gender use the upper part of the face location (generally the forehead area or the side of the head near the temple). For example, the signs *boy, husband, brother*, and *son* are produced in the forehead area. A probable explanation for male signs being produced in the forehead area is that men usually wore caps at the time these signs were developed. A probable explanation for female signs being produced in the cheek area relates to the ribbons used to tie bonnets worn by women at the time these signs were developed. As you learn ASL vocabulary, it is helpful to see that signs related in meaning often share common elements of production; that is, handshapes, locations, palm orientations, and/or movements.

Figure 6.19 shows the locations on the upper and lower part of the face that distinguish signs relating to females and males.

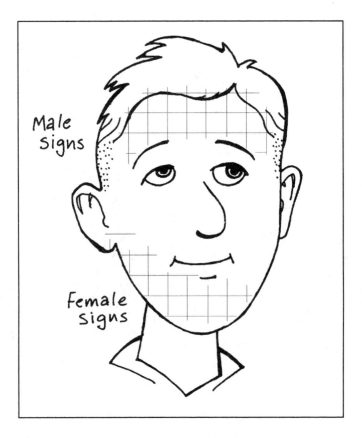

Fig. 6.19

2. How Are Signs Created?

The words that make up languages are created by the users of the languages when they have a need to express new concepts. In Unit 2, Learning ASL, the basic parts or parameters of signs, handshape, movement, location, and palm orientation were introduced. These are the building blocks of signs. Facial expression is also important to the meaning of many signs, and some linguists consider facial expression a fifth basic sign part.

When these four (or five) parts are combined, signs are created. Signs, therefore, are similar to words in spoken languages that are formed by combining consonant and vowel sounds. Signs, like spoken words, have meanings. So how do new signs come into ASL?

Users of ASL know what combinations of the basic sign parts may be combined to create new signs. Similarly in English, for example, all speakers recognize that "btd" is not an acceptable combination of letters/sounds. A new concept could not be given that "label" or "word." In English, the sound combinations that make words require at least one vowel (a, e, i, o, u). "Btd" is not a word but "bed" is an acceptable combination and it does have a meaning. Speakers of English recognize what it means when they hear it or see it written.

When there is a new concept that needs a sign, the users of ASL combine the basic sign parts (handshape, movement, location, and palm orientation) in acceptable combinations and a new sign is created. Often, there are several competing new signs that emerge from users. Over time, one or more of these new signs may become widely used and find its place in the ASL lexicon. Sometimes more than one sign is accepted; for example, see the three signs for computer shown in Figures 6.20, 6.21, and 6.22.

computer

Fig. 6.20

computer

Fig. 6.21

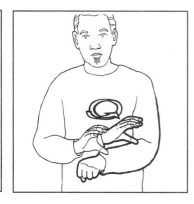

computer

Fig. 6.22

When ASL signers need to create a new sign, they often use an aspect of the new thing as part of the new sign; for example, how it works or looks. The ASL classifier system is one productive mechanism whereby new signs are created. Signers know that "flat-surfaced" objects may be represented with a "B" handshape and "round" objects may be represented with a "rounded claw" handshape. Signers know that if new signs are related in meaning to existing signs, the new signs may share aspects of the existing signs' basic parts. An example of this is signs representing emotion or emotional states. These signs share the chest location in the heart area. See Figures 6.23, 6.24, and 6.25 for *feelings, happy,* and *exciting.* Therefore, a new sign related to emotions or emotional states may be expected to share the heart/chest area as a location.

| *feelings* | *happy* | *exciting* |
| Fig. 6.23 | Fig. 6.24 | Fig. 6.25 |

Another productive avenue for sign development is what is called initialization. Initialized ASL signs have the handshape of the first letter of the English or French word that they share a meaning with. [Note: Langes des signes Francais (LSF) has had a significant influence on ASL due primarily to Laurent Clerc, a deaf teacher from Paris, France, who was the first deaf teacher of deaf students in the United States.] For example, the sign in ASL, which is derived from LSF *to-look-for,* is an initialized LSF sign; that is, this sign has the "C" handshape from the French word "chercher." Another example from LSF is the ASL sign *good.* This sign is the same as the French sign meaning "good" and has a "B" handshape from the French word "bon," meaning "good."

Using the first letter of the English word that shares the same meaning with an ASL sign probably occurs because minority languages surrounded by more powerful majority languages, as the situation is with ASL and English, will tend to borrow words from the majority language. This is a common phenomenon in bilingual language communities. Although borrowing (initialization) is a productive process in ASL, signs created via initialization will always find it harder to gain acceptance than signs created via mechanisms such as the ASL classifier system. Initialization is not the first choice for the creation of new signs and many initialized signs, especially those created by non-native signers, are rejected by the ASL community for many complex reasons. Some signs that are created through initialization, however, do become part of the ASL lexicon. Initialized signs that are accepted in modern ASL include *class, department,* and *family.* Note that these three signs share the common meaning of "group of" and, as shown in Figures 6.26, 6.27, and 6.28, their specific meanings are differentiated via handshape.

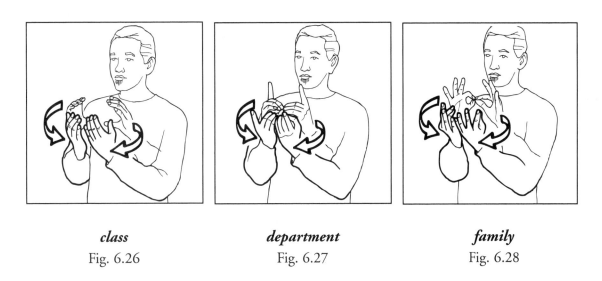

| *class* | *department* | *family* |
| Fig. 6.26 | Fig. 6.27 | Fig. 6.28 |

If you are interested in more information about mechanisms for developing ASL signs, it is recommended that you read the following article:

Bellugi, U., & Newkirk, D. (1981). Formal devices for creating new signs in American Sign Language. *Sign Language Studies, 30,* 1–35.

3. Deaf Children of Deaf Parents

About 10% of deaf children have deaf parents. These families generally have a special place within Deaf culture because the situation of Deaf parents with deaf children is considered a fortunate circumstance for a deaf child. Having Deaf parents means that the deaf child will grow up in an environment with access to a complete natural language and where being deaf is not considered a problem.

Deaf children born into families with Deaf parents, who are skilled in ASL, have the opportunity to acquire a natural language, ASL, similar to how hearing children learn spoken English. These deaf children are able to communicate easily with their parents in ASL, similar to how hearing children are able to easily communicate with their parents in spoken English.

Deaf children with hearing parents may receive significant benefits when their parents are advised early in their children's development to meet Deaf people and learn Deaf culture and community values, including the value of ASL. When hearing parents receive information that helps them to understand the benefits of connecting with the Deaf community for counsel and the benefits of learning ASL, their deaf children are given the opportunity to benefit from the support of the Deaf community. This can help contribute to a positive early childhood, both personally and socially, and to positive early educational experiences.

Readings

Azar, B. (1998). Sign language may help deaf children learn English. APA Monitor, 29 (4). Retrieved March 14, 2002, from American Psychological Association, APA Monitor Online: http://www.apa.org/monitor/apr98/ amer.html

Lane, H., Hoffmeister, R., & Bahan, B. (1996). Families with Deaf children. In: *A journey into the Deaf world* (Chap. 2, pp. 24–41). San Diego, CA: DawnSignPress.

Timberlake, B. (1997). One Family—Two Cultures. In A. Farb (Ed.), *Who speaks for the Deaf community: A Deaf American monograph* (Vol. 47, pp. 69–70). Silver Spring, MD: National Association of the Deaf.

4. Asking Personal Questions

The Deaf culture population is relatively small in numbers, and Deaf people tend to rely on other members of the culture to feel connected and supported. Deaf people feel a special bond with other Deaf people because they share common educational backgrounds and experiences in interacting with the larger hearing society in their family, school, work, and social lives.

For these reasons, Deaf people value knowing and making connections with other members of the Deaf culture and community. Because personal connections and relationships are important, Deaf people want to know other members of the Deaf community, how they are connected to Deaf culture and the Deaf community, where they went to school, and what their backgrounds, jobs, and personal life circumstances are.

Getting to know other members of the Deaf culture and community on a personal level is important. Therefore, asking about and telling about personal life circumstances is considered an appropriate topic of conversation.

As a learner of ASL, you may initially be uncomfortable with the personal nature of some questions you are asked; for example, questions related to marital status and your family. This is a difference in cultural perspectives and values between mainstream American culture and Deaf culture. It is important to recognize this cultural difference in perspective and not take offense if you are asked some questions that you consider personal in nature. No offense is intended. If a Deaf person you are becoming acquainted with asks you personal questions, you are seeing first hand the expression of a cultural value important to Deaf people. When you feel comfortable enough to share information about yourself on a personal level, you will be demonstrating your understanding and acceptance of this aspect of Deaf culture. You are learning ASL because you will or currently have some relationship to Deaf people. Understanding these values and how they are expressed within Deaf culture is an important part of learning and developing ASL communication skills.

Unit 6 Practice and Review Materials

1. Video Exercises

 – Sample Expressive Dialogue

 – Comprehension Practice

 – Expressive Practice Prompts

2. Grammar and Language, Culture, and Community Review Questions

3. Sign Vocabulary Illustrations

Sample Expressive Dialogue

Read the dialogue prompts below and then watch how each signer expresses these prompts on the video. Sign along with both Signer A and Signer B or with either Signer A or Signer B on the video. You may wish to practice this dialogue with a classmate outside of class time and your teacher may review this dialogue in class and ask you to sign this dialogue with a classmate.

Talking about Family

Signer A: Looking at a family photo, comment about Signer B's family

Signer A: Ask Signer B if he/she is married

Signer B: Answer in the negative

Signer A: Ask if Signer B has brothers and sisters

Signer B: Answer in the affirmative

Signer A: Ask how many brothers and sisters

Signer B: Answer with number of brothers and sisters

Signer A: Ask for names

Signer B: Answer from oldest to youngest using listing on the non-dominant hand (All names begin with the same first letter)

Signer A: Comment about siblings' names beginning with the same first letter

Signer B: Answer affirmatively

Signer A: Tell Signer B that he/she has a nice family

Signer B: Say "Thank you"

For the signing you observe, please write any helpful notes and questions you may have for your teacher.

Comprehension Practice 6.1

Watch the dialogue all the way through and then answer as many of the questions below as you can. If necessary, view the dialogue a second time to see whether you are able to understand more and answer any additional questions.

Discussing Marital Status

1. Which person is married?

2. What is the spouse's name?

3. What is the man's marital status?

4. How does the man express negation when he is asked if he is married?

5. Describe the man's current romantic situation, including the names.

6. When the man tells us about his current romantic involvements, what grammatical principle does he use to identify and name his girlfriends?

For the signing you observe, please write any helpful notes and questions that you may have for your teacher.

Comprehension Practice 6.2

Watch the dialogue all the way through and then answer as many of the questions below as you can. If necessary, view the dialogue a second time to see whether you are able to understand more and answer any additional questions.

Discussing Families

1. How many children does the woman have? How many boys and girls?

2. What are her children's names?

3. How many children does the man have and what are their names?

4. How does the man use space to differentiate among his children?

5. What ASL grammatical feature do the two signers use to discuss the names of their children?

6. How many brothers and sisters does the man have?

7. How does the woman express that she is impressed by the number of siblings the man has?

8. How many brothers and sisters does the woman have?

For the signing you observe, please write any helpful notes and questions that you may have for your teacher.

Comprehension Practice 6.3

Watch the dialogue all the way through and then answer as many of the questions below as you can. If necessary, view the dialogue a second time to see whether you are able to understand more and answer any additional questions.

Telling about Family

1. What is unique about the narrator's family?

2. What are the narrator's parents' names?

3. How many children do they have?

4. Describe how the narrator uses number incorporation and listing on his non-dominant hand to indicate the gender for his brothers and sisters.

5. What are the names and ages of the children in this family?

6. What are the jobs of the children in this family?

For the signing you observe, please write any helpful notes and questions that you may have for your teacher.

Expressive Practice Prompts

These Expressive Practice Prompts show you the types of questions and statements you should be able to express in ASL by the end of Unit 6. Your teacher may use these Expressive Practice Prompts in class. You should practice these with your practice partner and group outside of class as well.

1. Ask a classmate if he/she is married.

2. Express that you have children, how many, and their names and ages.

3. Ask a classmate how many children he/she has.

4. Ask a classmate how many brothers and sisters he/she has.

5. Express how many brothers and sisters you have, their names, and their ages.

6. Tell the class your friend's name.

7. Tell the class your parents' names.

8. Express that you are married.

9. Ask a classmate if his/her son or daughter has a boyfriend or girlfriend.

10. Express your sister's or brother's boyfriend/girlfriend's name. (You may substitute husband's/wife's name for boyfriend's/girlfriend's).

11. Count from 30 to 60 by 3's.

12. Count from 30 to 60 by 2's.

13. Ask a classmate the ages of his/her children.

14. Express the jobs of your parents.

15. Ask a classmate if his/her family members can sign.

Grammar and Language, Culture, and Community Review Questions

These questions will assist you as you read the Grammar and the Language, Culture, and Community sections in this unit.

1. Look at Figures 6.1, 6.2, and 6.3. What is happening to sign production when the two signs *female* and *to-be-married* are combined to form the compound sign *wife?*

2. When communicating about children in a family, how does a signer show the birth order of the children?

3. Look at Figures 6.5–6.8. What differences do you see in the formation of the signs?

4. When counting and communicating a number quantity in ASL (for example, how many children are in a family), what is the signer's palm orientation for the numbers 1 to 5? How is the palm orientation different for the numbers 1 to 5 when communicating time and age?

5. Often, signs that share a common element of meaning also share a common aspect of their production. What common aspect of production is shared for many of the signs related to "feelings"?

6. Describe three factors or mechanisms that may influence the creation of ASL signs.

7. Explain how deaf children born into families with Deaf parents are similar to hearing children born into families with hearing parents.

8. Explain why, in Deaf culture, asking personal questions and sharing background information is important.

Sign Vocabulary Illustrations

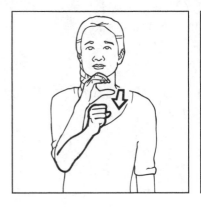 

age, *old*   ***baby***

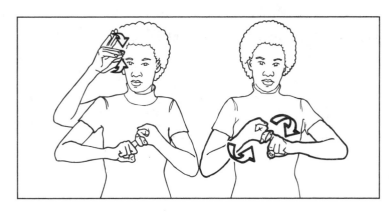 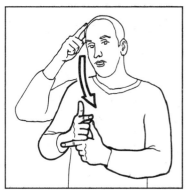

boyfriend   ***brother***

  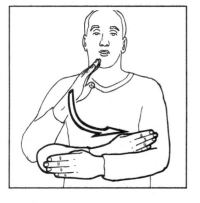

child   ***children***   ***daughter***

divorced

engaged

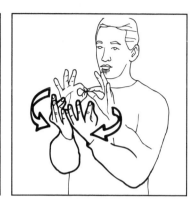

family

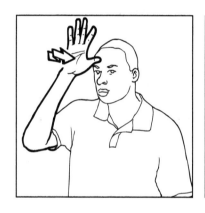

father

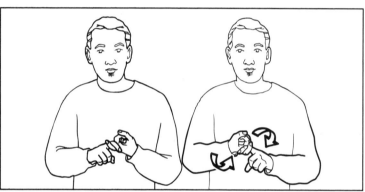

friend

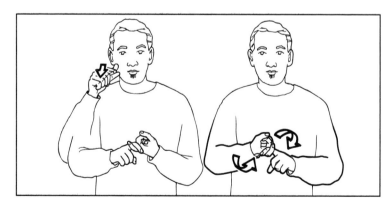

girlfriend

go-steady

have (possessive)

how-old

husband

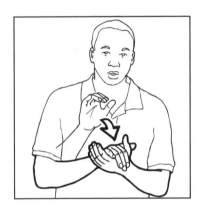

married

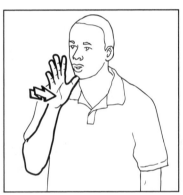

mother

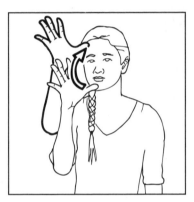

parents

pregnant

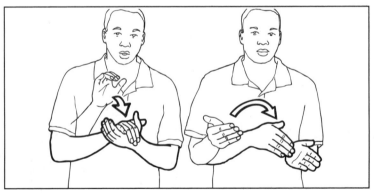

remarry

separated

single

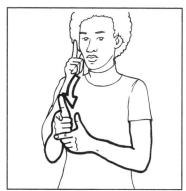

sister

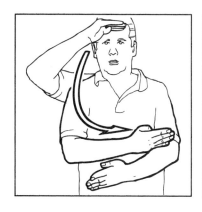

son

sweetheart

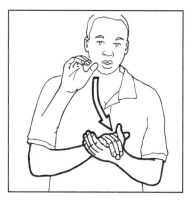

wife

Where People Live

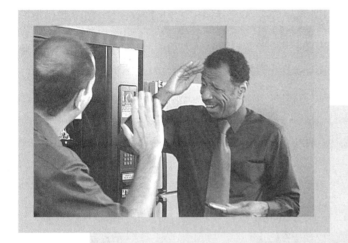

In this unit you learn to talk about where you were born and raised, where you live now, and forms of transportation. You also learn to ask how things are done. In addition, you learn how Deaf people make connections with other Deaf people and about types of schools for deaf and hard-of-hearing students.

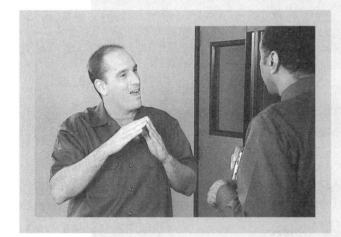

Unit 7 Overview

Learning Outcomes

1. Talk about where one was born, raised, and has lived

2. Talk about means of transportation

3. Ask how something is done or how something works

4. Learn how Deaf people make connections with one another

5. Learn about types of schools for deaf and hard-of-hearing students.

Vocabulary

house	*Boston*	*near*
big	*Chicago*	*far, distance*
small	*New-York* (state)	*car*
apartment	*New-York-City*	*to-drive*
building	*Buffalo* (city)	*train, railway*
dorm	*Rochester*	*bus*
to-live	*California*	*boat*
roommate	*Los-Angeles*	*go-by-boat*
which	*San-Francisco*	*airplane*
city/town, community	*Dallas*	*to-fly*
country	*Washington D-C*	*ride-in*
rural, country	*Seattle*	*bicycle/bike*
past	*born*	*motorcycle*
future	*grow-up*	*ride-on*
long-ago	*move*	*go-by-foot, walk*
recently	*from*	
Atlanta	*home*	

Unit 7 Overview

Grammar

1. Asking How Things Are Done

2. Subject and Object Incorporating Verbs

3. Use of Movement to Distinguish Noun/Verb Pairs

4. Use of Timeline for Expressing Past, Present, and Future Time

5. Non-Manual Signal for Proximity in Time or Space (cs)

Language, Culture, and Community

1. Opening Conversations with *"up-to-now see none"*

2. Closing Conversations with *"see-later"*

3. Meeting People

4. From Where? Versus Where Live Now?

5. Types of Schools for Deaf and Hard-of-Hearing Students

Practice and Review Materials

1. Video Exercises

    – Sample Expressive Dialogue

    – Comprehension Practice

    – Expressive Practice Prompts

2. Grammar and Language, Culture, and Community Review Questions

3. Sign Vocabulary Illustrations

1. Asking How Things Are Done

2. Subject and Object Incorporating Verbs

3. Use of Movement to Distinguish Noun/Verb Pairs

4. Use of Timeline for Expressing Past, Present, and Future Time

5. Non-Manual Signal for Proximity in Time or Space (cs)

1. Asking How Things Are Done

To ask how something is done, the sign **how** is produced with a wiggling movement of the dominant hand. This wiggling movement changes the meaning of the sign from the simple interrogative "how" as in "How are you?" to the meaning of "how something is done," called "how of manner." This form of the sign is used when asking questions about how someone does something or how something works. See Figures 7.1 and 7.2.

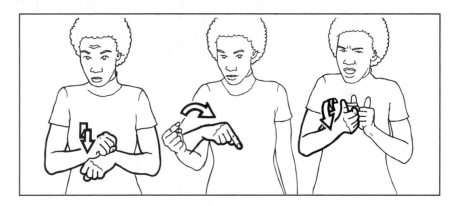

How do you come to work?
(How of Manner)
Fig. 7.1

How are you?
(Regular Interrogative)
Fig. 7.2

2. Subject and Object Incorporating Verbs

Some ASL verbs can indicate who does what to whom through the direction of their movements in space; that is, the subject (who does something) and the object of the verb (to whom something is done) are specified by the direction of movement to spatial reference points.

Using the verb **meet,** Figures 7.3–7.6 show the various paths along which verbs that incorporate subjects and objects may move.

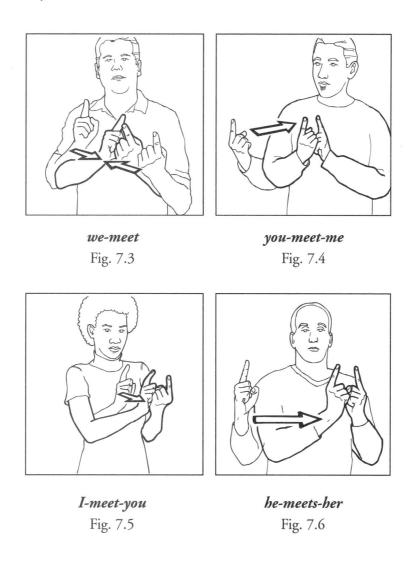

we-meet
Fig. 7.3

you-meet-me
Fig. 7.4

I-meet-you
Fig. 7.5

he-meets-her
Fig. 7.6

Other subject and object incorporating verbs you have learned include:

teach   *to-help*   *go-to*

3. Use of Movement to Distinguish Noun/Verb Pairs

Some ASL nouns and verbs share the same handshape, location, and orientation and are distinguished from each other by different movements. For these noun/verb sign pairs, nouns usually have repeated movement and verbs usually have single continuous movement. Figures 7.7–7.10 show these movement differences for two ASL noun/verb pairs.

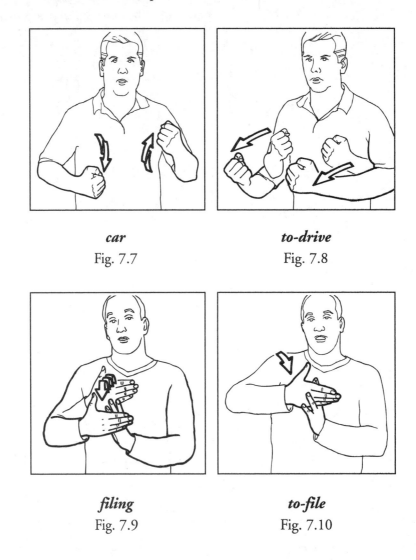

car
Fig. 7.7

to-drive
Fig. 7.8

filing
Fig. 7.9

to-file
Fig. 7.10

Other noun/verb pairs you have learned include the following:

airplane	*to-fly*
copying	*to-copy*

4. Use of Timeline for Expressing Past, Present, and Future Time

In ASL, past, present, and future time and communicating when events occur are expressed through use of the "timeline." This line runs from behind the signer forward to space in front of the signer. See Figure 7.11.

Timeline

Fig. 7.11

For signs that express past time, movements are back along this timeline; for example, *past, recently,* and *long-ago.*

Signs that express present or current time are produced in the space directly in front of the signer; for example, *now* and *today.*

For signs that express future time, movements are forward along this timeline; for example, *tomorrow* and *will/future.*

5. Non-Manual Signal for Proximity in Time or Space (cs)

ASL uses facial expressions and body postures called non-manual signals for many grammatical purposes. You have already learned how non-manual signals express questions. Non-manual signals are also used in ASL to express modifiers (adjectives and adverbs). A non-manual signal used to express that something is close in time to the present or two things are close together in space involves moving the shoulder of your dominant signing hand slightly, and moving the cheek and side of your mouth toward your shoulder. See Figure 7.12.

recently
Fig. 7.12

Unit 7 Language, Culture, and Community

1. Opening Conversations with *"up-to-now see none"*

2. Closing Conversations with *"see-later"*

3. Meeting People

4. From Where? Versus Where Live Now?

5. Types of Schools for Deaf and Hard-of-Hearing Students

1. Opening Conversations with *"up-to-now see none"*

In #3 of this Language, Culture, and Community section, the practice of "hugging" when friends or acquaintances meet each other after a period of separation is discussed. In conjunction with hugging, when Deaf community members have not seen each other for a long time, they will often open their conversation with the sign phrase ***up-to-now see none.*** This is comparable to the English expression "Long time no see" and it is used in a similar way. This sign phrase is illustrated in Figure 7.13.

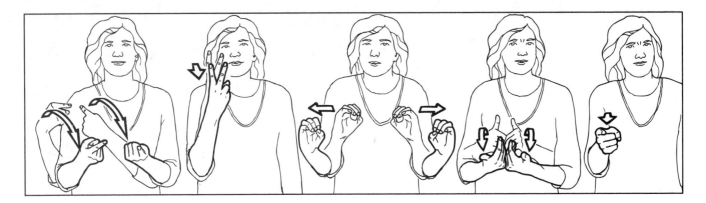

Long time no see. How have you been doing?
Fig. 7.13

2. Closing Conversations with *"see-later"*

In Unit 5, Work Duties, you learned that the signs ***thank-you/you're-welcome*** and ***ok*** may be used to close conversations. In Unit 4, Making Appointments, the signs ***see*** and ***later*** were introduced. These two signs may be combined to form the compound sign form ***see-later,*** which is used to close conversations between friends. This sign phrase may be used as a friendly conversation closer when there is a probability that the two signers will see one another at a future time. It also may be used when there is no definite expectation that the two signers will actually see each other at a later time. In this case, it is comparable to the English conversation closer of "so long." Use of the compound sign ***see-later*** to close a conversation is illustrated in Figure 7.14.

See you later.
Fig. 7.14

3. Meeting People

Although Deaf people are a minority group in American society, they often know many individuals across the United States and in other countries, because the Deaf World itself is indeed small. It is common within the Deaf community for people who are acquaintances to greet each other with a hug when they have not seen one another for a long time. When Deaf people first meet, they will usually give their full names and where they are from. If they attended a residential school for the deaf, they usually state the school they attended. A Deaf person whose parents are also Deaf is at the core of the Deaf world. Attending a residential school also marks a Deaf person as belonging to the inner circle of Deaf society. Deaf people who attended a mainstream school become a part of the Deaf community when they become active in the local Deaf community. Acceptance is further enhanced by becoming active in the national Deaf community by participating in clubs, sports, and other associations of Deaf people.

When Deaf people meet, exchanging the information discussed above forms the basis for initial conversations. When Deaf and hearing people meet, Deaf people assess the sign language skills of hearing persons and, based on this assessment, may ask questions related to the hearing person's connection to the Deaf community. (See #4 of this Language, Community, and Culture section for communication protocols related to introductions in ASL.)

4. From Where? Versus Where Live Now?

When Deaf people meet each other for the first time, they usually ask each other for their names and the question, "Where are you from?" The expected answer is the place where the Deaf person grew up and the place the new acquaintance considers "home." For example, if a Deaf person was born and grew up in New York City and as an adult has lived for many years in Chicago, the answer would be something like the following:

> *I was born and grew up in New York City. I went to school at Lexington School for the Deaf.*
> *Now I live in Chicago.*

Asking in ASL, "Where are you from?," therefore, is comparable to asking where you were born, where did you grow up, and what place do you consider home. Deaf people want to know where other Deaf people are from and their connection to the Deaf world.

Asking "Where do you live?" is a question about where the person lives now. Using the previous example, the answer would be the following:

> *I live in Chicago, but I grew up in New York City. I went to school at Lexington School*
> *for the Deaf.*

If Deaf people know that you are a hearing person and learning ASL, they will generally not ask you the question "Where are you from?" Because you are a hearing person, where you were born and grew up is not important to determining your connection to the Deaf world. They may ask you "Where do you live?" and it is appropriate for you to answer this question in the same way that you would answer it in English; for example, "I live in Rochester, NY." Deaf people also like to know whether people they meet are D/deaf or hearing. Fluent hearing ASL signers may sometimes not be immediately identified as hearing because their signing may appear native-like. In this case, a Deaf person may ask a fairly fluent hearing signer, "Where are you from?" Recognizing this question as a question that is trying to establish connections among Deaf people, the hearing signer would respond something like "I am hearing. I grew up in Rochester, NY." The Deaf person may then ask a fluent hearing ASL signer questions like, "How did you learn ASL?" "Wow, you are very skilled in ASL. Are your parents Deaf?" These questions are directed at discovering the hearing signer's connection to the Deaf world.

If you are learning ASL, you can expect to get questions like "Where are you learning ASL?" or "How did you learn ASL?" and "Who is your ASL teacher?" Deaf people will want to establish how and why you are learning ASL. They will want to know whether you have Deaf parents, relatives, neighbors or have other personal or professional reasons for learning ASL. It is important to understand these culturally determined patterns of questions when being introduced and how to respond appropriately.

5. Types of Schools for Deaf and Hard-of-Hearing Students

In 1817 in Hartford, Connecticut, Thomas Hopkins Gallaudet and Laurent Clerc founded the first school for deaf children in the United States, the American School for the Deaf (ASD). ASD, which is still in operation today, served a significant role in the development and standardization of ASL by bringing together a large number of deaf students in a residential school setting in which sign language was the primary means for instruction and communication. The ASD educational method of using ASL to teach deaf students became a model for U.S. schools for the Deaf that were founded during the late 1800s. If you have the opportunity to visit ASD and Gallaudet University, you will see that both have the same statue of Thomas Hopkins Gallaudet with Alice Cogswell, his first deaf student.

Residential schools are one type of educational programs for deaf and hard-of-hearing students in the United States. Most states in the United States have at least one residential school, but some have multiple residential schools; for example, California, New York, and North Carolina. In residential schools for the deaf today, students will typically live at the school in dormitories during the week, being transported home for weekends and returning to the school campus on Sunday afternoon or evening. Students living in the vicinity of a residential school typically attend classes at the school but live at home. In this case, the residential school is comparable to the next type of school program, the day school. Residential and day schools have comprehensive specialized educational programs and extra-curricular activities for deaf and hard-of-hearing students. These programs generally include instruction from certified teachers of the deaf, support services (for example, interpreters and note takers), opportunities for participation in athletics and other social activities with other students, and opportunities for attending nearby public schools as appropriate to the educational plans for each student.

Many large metropolitan areas have day school programs; for example, New York City and Chicago. Sometimes a day school is a separate school exclusively for deaf and hard-of-hearing students, but often a day school is part of a regular public school having a large population of deaf and hard-of-hearing students transported daily to the campus and living at home. Following trends in regular public school education, charter schools have begun to develop for deaf and hard-of-hearing students. Generally, charter schools are day schools with a specialized focus or philosophy.

A third type of educational placement that has become the most utilized placement is mainstreaming. Mainstreaming generally means that deaf and hard-of-hearing students attend regular public schools, have some or all of their classes with hearing students, and live at home. Mainstreaming varies from neighborhood schools to "center" schools, where students from a surrounding area are transported daily to one school and services are consolidated at this school. In center schools, deaf students may have specialized teachers of the deaf, interpreters, note takers, and other personnel working in this one center school, as well as options for instruction in classes with other deaf students or with hearing students.

Cutting across these program options are issues such as method of instruction and private versus public funding. Most residential schools are public, state funded schools in which some form of sign language is used in combination with other methods of communication as the primary means of instruction and communication. However, there are notable exceptions whereby some privately funded residential schools offer an "oral-only" approach to educating deaf students. In oral-only programs, all communication and instruction is conducted via spoken and written English, with no use of sign language. Two of the most well-known oral residential schools for deaf students are the Clarke School for the Deaf in Northampton, Massachusetts, and the Central Institute for the Deaf in St. Louis, Missouri.

Additional information for learning more about educational options for deaf and hard-of-hearing students can be found in the following reference:

Educational Options for Deaf and Hard of Hearing Students: Placement Considerations (http://clerccenter.gallaudet.edu/Clerc_Center/Information_and_Resources/Info_To_Go/ Educate_Children_(3_to_21)/Placement_Issues/Placement_Considerations.html)

Unit 7 Practice and Review Materials

1. Video Exercises

    – Sample Expressive Dialogue

    – Comprehension Practice

    – Expressive Practice Prompts

2. Grammar and Language, Culture, and Community Review Questions

3. Sign Vocabulary Illustrations

Sample Expressive Dialogue

Read the dialogue prompts below and then watch how each signer expresses these prompts on the video. Sign along with both Signer A and Signer B or with either Signer A or Signer B on the video. You may wish to practice this dialogue with a classmate outside of class time and your teacher may review this dialogue in class and ask you to sign this dialogue with a classmate.

Getting Reacquainted

Signers A and B: Greet each other

Signer A: Ask Signer B where he/she lives

Signer B: Respond and ask where Signer A lives

Signer A: Respond

Signer B: Ask Signer A if he/she was born in _____
(city)

Signer A: Respond affirmatively and ask if Signer B works

Signer B: Respond negatively and respond you go to school/college

Signer A: Ask if Signer B lives in an apartment

Signer B: Respond affirmatively, state that your apartment is close to your school, and ask if Signer A works

Signer A: Respond affirmatively

Signer B: Ask Signer A if his/her work is close to his/her home

Signer A: Respond negatively

Signer B: Ask Signer A how he/she goes to work

Signer A: Respond with mode of transportation used to go to work

Signer B: Tell Signer A that you use your bicycle or walk to school/college

For the signing you observe, please write any helpful notes and questions you may have for your teacher.

Comprehension Practice 7.1

Watch the dialogue all the way through and then answer as many of the questions below as you can. If necessary, view the dialogue a second time to see whether you are able to understand more and answer any additional questions.

Commuting to Work

1. What question opens the conversation?

2. What is the response?

3. Describe the man's commute to work.

4. Which classifier does the man use to represent the vehicle approaching his house?

5. Who has the longer commute? How much longer is it?

6. What does the facial expression used by the woman convey about the commute?

For the signing you observe, please write any helpful notes and questions that you may have for your teacher.

Comprehension Practice 7.2

Watch the dialogue all the way through and then answer as many of the questions below as you can. If necessary, view the dialogue a second time to see whether you are able to understand more and answer any additional questions.

Describing a New Home

1. The man in the blue shirt catches his friend at the snack machine. How does he get his friend's attention?

2. Describe the move the man in the purple shirt recently made.

3. When asking about the size of the house, what grammatical principle does the man in the blue shirt use to establish the contrast between "big" and "small"?

4. The man in the purple shirt answers that his house is large. Describe how he modifies the sign *"big"* and what this modification means.

5. How many rooms does the man's new house have?

6. What is preventing the man in the blue shirt from buying a house?

For the signing you observe, please write any helpful notes and questions that you may have for your teacher.

Comprehension Practice 7.3

Watch the dialogue all the way through and then answer as many of the questions below as you can. If necessary, view the dialogue a second time to see whether you are able to understand more and answer any additional questions.

Acquaintances Meet Again

1. Where did these two women meet before?

2. When the woman in the black blouse cannot remember her friend's name, her friend spells her name. What is her name?

3. The woman in the light-colored dress cannot remember her friend's name but she does remember one detail about her. What does she remember?

4. The woman in the light-colored dress fingerspells part of her friend's name. What does she spell?

5. What is the name of the woman wearing the black blouse?

6. Where does the woman in the light-colored dress live?

7. How does the woman in the black blouse describe the size of this city?

8. How does the woman in the light-colored dress feel about the city she lives in? What sign does she use to express her feeling?

For the signing you observe, please write any helpful notes and questions that you may have for your teacher.

Expressive Practice Prompts

These Expressive Practice Prompts show you the types of questions and statements you should be able to express in ASL by the end of Unit 7. Your teacher may use these Expressive Practice Prompts in class. You should practice these with your practice partner and group outside of class as well.

1. Express where you were born and grew up

2. Ask a classmate where he/she was born and grew up.

3. Ask a classmate whether his/her house is big or small and how many bedrooms and bathrooms it has.

4. Ask a classmate in which city/town he/she works.

5. Ask a classmate how he/she gets to work.

6. Express how many rooms your house has.

7. Express that you don't live in an apartment.

8. Express where you are from.

9. Ask a classmate when he/she moved to _____.
    (name city)

10. Ask a classmate whether he/she lives in the city or the country.

11. Express what color your car is and that you don't like this color.

12. Express that you moved to _____ recently.
    (name city)

13. Ask a classmate if he/she was born in _____.
    (name city)

14. Express that your roommate was born in Los Angeles and recently moved to Seattle.

15. Express that you flew to Washington, D.C. for a meeting.

16. Ask a classmate in which building he/she works.

17. Ask a classmate his/her address.

18. Express the three cities you like best.

19. Express that you have an apartment in New York City and a house in Los Angeles.

20. Express how you come to class.

21. Ask a classmate if he/she rides a bus to class.

22. Ask a classmate if he/she lives near a university.

Grammar and Language, Culture, and Community Review Questions

These questions will assist you as you read the Grammar and the Language, Culture, and Community sections in this unit.

1. What movement of the dominant hand changes the sign **how** from a simple interrogative to the sign meaning "how something is done"?

2. Some verbs in ASL can include the subject (who did it) and the object (to whom it was done). Explain how this happens with some ASL verb signs.

3. What distinguishes the verb **to-drive** from the noun **car?**

4. What grammatical device is used in ASL to show that events occur in past, present, or future time?

5. Look at Figure 7.12. Describe the non-manual signal that is being used to show that something is close in time or space.

6. Describe a circumstance when the sign phrase **up-to-now see none** may be used between friends.

7. Describe how the compound sign **see-later** is used in two different circumstances between friends.

8. When Deaf people meet hearing people, what types of questions will they customarily ask and why do they ask these questions?

9. When Deaf people meet each other, they will usually exchange their full names, where they are from, and where they went to school. Why is this a cultural value?

10. Name three types of educational placements for deaf and hard-of-hearing students and explain how they differ from one another.

Sign Vocabulary Illustrations

airplane

apartment

Atlanta

bicycle/bike

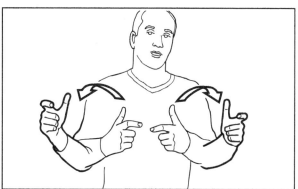

big

boat

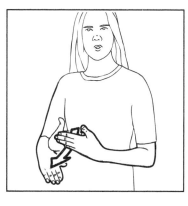

born

Boston

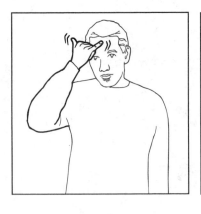

Buffalo (*city*)

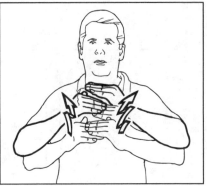

building

bus

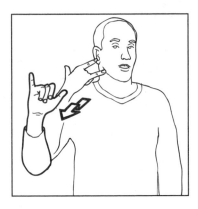

California

car

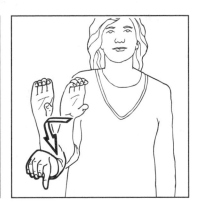

Chicago

city/town, *community*

country

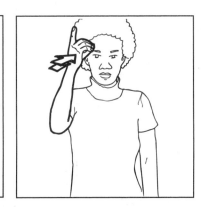

Dallas

dorm

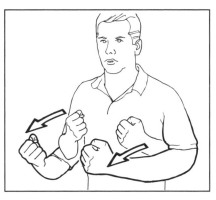

to-drive

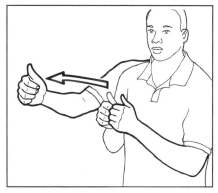

far, *distance*

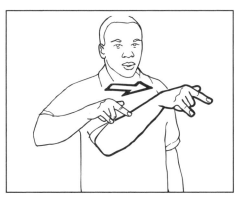

to-fly

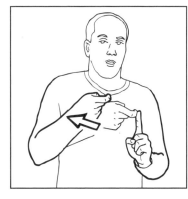

from

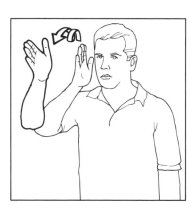

future

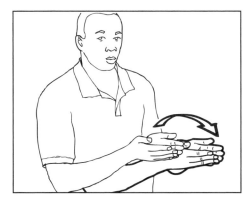

go-by-boat

go-by-foot, *walk*

grow-up

home

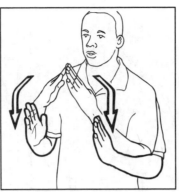

house

to-live (1)

to-live (2)

long-ago

Los-Angeles

motorcycle

move

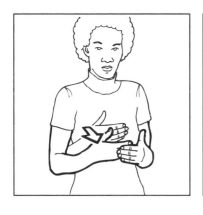

near

New-York (state)

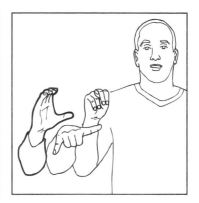

New-York-City (1)

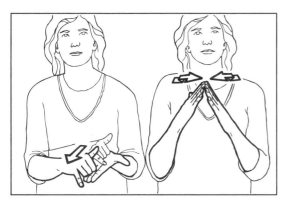

New-York-City (2)

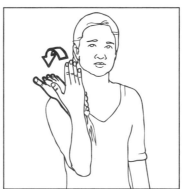

past

recently

ride-in

ride-on

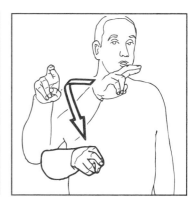

Rochester

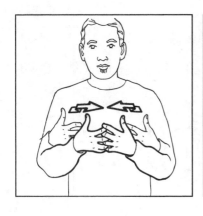

roommate

rural, country

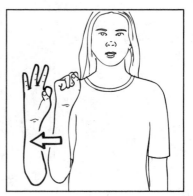

San-Francisco

Seattle

small

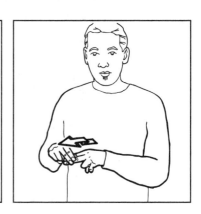

train, railway

Washington D-C

which

Time and Activities

In this unit you learn to discuss activities, including when they occur. You learn to express past, present, and future and how these time concepts are incorporated within signs for day, week, month, and year. Also, you review and are introduced to additional strategies for requesting clarification and you learn about social events and diversity within the Deaf community.

Unit 8 Overview

Learning Outcomes

1. Discuss activities, including when they occur

2. Use time signs in appropriate order

3. Express the months of the year and years

4. Request clarification when something is not understood

5. Learn about social events and diversity within the Deaf community

Vocabulary

week	*time-off, off-from-work*	*running*
last-week	*vacation*	*newspaper/print*
next-week	*go-out-to*	*shopping*
month	*movie, film*	*studying*
last-month	*theatre, drama, play*	*homework*
next-month	*restaurant*	*autumn/fall*
year	*church*	*winter*
last-year	*store* (business)	*spring* (season)
next-year	*temple*	*summer*
weekend	*oversleep*	*all-year*
birthday	*bowling*	*quarter* (academic year)
start, begin	*take-care-of*	*semester*
end, complete	*reading*	*how-long*
finish, done	*to-exercise, work-out*	*approximately, about*
	walking	*up-to-now, since*

Note: For how to express months of the year, and years, see Language, Culture, and Community section, #2 and #3, in this unit.

Unit 8 Overview

Grammar

1. More on Using the Timeline
2. Order for Time Signs
3. Time First in Sign Word Order
4. More on Number Incorporation with Time Signs
5. Use of Rhetorical Question Structure
6. Expressing Wh-Questions without Using Interrogative Signs

Language, Culture, and Community

1. Review and Additional Techniques for Requesting Clarification
2. Expressing Months of the Year
3. Expressing Years
4. Social Events and Diversity in the Deaf Community

Practice and Review Materials

1. Video Exercises
   - Sample Expressive Dialogue
   - Comprehension Practice
   - Expressive Practice Prompts
2. Grammar and Language, Culture, and Community Review Questions
3. Sign Vocabulary Illustrations

1. More on Using the Timeline

As explained in Unit 7, Where People Live, the timeline is a line that runs from the space behind the signer forward to the space in front of the signer.

In this unit, the timeline is incorporated within the signs meaning *last-week, next-week, last-month, next-month, last-year*, and *next-year.* Consistent with what was explained in Unit 7, these signs move backward along the timeline to indicate past tense and forward along the timeline to indicate future tense. See Figures 8.1–8.4 for examples of use of the timeline.

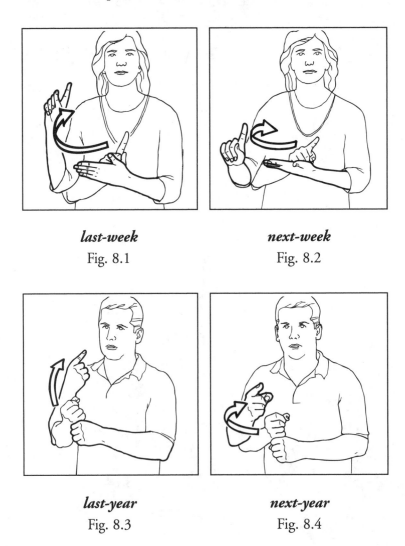

last-week
Fig. 8.1

next-week
Fig. 8.2

last-year
Fig. 8.3

next-year
Fig. 8.4

2. Order for Time Signs

ASL follows a principle of "from most general to most specific." This principle is applied to ASL "time signs"; that is, in explaining when an event occurred or will occur, ASL presents time concepts in an order from the most general to the most specific. For example, suppose that you wish to tell a friend that you will be exercising at 7:00 a.m. on Wednesday morning next week. In ASL, these units of time are ordered as follows: next week, Wednesday, morning, at 7:00. "Next week" is the most general time concept, the day of the week is more specific, then the time period of the day (morning) is more specific, and the exact time of the event is the most specific. Therefore, the signs *next-week, Wednesday, morning,* and *at-7:00* follow the order from most general to most specific. Figure 8.5 shows how this sequence of time signs would be communicated. (Also, see Grammar #3 in this unit.)

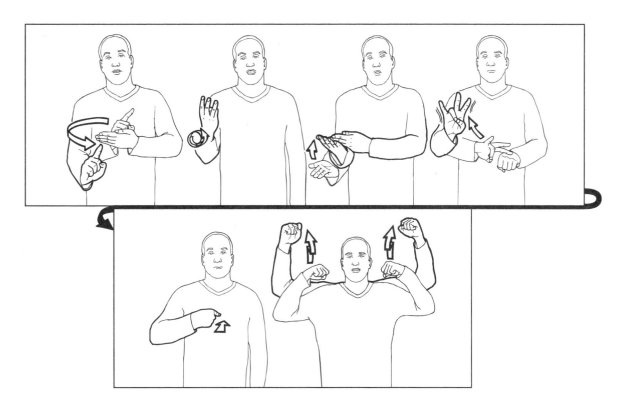

I will be exercising next Wednesday morning at 7:00.

Fig. 8.5

3. Time First in Sign Word Order

In English, verbs are inflected to show time or tense; for example "work" becomes "worked" to indicate past tense. ASL shows tense in a different way. In ASL, the verbs themselves are not inflected. Instead, ASL uses time adverbials to make the time or tense clear in the beginning of a sentence. ASL time adverbial signs include *yesterday, today, tomorrow, night, this-morning,* and *next-week.* When the time being referred to needs to be clear, these signs and sign phrases are expressed first in ASL sentences. For example, to express the idea that you were late to work yesterday, you would sign:

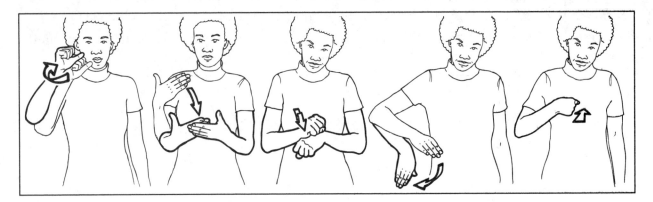

I was late to work yesterday.

Fig. 8.6

Notice that the time adverbial *yesterday* is expressed at the beginning of the ASL sentence. This makes it clear that the event being discussed occurred in the past. Because English inflects verbs for tense, time adverbials can be placed at the beginning, middle, or end of sentences. For ASL, the preferred placement of time adverbials is at the beginning of sentences. It may require you some practice to become accustomed to this requirement to express "time first" for ASL word order.

4. More on Number Incorporation with Time Signs

In Unit 4, Making Appointments, Grammar #1, you were introduced to number incorporation with time adverbials. You learned that number handshapes can be incorporated with signs such as **minute** and **hour.** In this unit, other signs that can incorporate number are introduced. The signs meaning **week, month,** and **year** can incorporate a number handshape to specify the number of weeks, months, and years. A few examples of this are illustrated in Figures 8.7–8.12. Your instructor will show you additional examples of number incorporation with time adverbials and how number incorporation and use of the timeline can be combined when expressing time adverbials.

Note: Number handshapes up to 9 may be incorporated with signs meaning **week** and **month.** With the sign **year,** only handshapes up to 5 may be incorporated.

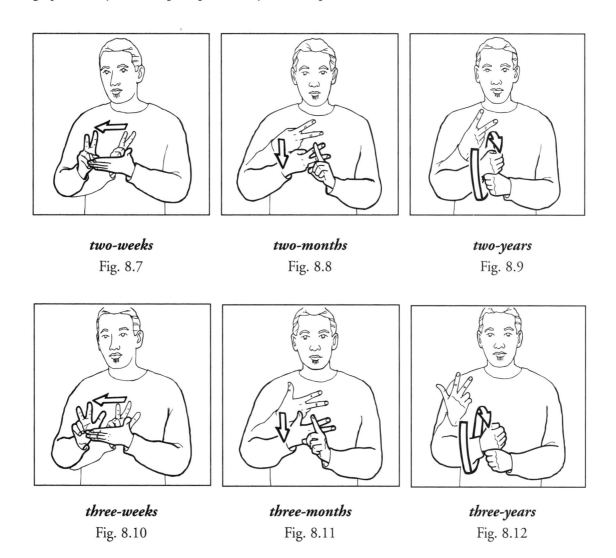

two-weeks	*two-months*	*two-years*
Fig. 8.7	Fig. 8.8	Fig. 8.9
three-weeks	*three-months*	*three-years*
Fig. 8.10	Fig. 8.11	Fig. 8.12

5. Use of Rhetorical Question Structure

ASL uses the rhetorical question structure to make statements and introduce topics in a discourse. The first part of the rhetorical question structure uses raised eyebrows and head tilted slightly back, with the wh-question sign occurring at the end of the question part of the expression. After a slight pause, the signer shifts head and body to the neutral signing position and the "answer" to the question is supplied by the signer. Figures 8.13 and 8.14 show examples of ASL rhetorical questions.

I will not work next week because I will be on vacation.

Fig. 8.13

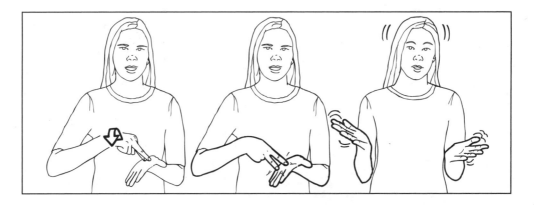

And this is what it all means.

Fig. 8.14

6. Expressing Wh-Questions without Using Interrogative Signs

In Unit 1, Introducing Ourselves, you were introduced to wh-questions; for example, asking someone his/her name using the interrogative sign *what* (see Figure 8.15).

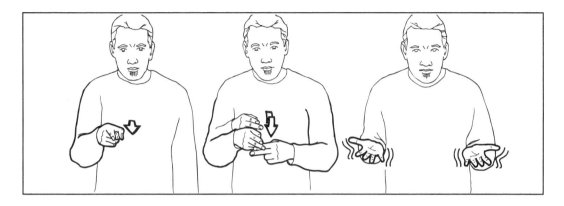

What is your name?
Fig. 8.15

Sometimes, wh-questions may be expressed without an interrogative sign. For example, when asking someone what time it is, a signer may use the sign *time* with wh-question expression (see Figure 8.16).

What time is it?
Fig. 8.16

Unit 8 Language, Culture, and Community

1. Review and Additional Techniques for Requesting Clarification

2. Expressing Months of the Year

3. Expressing Years

4. Social Events and Diversity in the Deaf Community

1. Review and Additional Techniques for Requesting Clarification

When two people engage in conversation, it is quite common that information is not understood and needs to be clarified. This may be especially true when discussing the time when events occur. When you do not understand something that is signed to you, there are ASL techniques for requesting clarification. In #2 and #3 of the Unit 2 Language, Culture, and Community section, three techniques for requesting clarification were discussed: (a) Wh-question expression, (b) ***don't-understand, again*** (see Figure 2.19), and (c) ***fingerspell again slow*** (see Figure 2.20). Figures 8.17 and 8.18 show two additional techniques for requesting clarification. Your instructor will demonstrate these and other common ASL techniques for requesting clarification when you do not understand.

When something is fingerspelled   **When something is signed**

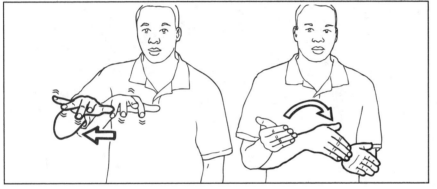

Spell again.   **What did you say?**

Fig. 8.17   Fig. 8.18

2. Expressing Months of the Year

Months of the year are fingerspelled fully if they have five or fewer letters; that is, ***M-a-r-c-h, A-p-r-i-l, M-a-y, J-u-n-e,*** and ***J-u-l-y.*** Months that contain more than five letters are fingerspelled as abbreviations, that is, ***J-a-n, F-e-b, A-u-g, S-e-p-t, O-c-t, N-o-v,*** and ***D-e-c.***

3. Expressing Years

In ASL, years are most often expressed in two-number units. For example, the year 1983 would be expressed with the number combinations 19 and 83 (see Figure 8.19). When years include a zero, the year is expressed with three-number units; for example, 1905 is expressed as 19, 0, and 5 (Figure 8.20 shows this example). When years include a double zero, for example 2003, the year is expressed as a four-number unit. Figure 8.21 shows this example. The years 2010 to 2099 are expressed in two-number units in the same way that 1983 is expressed (see Figure 8.22).

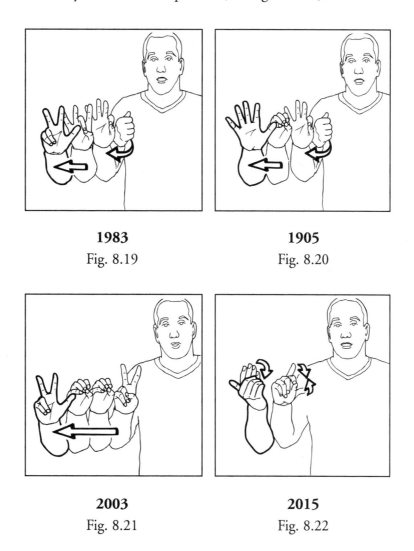

1983
Fig. 8.19

1905
Fig. 8.20

2003
Fig. 8.21

2015
Fig. 8.22

4. Social Events and Diversity in the Deaf Community

Deaf community events are an important part of Deaf culture. Deaf people seek the company and friendship of other members of the Deaf community. This social network provides support and encouragement for participation in Deaf community social and political activities. Deaf clubs in many cities, state Associations of the Deaf, the National Association of the Deaf (NAD), and other local, state, and national organizations within the Deaf community provide a network for social and political activities for community members. Many churches encourage and support the participation of deaf and hard-of-hearing persons by providing interpreters for services and other church-sponsored events. In addition, there are churches whose membership is predominantly deaf and whose ministers or pastors may also be deaf. These churches also are a source of support for Deaf community social and political activities.

With the advent of the American with Disabilties Act (ADA) (http://www.ada.gov), deaf Americans have gained access to public and private business and social services and events. For example, the ADA has led to movie theaters providing open-captioned movies in their schedules so that deaf and hard-of-hearing persons may attend first-run movies. Also, theaters in major cities often provide interpreted performances of their plays for deaf and hard-of -hearing theatergoers. The social calendars of members of the Deaf community can be rather full. One weekend might be consumed by a local, state, or regional Deaf bowling tournament sponsored by the U.S.A. Deaf Sports Federation (USADSF) (http://www.usdeafsports.org/). Another weekend might include attending a performance of a local or national Deaf theatre group on Friday evening, a Saturday euchre tournament at the local Deaf club, and a Sunday matinee open-captioned movie. At all of these events, networking and social interaction will be high on the agenda. Catching up on news, talking to friends, asking for advice, and learning from and supporting other members of the Deaf community are important functions served through the Deaf community's vibrant social network.

The Deaf community is made up of diverse ethnic, racial, and religious groups as well. Within the larger Deaf community there are organizations for Deaf people who are African American, Hispanic, Jewish, gay/lesbian, and women, among others. These groups provide social contact, networking, and support to members who share common interests and experiences because of their additional group identifications. Although the Deaf community is diverse, many deaf and hard-of-hearing persons report a strong sense of identification with Deaf culture that crosses their ethnic, racial, sexual, gender, and religious identities or affiliations.

1. Video Exercises

    – Sample Expressive Dialogue

    – Comprehension Practice

    – Expressive Practice Prompts

2. Grammar and Language, Culture, and Community Review Questions

3. Sign Vocabulary Illustrations

Sample Expressive Dialogue

Read the dialogue prompts below and then watch how each signer expresses these prompts on the video. Sign along with both Signer A and Signer B or with either Signer A or Signer B on the video. You may wish to practice this dialogue with a classmate outside of class time and your teacher may review this dialogue in class and ask you to sign this dialogue with a classmate.

Talking about Work

Signer A: Ask where Signer B works

Signer B: Tell where you work

Signer A: Ask how long Signer B has been working there

Signer B: Tell how many years

Signer A: Express appropriate feedback

For the signing you observe, please write below any helpful notes and questions you may have for your teacher.

Comprehension Practice 8.1

Watch the dialogue all the way through and then answer as many of the questions below as you can. If necessary, view the dialogue a second time to see whether you are able to understand more and answer any additional questions.

Explaining an Absence

1. The man in the blue shirt opens the conversation by asking a question involving a past event. What grammatical principle does he use to indicate that he is referring to a past event?

2. What reason does the man in the green shirt give for missing the meeting?

3. What did the man in the green shirt do that day?

4. The man in the green shirt describes what he did on his day off. How does he structure this short narrative?

5. The man in the green shirt abruptly changes the focus of the conversation. Describe how he does this and what is he interested in learning about.

6. How does the man in the green shirt use space to inquire about the meeting?

7. How do we know the man in the blue shirt dislikes meetings?

For the signing you observe, please write any helpful notes and questions that you may have for your teacher.

Comprehension Practice 8.2

Watch the dialogue all the way through and then answer as many of the questions below as you can. If necessary, view the dialogue a second time to see whether you are able to understand more and answer any additional questions.

Requesting a Change in Schedule

1. What schedule change does the man wish to make?

2. Why does the man need to request this work schedule change?

3. How does the man indicate that he wants to change his schedule for more than one work day?

4. For this new work schedule, what times does the woman suggest that the man should arrive at work and leave work?

5. What grammatical principle does the woman use when the expressing the times the man should arrive at and leave work?

For the signing you observe, please write any helpful notes and questions that you may have for your teacher.

Comprehension Practice 8.3

Watch the dialogue all the way through and then answer as many of the questions below as you can. If necessary, view the dialogue a second time to see whether you are able to understand more and answer any additional questions.

Describing the Weekend

1. In the opening of the narrative, what does the narrator tell us?

2. What did the narrator and a friend do on Friday night? What is his friend's name?

3. What did the narrator do on Saturday morning? How did he feel about this activity?

4. What did the narrator do on Saturday evening? Be specific.

5. What is the first thing the narrator did on Sunday morning and at what time?

6. After the first Sunday activity, describe the rest of the narrator's Sunday activities.

For the signing you observe, please write any helpful notes and questions that you may have for your teacher.

Comprehension Practice 8.4

Watch the dialogue all the way through and then answer as many of the questions below as you can. If necessary, view the dialogue a second time to see whether you are able to understand more and answer any additional questions.

New in Town

1. How does the woman in the black blouse gain attention to initiate the conversation with the man?

2. What does the woman in the black blouse ask? Why doesn't she know this information?

3. What is the man's response?

4. The man uses the sign *to-ask.* Describe how he uses subject-object incorporation in this sign and state what it means.

5. What does the woman in the purple blouse explain? Be specific with the details she provides.

6. Explain the importance of asking if there is a large crowd of Deaf people attending this community activity.

7. Where is the place that these people are discussing?

8. What do you notice about how the woman in the purple blouse fingerspells the name of this place?

For the signing you observe, please write any helpful notes and questions that you may have for your teacher.

Expressive Practice Prompts

These Expressive Practice Prompts show you the types of questions and statements you should be able to express in ASL by the end of Unit 8. Your teacher may use these Expressive Practice Prompts in class. You should practice these with your practice partner and group outside of class as well.

1. Ask a classmate if he/she went to a play last night.

2. Tell a classmate the current quarter/semester of the school year.

3. Tell a classmate you are going to a movie this Friday night.

4. Ask a classmate if he/she enjoys bowling.

5. Tell a classmate you enjoy sleeping in on Saturday morning.

6. Tell a classmate you enjoyed going out to eat with your husband or wife this past Friday. (Boyfriend, girlfriend, or friend may be substituted.)

7. Ask a classmate what he/she did last weekend.

8. Ask a classmate the date of his/her birthday.

9. Express the seasons of the year.

10. Tell a classmate three activities you enjoy doing on the weekend.

11. Ask a classmate if he/she exercised yesterday.

12. Express the months of the year.

13. Ask a classmate where he/she went on vacation last summer.

14. Tell a classmate you don't want to exercise because it is boring.

15. Tell a classmate to meet you at the meeting at 3 p.m.

Expressive Practice Prompts (continued)

16. Ask a classmate when he/she will have some time off from work.

17. Tell a classmate your favorite restaurant and when you go there.

18. Tell the class how long you have been married.

19. Tell the class what time you start and end work.

Grammar and Language, Culture, and Community Review Questions

These questions will assist you as you read the Grammar and the Language, Culture, and Community sections in this unit.

1. How are the meanings of "future time" and "past time" communicated in the signs shown in Figures 8.1–8.4?

2. What is the general organizing principle for telling when an event will occur? Give an example of this principle.

3. How do ASL signers express tense (past, present, or future)? How does this differ from English?

4. How is the specific number of weeks, months, and years indicated in Figures 8.7–8.12?

5. Explain how signers make statements using question signs (interrogatives), for example, who, what, when, how?

6. Study Figures 8.15 and 8.16. How is "a question" being communicated differently in these examples?

7. When something is fingerspelled and you miss or do not understand the spelling, how should you request clarification?

8. Which months of the year are abbreviated in ASL?

9. When a year has double zeros (for example, 2005), how is the year expressed in ASL?

10. Name two major, national organizations that play an important role in the social and political activities of Deaf people.

11. What functions are served by the clubs, organizations, and events within the Deaf community?

12. What federal law helped the Deaf community gain access to public and private business and social events?

Sign Vocabulary Illustrations

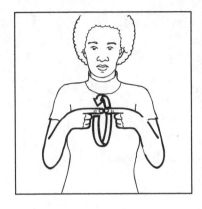

all-year

approximately, about

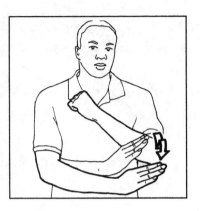

autumn/fall

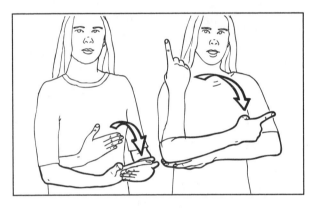

birthday (1)

birthday (2)

bowling

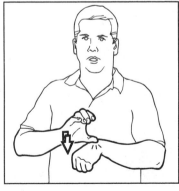

church

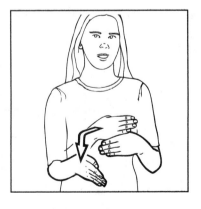

end, complete

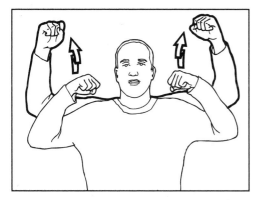

to-exercise, *work-out*

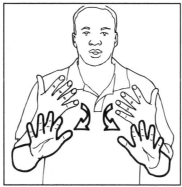

finish, *done*

go-out-to

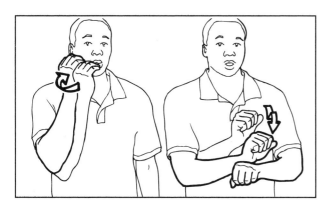

homework

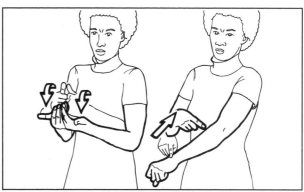

how-long

last-month

last-week

last-year

month

movie, *film*

newspaper/print

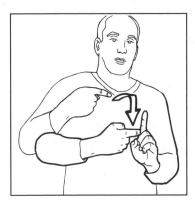

next-month

next-week

next-year

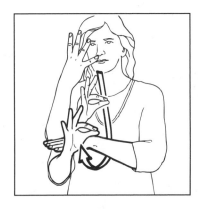

oversleep

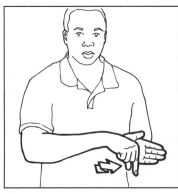

quarter (academic year)

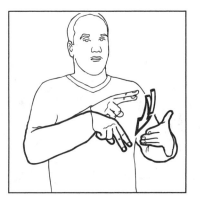

reading

restaurant

running

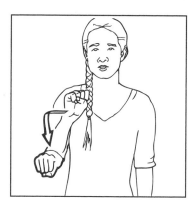

semester

shopping

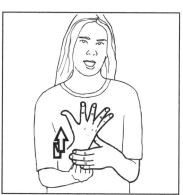

spring (season)

start, *begin*

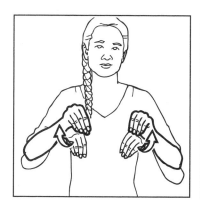

store (business)

studying

summer

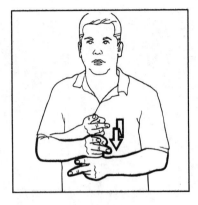

take-care-of

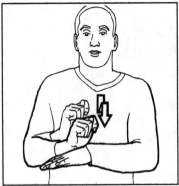

temple

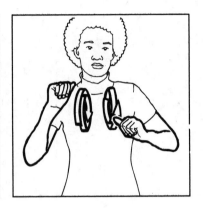

theatre, *drama, play*

time-off, *off-from work*

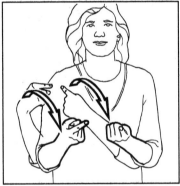

up-to-now, *since*

vacation

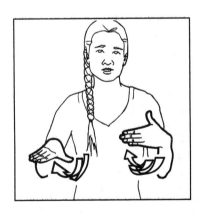

walking

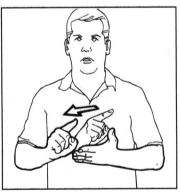

week

weekend

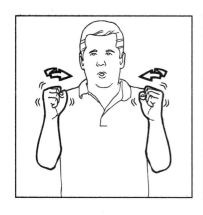
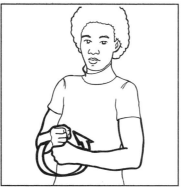

winter   *year*

Asking for Assistance

In this unit you learn to make formal, informal, and command requests. Several grammar principles introduced in previous units are further elaborated and practiced, and the "metaphor of silence" as it has been applied to Deaf people is discussed.

Unit 9 Overview

Learning Outcomes

1. Make formal, informal, and command requests

2. Distinguish noun/verb pairs

3. Use subject and object incorporating verbs

4. Produce a topic/comment sentence

5. Use instrumental classifiers

6. Learn about the "metaphor of silence" as it has been applied to Deaf people

---

Vocabulary

open-door	*noisy*	*don't-mind*
close-door	*quiet,* silent, calm	*hand-to*
window	*light* (electric)	*to-show*
open-window	*turn-light-on*	*tell*
close-window	*turn-light-off*	*I-D/identification*
key	*dim-the-light*	*picture,* photograph
to-lock	*dark*	*look-at*
locked	*bright,* clear	*bring*
open-book	*for*	*use,* wear
close-book	*what-for*	

Grammar

1. More on Noun/Verb Pairs

2. More on Subject and Object Incorporating Verbs

3. More on Topic/Comment Sentence Structure

4. Instrumental Classifiers

Unit 9 Overview

Language, Culture, and Community

1. Making Requests Appropriately

2. The Metaphor of Silence

Practice and Review Materials

1. Video Exercises

   – Sample Expressive Dialogue

   – Comprehension Practice

   – Expressive Practice Prompts

2. Grammar and Language, Culture, and Community Review Questions

3. Sign Vocabulary Illustrations

1. More on Noun/Verb Pairs
2. More on Subject and Object Incorporating Verbs
3. More on Topic/Comment Sentence Structure
4. Instrumental Classifiers

1. More on Noun/Verb Pairs

In Unit 7, Where People Live, noun/verb sign pairs were introduced. These are sign pairs for which the noun is derived from the verb; that is, a change from single, continuous movement for verb signs to repeated, shorter movement for noun signs, with other sign parts (handshape, location, and orientation) remaining the same. Examples of noun/verb sign pairs in this unit include the following:

Nouns	Verbs
door	*open-door* and *close-door*
window	*open-window* and *close-window*
key	*to-lock* and *unlock*
book	*open-book* and *close-book*
light	*turn-light-on* and *turn-light-off*

Figures 9.1, 9.2, and 9.3 show *door, open-door,* and *close-door.*

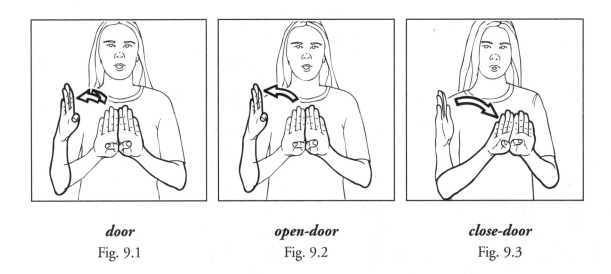

door	*open-door*	*close-door*
Fig. 9.1	Fig. 9.2	Fig. 9.3

2. More on Subject and Object Incorporating Verbs

In Unit 7, Where People Live, subject and object incorporating verbs were discussed and shown. As stated in Unit 7, these verb signs may indicate the subject (who did it), the verb (what is being done), and the object (to whom it was done) all in one sign. The locations where the verb sign begins and ends and the direction of the movement are important to indicating the subject (beginning location in the signing space) and object (ending location in the signing space). Examples of these types of verbs in this unit are show in Figures 9.4–9.10.

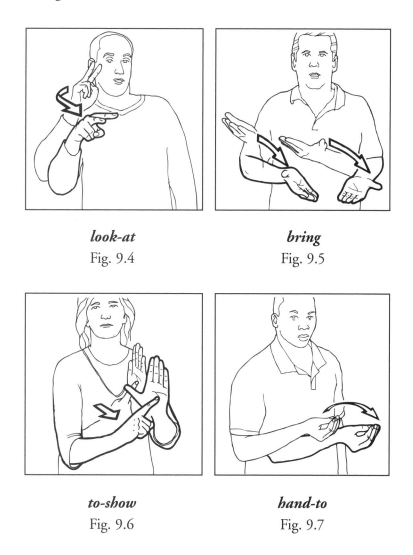

look-at
Fig. 9.4

bring
Fig. 9.5

to-show
Fig. 9.6

hand-to
Fig. 9.7

Examples of this with *to show* are illustrated below:

I show you.
Fig. 9.8

You show me.
Fig. 9.9

He/She shows him/her.
Fig. 9.10

3. More on Topic/Comment Sentence Structure

In Unit 5, Work Duties, Topic/Comment Structure was introduced. This structure may be used when making requests. For example, to communicate "Please hand me that paper" ASL (a) marks the topic *paper there* with raised eyebrows and upper torso raised and held slightly back, (b) followed by marking the comment (request) *please hand-to-me* with a slight pause, lowering of the eyebrows, and resuming a normal, neutral posture. This sentence is illustrated in Figure 9.11.

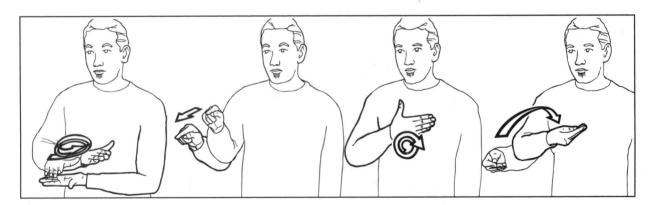

Please hand me that paper.
Fig. 9.11

4. Instrumental Classifiers

In Unit 5, Work Duties, classifiers as a general topic and whole entity classifiers as one type of classifier were introduced. In this unit, instrumental classifiers are introduced.

It is important to remember that in many circumstances classifiers function as predicates; that is, they express the "verb" portion of a sentence. Instrumental classifiers show how something is being held and used. In the handshape and movement of the verb, an aspect of the object being held and used is evident. Another way to think about this is that there is agreement between the verb and the object of the verb, which is shown in the handshape and movement of the verb sign. For example, suppose I want to express "pick up a piece of paper." The verb sign **pick-up** will be produced with the thumb and index finger pinching together with the motion of picking up as if actually picking up one sheet of paper. If I want to express "pick up a stack of paper," the verb sign **pick-up** uses two hands in an inverted "C" handshape as if grasping a thick stack of paper and lifting it up. If I wanted to express "pick up a ball," depending on the size of the ball I would use one hand or two hands and the hand-shape conforms to the size and shape of the ball being picked up. These three forms of the verb sign **pick-up** using three different instrumental classifier handshapes are illustrated in Figures 9.12–9.14.

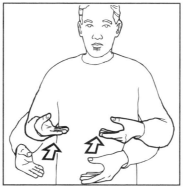
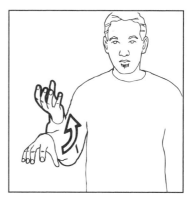

pick-up-piece-of-paper   *pick-up-stack-of-paper*   *pick-up-tennis-ball*
Fig. 9.12   Fig. 9.13   Fig. 9.14

Unit 9 Language, Culture, and Community

1. Making Requests Appropriately

2. The Metaphor of Silence

1. Making Requests Appropriately

In this unit, you learn to make requests in ASL. The structure of your request and the signs you use depend on the degree of formality involved with the situation and the person(s) you are addressing. In a formal situation, such as a meeting or when making a request to someone you are not familiar with, it is considered polite to fully explain a reason and use the phrase ***please for+me.*** In addition, when Deaf people address hearing people, they will also often make formal requests by stating a reason and signing ***please*** and the request, with the phrase ***for+me*** not included. Figure 9.15 shows a formal request.

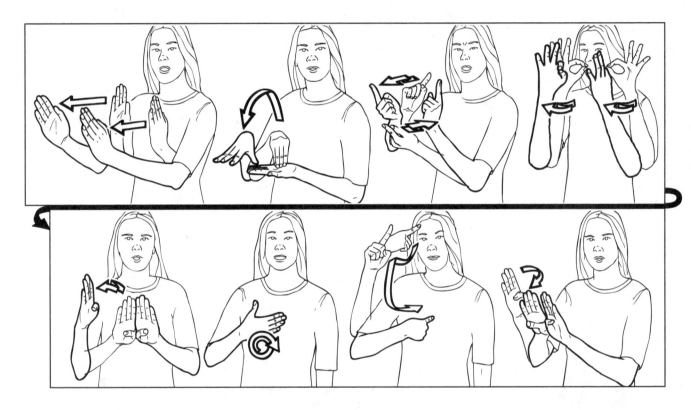

There is a lot of noise in the hallway. Would you be so kind as to close the door for me?
(Formal Request)
Fig. 9.15

In informal situations such as addressing a friend, co-worker, or family member, it is appropriate to use a less formal request. Informal requests may or may not be preceded by a brief reason and will usually include ***for+me.*** Informal requests may also simply use ***please,*** with no reason stated. In addition, ***don't-mind*** is frequently used to make informal requests. Figures 9.16 through 9.18 demonstrate informal requests.

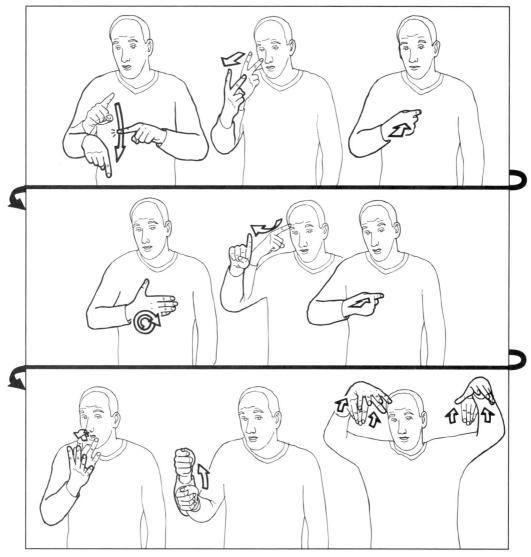

I can't see. Would you get the light for me?
(Informal Request)
Fig. 9.16

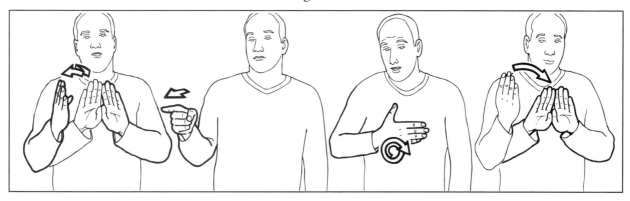

Please close the door.
(Informal Request)
Fig. 9.17

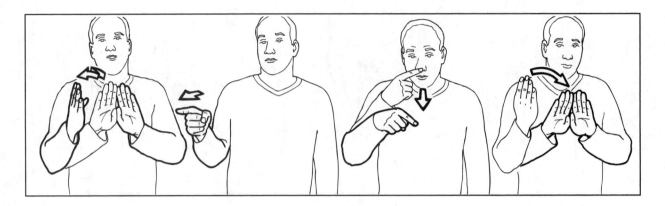

Please close the door.
(Informal Request)
Fig. 9.18

In situations where there is urgency or when it may be appropriate to make a command request, the signs will be produced with greater force and phrases such as ***please for+me*** and ***don't-mind*** are not used. Figure 9.19 shows a command request.

Bring your books tomorrow.
(Command)
Fig. 9.19

2. The Metaphor of Silence

"Deaf people cannot hear, right?" Not exactly. Many deaf people can hear sounds to varying degrees. They do not live in "a world of silence," although, to paraphrase Padden and Humphries (1988, p. 91), the metaphor of silence is a pervasive one for hearing people and is used by Deaf people as well as a self-reference. Publications and organizations in the Deaf world use references to silence; for example, *The Silent Worker* and *Silent News* newspapers and the Pacific Silent Club and the Silent Oriole Club. Although Deaf people make use of this silence metaphor, their lives are far from soundless, and they know quite a bit about sound. As students in schools for the deaf, they experiment with vocal sounds and use their voices to gain attention. Many Deaf people have had hours of formal practice learning to use speech and listening to communicate. This formal instruction and what deaf children learn informally about sound form a basis for deaf individuals' understanding and use of sound.

Deaf children learn that particular bodily functions are accompanied by sounds and that these sounds, whether they can "hear" them or not, must be "controlled" to avoid social embarrassment. They learn that walking makes sounds when they are "caught" trying to sneak out of their dorm rooms in the middle of the night by their hearing houseparent or when they are reprimanded by their teacher for "shuffling their feet." They learn that setting things down or closing doors can make loud sounds that will get a reaction from some hearing people. By making loud sounds and seeing the reaction of their hearing and hard-of-hearing peers, friends, and teachers, Deaf children learn the function of sound and learn to use sound in ways unique to Deaf culture. Even into adult life, these "lessons in sound" may continue when Deaf mothers or fathers are chided by their hearing children to "stop reaching in the popcorn box so noisily" while in the movie theatre.

Deaf people definitely do not live in a world of silence. Some deaf people can hear and appreciate music. Many, with hearing aids, can hear environmental sounds such as airplanes, horns honking, and the whir of machinery. Don't think "the noisy office" will be a good place to stick Deaf Smith. Deaf Smith may be more annoyed by the constant noise or vibration than Hearing Jones because Hearing Jones has more practice blocking out background sounds. For an excellent treatment of this subject, read "The Meaning of Sound" by Padden and Humphries (1988).

Reference

Padden, C., & Humphries, T. (1988). Chapter 6: The meaning of sound. In *Deaf in America: Voices from a culture* (pp. 91–109). Cambridge, MA: Harvard University Press.

1. Video Exercises

    – Sample Expressive Dialogue

    – Comprehension Practice

    – Expressive Practice Prompts

2. Grammar and Language, Culture, and Community Review Questions

3. Sign Vocabulary Illustrations

Sample Expressive Dialogue

Read the dialogue prompts below and then watch how each signer expresses these prompts on the video. Sign along with both Signer A and Signer B or with either Signer A or Signer B on the video. You may wish to practice this dialogue with a classmate outside of class time and your teacher may review this dialogue in class and ask you to sign this dialogue with a classmate.

Making a Request

Signer A: Gain attention

Signer B: Respond appropriately

Signer A: Ask politely and informally that the door be opened

Signer B: Respond that you cannot open the door because the door is locked and you do not have a key

Signer B: State that you will go to the secretary to get key

Signer A: Respond appropriately

For the signing you observe, please write below any helpful notes and questions you may have for your teacher.

Comprehension Practice 9.1

Watch the dialogue all the way through and then answer as many of the questions below as you can. If necessary, view the dialogue a second time to see whether you are able to understand more and answer any additional questions.

Locked Out of the Office

1. What is the woman's problem?

2. What does the campus safety officer ask for at first?

3. What differences does the campus safety officer notice between what the woman provides and the woman herself?

4. How does the woman explain these differences?

5. What is the woman's name?

6. What do you notice about how the woman spells her name when she makes the letter "e"? Can you explain why she forms her "e" in this manner?

For the signing you observe, please write any helpful notes and questions that you may have for your teacher.

Comprehension Practice 9.2

Watch the dialogue all the way through and then answer as many of the questions below as you can. If necessary, view the dialogue a second time to see whether you are able to understand more and answer any additional questions.

Using a Copy Machine

1. What does the woman ask?

2. What reason does the man give for not knowing how to use the copy machine?

3. What four features of the machine does the woman describe?

4. What additional question about using the machine does the man ask?

5. In answering the man's last question, the woman uses several classifiers. Identify and discuss the meanings for two of the classifiers that she uses.

For the signing you observe, please write any helpful notes and questions that you may have for your teacher.

Comprehension Practice 9.3

Watch the dialogue all the way through and then answer as many of the questions below as you can. If necessary, view the dialogue a second time to see whether you are able to understand more and answer any additional questions.

Locked Out of the House

1. When did the incident happen?

2. Briefly summarize the main ideas expressed in this story.

3. Describe the classifier the woman uses to indicate that she and her son approached the house.

4. What does the woman notice and then use to break the window?

5. Identify two instrumental classifiers the woman uses in her description of the incident.

6. The woman uses *cl:index* with both hands to describe the shape of two objects. What are these two objects and what are their shapes?

7. How will the woman prevent this from happening again?

For the signing you observe, please write any helpful notes and questions that you may have for your teacher.

Comprehension Practice 9.4

Watch the dialogue all the way through and then answer as many of the questions below as you can. If necessary, view the dialogue a second time to see whether you are able to understand more and answer any additional questions.

Requesting a New Printer

1. The woman is focused on something at her desk. How does the man initially gain her attention?

2. Before the man sits down, he signs ***"Don't-mind short discussion."*** What does this mean? What type of request is he making?

3. The woman uses a classifier in responding to the man's initial request. Identify this classifier and describe what it means.

4. After the man sits down, what request does he make first? Why does he make this request?

5. What is the man's concern? What does he need? Be specific. Describe in detail what the problem is and exactly what type of new equipment he is asking for.

6. What solution does the woman offer? What is the name of the other person mentioned in the solution the woman offers?

7. Explain the mood that occurs in the conversation.

For the signing you observe, please write any helpful notes and questions that you may have for your teacher.

Expressive Practice Prompts

These Expressive Practice Prompts show you the types of questions and statements you should be able to express in ASL by the end of Unit 9. Your teacher may use these Expressive Practice Prompts in class. You should practice these with your practice partner and group outside of class as well.

1. Ask a classmate to help you move a table from one location to another in the room.

2. Give a reason and ask a classmate to close a window.

3. Ask a classmate if his/her car is locked.

4. Tell a classmate that you forgot to lock your car.

5. Give a reason and ask a classmate to close the door.

6. Ask a classmate to give a paper to each person in the class.

7. Ask a classmate to show you his/her ID.

8. Express that the lights are dim and to please make them brighter.

9. Express three ways you use your ID.

10. Express to someone that you forgot his/her name and ask him/her to tell you his/her name again.

11. Explain how you use a copy machine to make copies.

12. Tell a classmate to look at you.

13. Express that you cannot enter the room because you left your keys at home.

14. Ask a classmate to turn off the lights when class is finished.

15. Ask a classmate whether his/her ID picture is black and white or color.

Expressive Practice Prompts (continued)

16. Express two ways to get in the house when you are locked out.

17. Express that print on the projected image is not clear. Ask that it be made clear, pause, and express satisfaction that it is now clear.

18. Give a reason and ask a classmate to go to the light switch and flip the switch to turn on the lights.

19. Ask a classmate to give you the phone book because you need to look up a phone number.

20. Ask a classmate if he/she brought his/her homework to class.

Grammar and Language, Culture, and Community Review Questions

These questions will assist you as you read the Grammar and the Language, Culture, and Community sections in this unit.

1. For ASL noun/verb pairs, explain the difference in production of the noun and the verb.

2. Explain how the sign *hand-to* can communicate the subject (who handed something) and the object (to whom something was handed).

3. What non-manual signals show that a topic/comment sentence is being communicated?

4. Explain how handshapes are modified to "agree" with the object being "handled" when used for instrumental classifiers.

5. Name and explain the three types of requests introduced in this unit.

6. Explain why it is incorrect to consider that most deaf people live in a completely "silent world."

7. How do deaf children learn about sound, both formally and informally?

Sign Vocabulary Illustrations

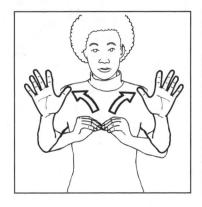

bright, clear

bring

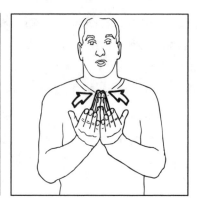

close-book

close-door

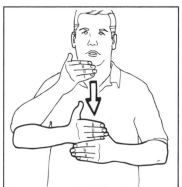

close-window

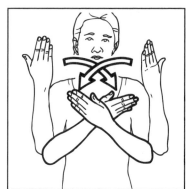

dark

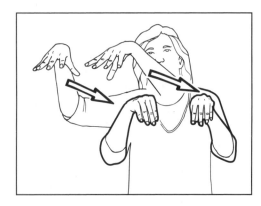

dim-the-light

don't-mind

for

hand-to

I-D/identification

key

light (electric)

to-lock

locked

look-at

noisy

open-book

open-door

open-window

picture, *photograph*

quiet, *silent, calm*

to-show

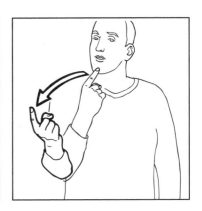

tell

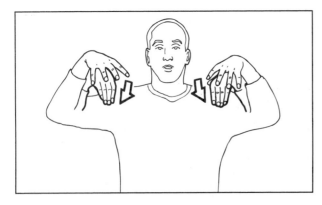

turn-light-off

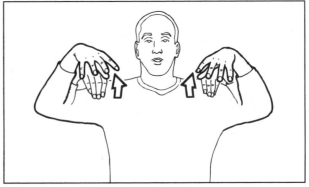

turn-light-on

use, *wear*

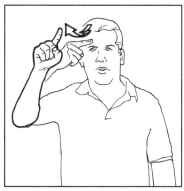

what-for

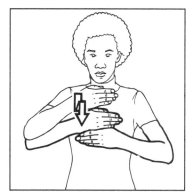

window

Discussing Weather

In this unit you learn to report and comment on common weather conditions found in various parts of the United States. Also, you learn to show relative locations for areas of the United States, signs for U.S. cities and states, and map directions versus real orientation.

Unit 10 Overview

Learning Outcomes

1. Report weather forecasts, including degrees of weather conditions from mild to severe

2. Express feelings about weather conditions

3. Show relative locations when referring to areas of the United States

4. Express signs for U.S. cities and states

5. Express map directions versus real orientation

Vocabulary

snow	*dry*	*strange, odd*
rain	*minus, negative*	*north*
wind	*plus, negative*	*south*
cloudy	*inside*	*east*
sun	*outside*	*west*
weather	*always*	*middle-of, center*
good	*often*	*thereabouts*
bad	*sometimes*	*to-plow*
thunder	*never*	*to-rake*
lightning	*more*	*to-paint*
temperature (climate)	*less, reduce*	*to-play*
cold	*tend-to*	*to-plant*
hot	*predict, forecast*	*to-shovel*
cool (climate)	*warn*	*grow*
warm	*open*	*#if*
61 to *100* *	*closed, to-close*	*suppose*
freeze	*careful*	
humid	*fast*	

* Signs for **61** to **100** are not included in the Unit 10 Sign Vocabulary Illustrations section of this *ASL at Work Student Text.*

Unit 10 Overview

Grammar

1. More on Use of Space for Contrasting and Comparing

2. More on Modifying Sign Movement for Degree

3. Incorporation of Timeline with Sign Movement for Frequency of Occurrence

4. Conditional Sentence Structure

5. More on Use of Non-Manual Signals (oo, mm, cha, ee, th) for Expressing Adverbs and Adjectives

6. Numbers that "Rock and Roll"

Language, Culture, and Community

1. U.S. State Signs and Fingerspelled Abbreviations

2. Signs for Major U.S. Cities

3. Map Directions versus Real Orientation

Practice and Review Materials

1. Video Exercises
   - Sample Expressive Dialogue
   - Comprehension Practice
   - Expressive Practice Prompts

2. Grammar and Language, Culture, and Community Review Questions

3. Sign Vocabulary Illustrations

1. More on Use of Space for Contrasting and Comparing

2. More on Modifying Sign Movement for Degree

3. Incorporation of Timeline with Sign Movement for Frequency of Occurrence

4. Conditional Sentence Structure

5. More on Use of Non-Manual Signals (oo, mm, cha, ee, th) for Expressing Adverbs and Adjectives

6. Numbers that "Rock and Roll"

1. More on Use of Space for Contrasting and Comparing

In Unit 3, People at Work, Contrasting and Comparing was introduced. As discussed in Unit 3, when making comparisons signers establish absent referents (persons, places, or things) to the sides of the signing space. When making comparisons:

- The first referent is established on the non-dominant hand side of the signer.

- The second referent is established on the dominant hand side of the signer.

- When pointing or referring to each referent, the signer shifts his/her body and head slightly in the direction of the referent established on each side of the signing space.

Figure 10.1 on the next page shows an example of the use of space for contrasting and comparing.

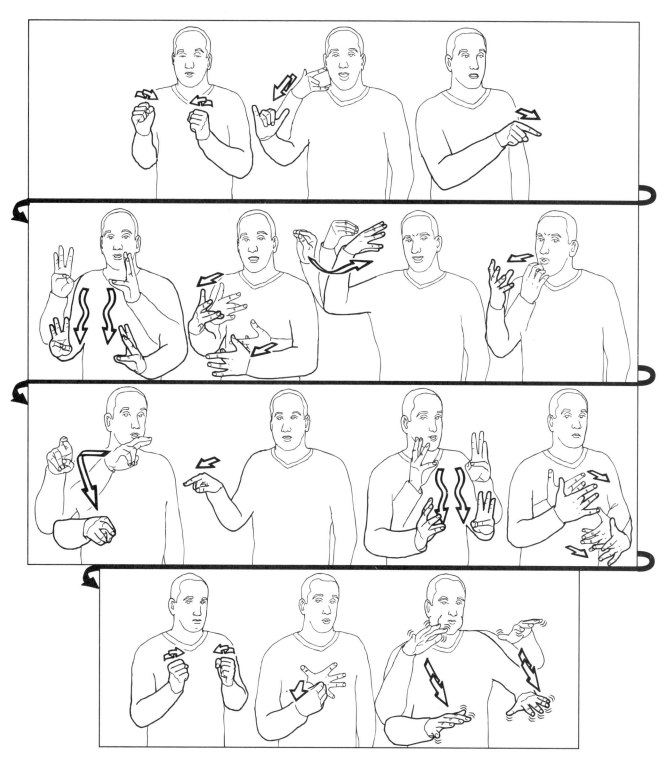

**The weather in California in winter is generally sunny and warm,
while the weather in Rochester is cold and snowy.**

Fig. 10.1

2. More on Modifying Sign Movement for Degree

In Unit 5, Work Duties, sign movement modification and non-manual signals for degree were introduced. Sign movement changes and non-manual signals (see #3 in this Grammar section) are used to modify verbs like ***to-rain*** to indicate that it is raining very hard or very lightly. These meanings are illustrated in Figures 10.2 and 10.3.

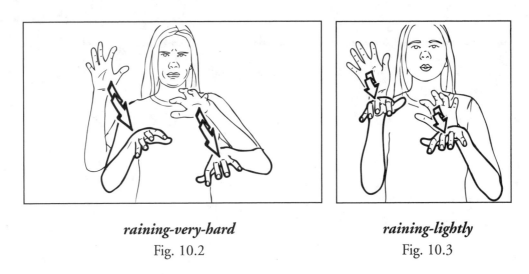

raining-very-hard	***raining-lightly***
Fig. 10.2	Fig. 10.3

Other weather conditions introduced in this unit that may be modified in this way include ***cold*** and ***hot;*** see Figures 10.4 and 10.5.

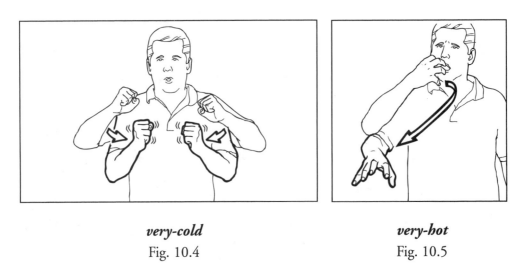

very-cold	***very-hot***
Fig. 10.4	Fig. 10.5

3. Incorporation of Timeline with Sign Movement for Frequency of Occurrence

In Unit 7, Where People Live, the Timeline was introduced. In this unit the timeline is combined with the handshape for the sign meaning ***to-repeat*** or ***again*** to create signs that express how frequently something occurs. Figures 10.6–10.8 show these signs.

something-occurs-very-frequently
Fig. 10.6

something-occurs-occasionally
Fig. 10.7

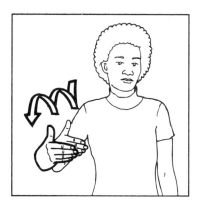

something-occurs-infrequently
Fig. 10.8

4. Conditional Sentence Structure

Similar to English, conditional sentences in ASL consist of two parts, the conditional clause and the consequence or result. In ASL, the conditional clause includes the non-manual signal of raised eyebrows with head tilted forward. There is a slight pause in signing between stating the condition and the result. The result or consequence part of the sentence may be either a statement or a question and it is accompanied by non-manual signals appropriate for either statements or questions. In ASL, the condition is stated first, followed by the result. English conditional sentences have more flexible word order, with either the condition or the result stated first.

Conditional statements in English usually begin with the word "if." In ASL, conditional statements may be communicated by signers using only the conditional non-manual signal described above, or they may add this non-manual signal to the fingerspelled loan sign *"#if"* or the sign *suppose.* Figure 10.9 below shows a conditional statement using the fingerspelled loan sign *#if* and Figure 10.10 on the next page shows a conditional statement using the sign *suppose.*

If the temperature hits 100 degrees in Buffalo, what would you do?

Fig. 10.9

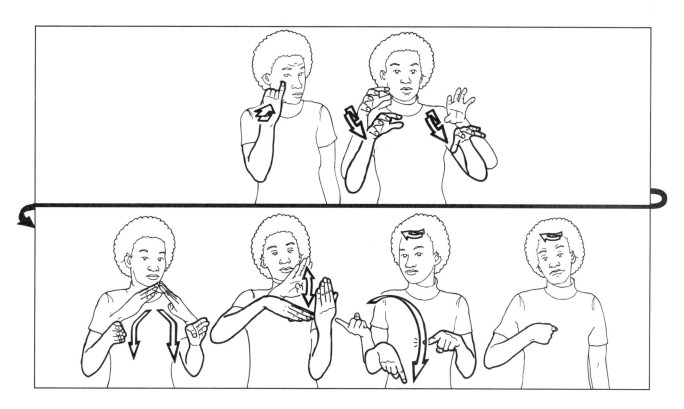

Suppose it rains, I can't paint my house.

Fig. 10.10

5. More on Use of Non-Manual Signals (oo, mm, cha, ee, th) for Expressing Adverbs and Adjectives

In Unit 7, Where People Live, the non-manual signal for close in time or space (cs) was introduced. In this unit, additional non-manual signals used to add meaning to signs are introduced and practiced. The non-manual signal "oo" indicates very small or thin. The non-manual signal "mm" indicates something is normal or happens with regularity. The non-manual signal "cha" indicates something is abnormally large or tall, the non-manual signal "ee" indicates something is happening with intensity, and the non-manual signal "th" indicates something is happening carelessly. All of these non-manual signals are formed with the lips, tongue, and eyes. Figures 10.11–10.15 show these non-manual signals and the meanings they add to signs.

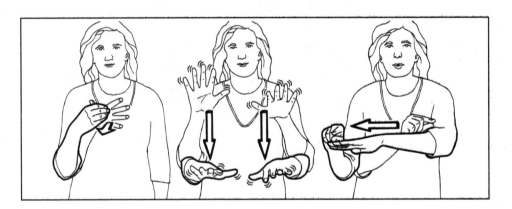

The snow cover is very thin.
"oo"
Fig. 10.11

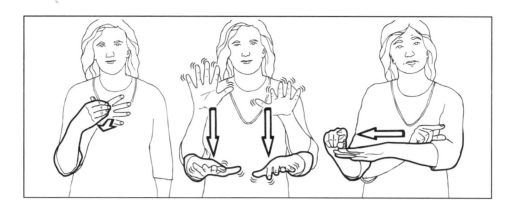

The snow cover is moderately thick.
"mm"
Fig. 10.12

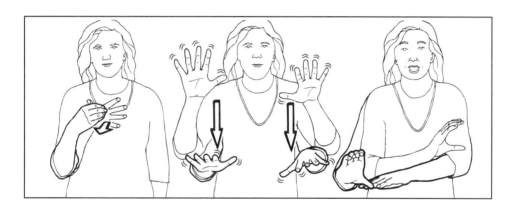

The snow cover is very thick.
"cha"
Fig. 10.13

Driving carefully.
"ee"
Fig. 10.14

Driving carelessly.
"th"
Fig. 10.15

6. Numbers that "Rock and Roll"

Signs for the numbers from *67* to *99* have unique production characteristics. You learned in Unit 6, Sharing Personal Information, that signs from *26* through *66* follow regular production patterns. For example, *45* is simply the sign *4* and *5* with palm orientation forward and a slight movement to the side between the numbers. Number signs between *26* and *66* are produced in this same manner, except for the double numbers *22, 33, 44, 55,* and *66,* which have a palm orientation facing down. In addition, the numbers *77, 88,* and *99* are produced with palm orientation facing down.

However, some number signs between *67* and *98* really "rock"; that is, the production of these numbers requires a twisting or rocking motion of the wrist and hand. Don't worry! They are easy to learn because they follow a pattern that is based on "low to high" or "high to low." What does that mean? You have learned that touching your thumb to your little finger means *6,* thumb to ring finger means *7,* thumb to middle finger means *8,* and thumb to index or first finger means *9.* Six is a lower number than seven. It is not only lower numerically, but also formed by touching your thumb to the "lowliest finger," your pinky! Thus, when you sign *67* your hand starts "low" and twists or rocks "up" to the higher number. Figure 10.16 on the next page shows *69* and the twisting motion from "lower to higher" for this number. The numbers *67* and *68* would follow this production pattern because these numbers combine a "lower" with a "higher" number. This same principle holds true for numbers in the 70's and 80's. The complete set of numbers that follow this "lower-to-higher" pattern are *67, 68, 69, 78, 79,* and *89.*

The opposite production pattern holds for numbers that combine a higher number with a lower number. For example, for **96,** the **9** is a higher number than the **6** and **9** involves the "mighty" index finger versus the **6,** which uses the lowly pinky finger. Thus, when you sign **96** your hand starts high on the **9** and rolls down low on the **6.** Figure 10.17 shows **96** and the rolling motion from higher to lower for this number. The numbers **97** and **98** follow this same production pattern because these numbers combine a higher with a lower number. This pattern holds true for numbers in the 70's and 80's as well. The complete set of numbers that follow this higher-to-lower pattern are **76, 86, 87, 96, 97,** and **98.**

Practice the two sets of "rockin 'n' rollin" numbers discussed above. If you remember the patterns it should be a snap.

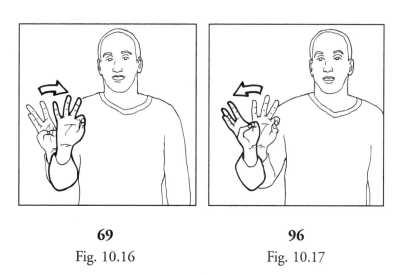

69

Fig. 10.16

96

Fig. 10.17

Unit 10 Language, Culture, and Community

1. U.S. State Signs and Fingerspelled Abbreviations

2. Signs for Major U.S. Cities

3. Map Directions versus Real Orientation

1. U.S. State Signs and Fingerspelled Abbreviations

Some U.S. states have signs that are widely used by ASL signers. Among these are *California, Texas, New-York, Colorado,* and *Arizona.* Other states are commonly abbreviated using both the older and the newer forms of Post Office abbreviations. Older forms include *F-l-a* (Florida), *M-i-n-n* (Minnesota), *W-i-s-c* (Wisconsin), *C-o-n-n* (Connecticut), and newer forms include *P-a* (Pennsylvania), *N-c* (North Carolina), *S-c* (South Carolina), and *N-m* (New Mexico). Also, in some signing communities, there may be a sign for the state that is used locally, but is not used on a nationwide basis. It is best to check with local signers for state signs and abbreviations that are used and understood within your local signing community.

2. Signs for Major U.S. Cities

Major U.S. cities commonly have signs or fingerspelled abbreviations that are widely used among ASL signers. Cities with signs used on a nationwide basis include *New-York, L-a* (Los Angeles), *S-f* (San Francisco), *Chicago, Houston, Atlanta, Buffalo, Detroit,* and *Seattle.* Some cities share the same sign; for example, *Rochester* (NY) and *Richmond* (VA) both use an "R" handshape with a movement that looks like a 7 being drawn in the air. Many other cities have name signs that will be used by signers in a local signing community but are not widely known or used outside of those communities. Like state signs, it is best to check with local signers for city sign names used and understood in your local signing community.

3. Map Directions versus Real Orientation

When discussing compass directions without reference to real places or locations, signers use the signing plane in front of them to indicate north, south, east, and west. *North* is signed with the N handshape moving up in space, *south* is signed with the S handshape moving down in space, *east* is signed with the E handshape moving to the signer's right, and *west* is signed with the W handshape moving to the signer's left. When referencing a direction with regard to a real location, the signs *north, south, east,* and *west* move in the actual direction of north, south, east, or west depending on the direction the signer is facing.

Unit 10 Practice and Review Materials

1. Video Exercises

    – Sample Expressive Dialogue

    – Comprehension Practice

    – Expressive Practice Prompts

2. Grammar and Language, Culture, and Community Review Questions

3. Sign Vocabulary Illustrations

Sample Expressive Dialogue

Read the dialogue prompts below and then watch how each signer expresses these prompts on the video. Sign along with both Signer A and Signer B or with either Signer A or Signer B on the video. You may wish to practice this dialogue with a classmate outside of class time and your teacher may review this dialogue in class and ask you to sign this dialogue with a classmate.

Talking About Weather

(Situation: Signer B is reading the weather section of the newspaper. Signer A begins the conversation with a statement about today's weather conditions.)

Signer A: Make a statement about the weather being bad today

Signer B: Agree and make a statement that the weather will improve tomorrow

Signer A: Ask to confirm that Signer B's statement is true

Signer B.   Show the newspaper as proof

Signer A: Express that the weather has been hot for several days and now it will finally change

Signer B: Express that you prefer cool, sunny weather

Signer A: Express that you prefer the same weather conditions and express dislike for hot, humid, and rainy weather

Signer B: Express your agreement with Signer A

For the signing you observe, please write any helpful notes and questions that you may have for your teacher.

Comprehension Practice 10.1

Watch the dialogue all the way through and then answer as many of the questions below as you can. If necessary, view the dialogue a second time to see whether you are able to understand more and answer any additional questions.

Discussing Spring Activities

1. What does the woman ask the man to do? What do they see?

2. What reasons does the woman give for looking forward to spring?

3. Which one of the woman's reasons surprises the man?

4. What does the woman plan to plant?

5. What grammatical principle does the woman use when describing her plans for this year?

6. What did the woman plant last year that did not grow well? Explain what happened and why.

7. What change would the woman like to see this year?

For the signing you observe, please write any helpful notes and questions that you may have for your teacher.

Comprehension Practice 10.2

Watch the dialogue all the way through and then answer as many of the questions below as you can. If necessary, view the dialogue a second time to see whether you are able to understand more and can answer any remaining questions.

Discussing Weather

1. What does the first woman express about the weather?

2. What detail does the second woman clarify?

3. What does the first woman plan to do after work?

4. After looking out the window, why is the second woman excited?

5. Describe the snow conditions. What signs and sign principles does the second woman use to describe these conditions?

6. What does the second woman plan to do after work?

For the signing you observe, please write any helpful notes and questions that you may have for your teacher.

Comprehension Practice 10.3

Watch the dialogue all the way through and then answer as many of the questions below as you can. If necessary, view the dialogue a second time to see whether you are able to understand more and answer any additional questions.

Discussing an Ideal Climate

1. What are these two women discussing and what is different about how they discuss this topic?

2. What is the meaning of the sign *feel* used in this dialogue?

3. These two women are discussing their preferred climates. Describe in detail the first climate you see discussed, including geographical area, temperature, and weather conditions.

4. Describe in detail the preferred climate of the woman wearing the black blouse.

5. In discussing the preferred climate of the woman wearing the black blouse, the woman wearing the light purple blouse asks a clarifying question. What does she ask?

6. Both women use a sign that indicates that the weather conditions they are describing are typical for the regions they describe. What sign do they use that indicates this?

7. Give two different examples of how the use of space clarifies the information provided by both women.

8. How does the woman wearing the black blouse indicate the relationship between Miami and Orlando, Florida?

For the signing you observe, please write any helpful notes and questions that you may have for your teacher.

Comprehension Practice 10.4

Watch the narrative all the way through and then answer as many of the questions below as you can. If necessary, view the narrative a second time to see whether you are able to understand more and answer any additional questions.

Describing a Storm

1. When did this incident happen?

2. Did the narrator have any warning about this weather event?

3. What does the narrator describe happening after she initially went to sleep?

4. What classifier does the narrator use when she tells us her children came to her bedside in the middle of the night?

5. Her children are frightened. At first the narrator dismisses their concern. Finally she gets up to look out the window. Describe what she sees.

6. The narrator tells us what she does as a safety precaution. Describe what she does and who is involved.

7. In the description above, the narrator uses a grammatical principle indicating how many people were involved in this safety precaution. Name and describe the grammatical principle she uses.

8. Describe what the narrator sees when she opens the door the next morning.

9. When the narrator describes the aftermath of the storm, she tells us that both school and work were closed on the day after the storm. What grammatical principle does she use?

For the signing you observe, please write any helpful notes and questions that you may have for your teacher.

Expressive Practice Prompts

These Expressive Practice Prompts show you the types of questions and statements you should be able to express in ASL by the end of Unit 10. Your teacher may use these Expressive Practice Prompts in class. You should practice these with your practice partner and group outside of class as well.

1. Ask a classmate whether it is warmer or colder outside now.

2. Express which season of the year you like best and why.

3. Give a brief weather report for the weather today and tomorrow.

4. Report on the different regions of the country and the types of weather/climate-related problems each has.

5. Tell the class what your ideal weather would be like.

6. Comment about how strange the weather has been today. Compare two periods of the day, such as morning and afternoon.

7. Tell the class that it was difficult to drive to work this morning because it was foggy.

8. Caution the class that when they drive home this afternoon they will need to be careful because there is a forecast for freezing rain.

9. Say you don't mind living in an area that has hurricanes once in a while, but you would never live in an area that has tornadoes.

10. Say you don't mind living in an area that is cold once in awhile, but you would never live in an area that is often hot.

11. Ask a classmate whether it is colder outside today than yesterday.

12. Ask a classmate in what season of the year he/she was born.

13. Ask a classmate what the weather will be like tomorrow.

Expressive Practice Prompts (continued)

14. Ask a classmate what the weather will be like this weekend.

15. Ask a classmate what the temperature is inside the classroom.

16. Express the activities that you do during each season.

17. Express what you like to do outside when the weather is good.

18. Tell about the types of bad weather conditions in one area of the United States.

19. Announce to the class that because of a heavy snow storm schools will be closed.

20. Ask a classmate what he/she thinks the weather will be like during the summer this year.

Grammar and Language, Culture, and Community Review Questions

These questions will assist you as you read the Grammar and the Language, Culture, and Community sections in this unit.

1. Explain how signers use the signing space to make comparisons.

2. How are signs modified with movement and non-manual signals to indicate degree or emphasis?

3. Describe how the timeline is being used in Figures 10.6–10.8 to indicate future time.

4. Explain the non-manual signals (including facial expression and head position) that accompany a conditional clause in ASL.

5. What do the non-manual signals represented as follows indicate?
   A. "oo"
   B. "mm"
   C. "cha"
   D. "ee"
   E. "th"

6. Some number signs between **61** and **100** use a rocking motion when they are formed. Give three examples of each characteristic below for the number signs between **61** and **100** that use the following motions:
   A. Do not use any rocking motion when made
   B. Hand/wrist rotates/twists upward
   C. Hand/wrist rotates/twists downward

7. Some states have signs that are used widely among ASL signers. Other states tend to be abbreviated. Name two examples of states within each group below:
   A. States that are represented by signs
   B. States represented by older Post Office abbreviations
   C. States represented by two-letter Post Office abbreviations

8. Name three major U.S. cities that have signs commonly used among ASL signers.

9. When referencing a real location, what determines the direction of movement for ***north, south, east,*** and ***west?***

Sign Vocabulary Illustrations

always

bad

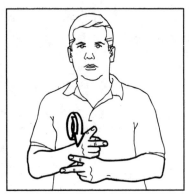

careful

closed, to-close

cloudy

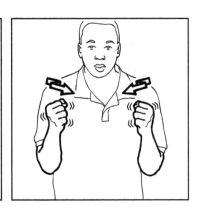

cold

cool (climate)

dry

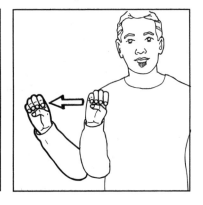

east

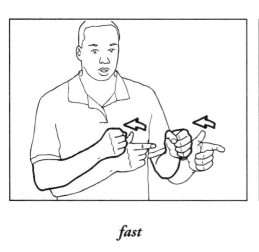

fast

freeze

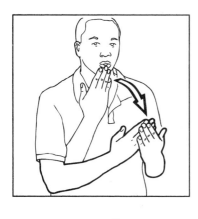

good

grow

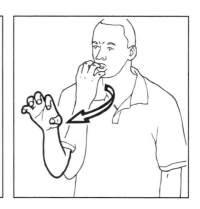

hot

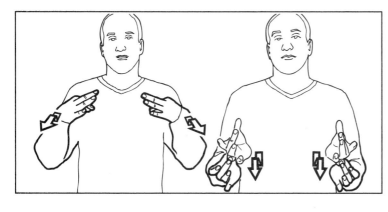

humid

#if

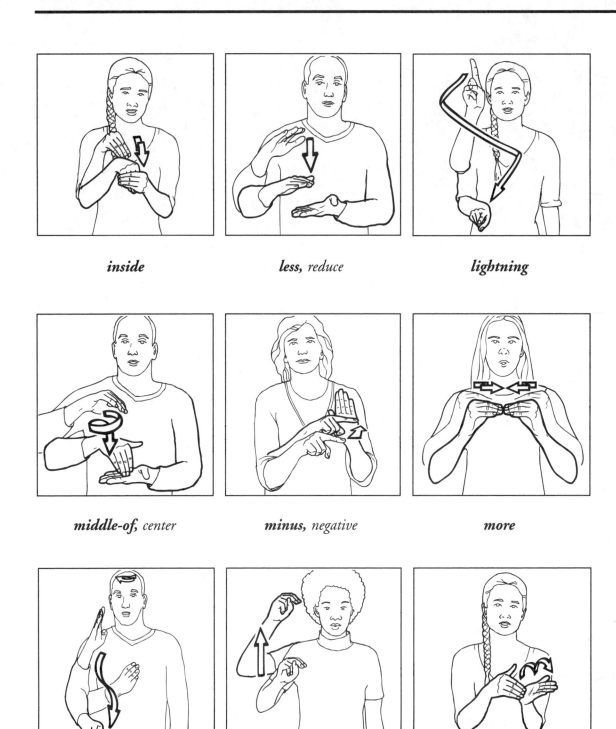

inside

less, *reduce*

lightning

middle-of, *center*

minus, *negative*

more

never

north

often

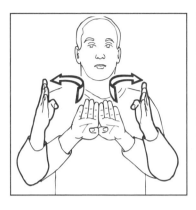

open

outside

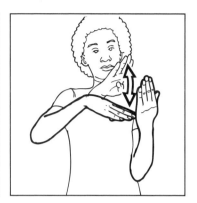

to-paint

to-plant

to-play

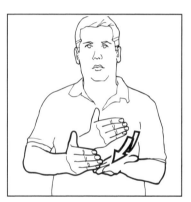

to-plow

plus, *positive*

predict, *forecast*

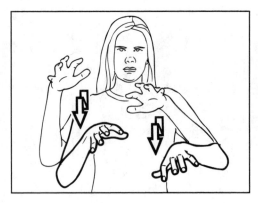

rain   *to-rake*   *to-shovel*

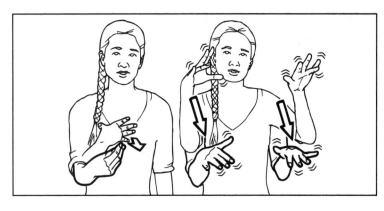

snow   *sometimes*

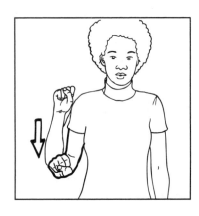

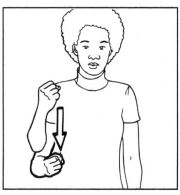

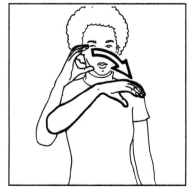

south (1)   *south* (2)   *strange,* odd

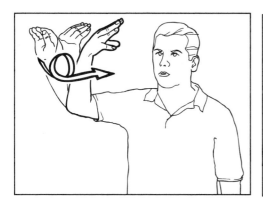

sun

suppose

temperature (climate)

tend-to

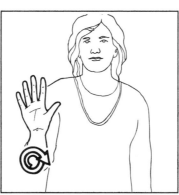

thereabouts

thunder

warm

warn

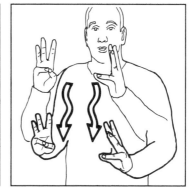

weather (1)

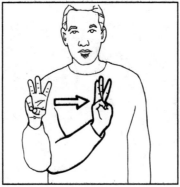

weather (2) **west** (1) **west** (2)

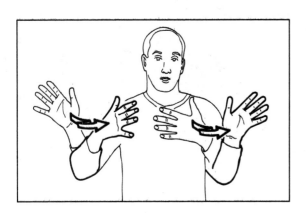

wind

Schedules and Events

In this unit you learn to discuss routine work and social activities, including meetings and workshops that people attend. You also learn about the importance of networking within the Deaf community, about the interpreting profession, and about how meetings are conducted when there are both deaf and hearing participants.

Unit 11 Overview

Learning Outcomes

1. Discuss routine work and social activities, including meetings and workshops

2. Modify sign movements in combination with the timeline for frequency of occurrence

3. Understand the importance of networking in the Deaf community

4. Become acquainted with the interpreting profession

5. Learn principles for meetings involving both deaf and hearing participants

---

Vocabulary

every-morning, mornings	*to-plan*
every-afternoon, afternoons	*topic/title*
every-night, nights	*attend, go-to*
every-Monday, Mondays	*to-contact*
every-Tuesday, Tuesdays	*interesting*
every-Wednesday, Wednesdays	*boring*
every-Thursday, Thursdays	*popular*
every-Friday, Fridays	*agree*
every-Saturday, Saturdays	*disagree*
every-Sunday, Sundays	*show-up, appear*
every-week, weekly	*arrive*
every-month, monthly	*conflict*
every-year, yearly, annually	*interpreter*
Monday-through-Friday	*lecture, speech*
advertise	*interpret*
announce, declare	*listen*
to-post	*cancel*
inform	*decide*
information	*postpone, delay*
workshop, seminar	*move-closer-to-present-time*

Unit 11 Overview

Grammar

1. More on Horizontal and Vertical Sweep for Plural

2. Sign Movement Repetition for Plural

3. More on Number Incorporation with Time Signs

4. Listing on the Non-Dominant Hand for Specifying Weeks in a Month

Language, Culture, and Community

1. Opening Conversations with *"fine,"* *"what's-up,"* and *"hear"*

2. Deaf Community Networking

3. Interpreting and Interpreters

4. Meetings Involving Deaf and Hearing Participants

Practice and Review Materials

1. Video Exercises
   - Sample Expressive Dialogue
   - Comprehension Practice
   - Expressive Practice Prompts

2. Grammar and Language, Culture, and Community Review Questions

3. Sign Vocabulary Illustrations

1. More on Horizontal and Vertical Sweep for Plural

2. Sign Movement Repetition for Plural

3. More on Number Incorporation with Time Signs

4. Listing on the Non-Dominant Hand for Specifying Weeks in a Month

1. More on Horizontal and Vertical Sweep for Plural

In Unit 2, Learning ASL, use of horizontal and vertical sweep for plural was introduced with the pronouns *you-all, they,* and *these.* Horizontal sweep is also used with the signs *morning, afternoon,* and *night* to communicate *every-morning, every-afternoon,* and *every-night.* Vertical sweep is used with signs for days of the week to communicate *every-Monday, every-Tuesday,* and so forth. Figures 11.1–11.4 show the use of horizontal and vertical sweep with some of these time signs.

every-morning
Fig. 11.1

every-night
Fig. 11.2

every-Monday
Fig. 11.3

every-Tuesday
Fig. 11.4

2. Sign Movement Repetition for Plural

Signs can be repeated to indicate plural. For ***every-week,*** the hands move down with each repeated movement. For ***every-month*** and ***every-year,*** the hands move forward with each repeated movement. These signs are illustrated in Figures 11.5–11.7.

every-week
Fig. 11.5

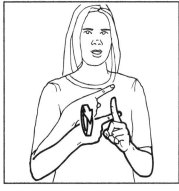

every-month
Fig. 11.6

every-year
Fig. 11.7

3. More on Number Incorporation with Time Signs

In Unit 4, Making Appointments, and Unit 8, Time and Activities, you were introduced to number incorporation with time signs. You learned that number handshapes can be incorporated with signs such as *minute* and *hour* to specify how many minutes or hours. Also, you may incorporate a number handshape with *week, month,* and *year* to specify the number of weeks, months, and years. A number handshape can also be incorporated with *every-week, every-month,* and *every-year* to specify that an activity occurs at intervals such as every 2 weeks, every 3 months, or every 5 years. Examples of the above are illustrated in Figures 11.8–11.10.

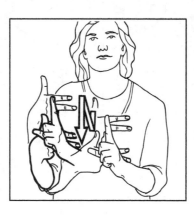

every-two-weeks
Fig. 11.8

every-three-months
Fig. 11.9

every-five-years
Fig. 11.10

4. Listing on the Non-Dominant Hand for Specifying Weeks in a Month

In Unit 5, Work Duties, listing on the non-dominant hand was introduced and in Unit 6, Sharing Personal Information, using listing on the non-dominant hand to show the rank order of members of one's family was introduced. In this unit, we see the use of the non-dominant hand to refer to specific weeks in a month. Depending on the number of weeks in the month, the fingers of the non-dominant hand are held in either a 4 handshape or a 5 handshape. Each finger represents one of the weeks of a month, as arranged on a calendar. The index finger of the dominant hand points to, touches, and moves along one of the fingers of the non-dominant hand, indicating which particular week in the month is being specified. In this way, signers can communicate, for example, that they are planning a vacation to occur in the third week of July. Figures 11.11 and 11.12 show use of listing on the non-dominant hand to specify the third week of a 5-week month and the second week of a 4-week month.

third week of a 5 week month

Fig. 11.11

second week of a 4 week month

Fig. 11.12

Unit 11 Language, Culture, and Community

1. Opening Conversations with *"fine,"* *"what's-up,"* and *"hear"*

2. Deaf Community Networking

3. Interpreting and Interpreters

4. Meetings Involving Deaf and Hearing Participants

1. Opening Conversations with *"fine," "what's-up,"* and *"hear"*

In previous units, you learned several ways that conversations may be opened. When a signer has been looking for someone for a long time and finally runs into this person, he/she may use the sign *fine* with one sharp down and away movement to open the conversation. This conversation opener means something like "Finally, I run into you. I need to tell you something." Figure 11.13 shows the use of *fine* to open a conversation.

Finally, I run into you. You know we have a meeting tomorrow. Right?
Fig. 11.13

In this unit, Language, Culture, and Community information #2 explains the Deaf cultural value of keeping people informed. One conversation opener that is related to this value is the use of the sign *what's-up.* People will often greet each other with this sign. It can have the general meaning of "How are you?" and often signers will reply with the sign *fine,* produced with a tapping motion on the chest area. However, if the signer who is greeted with *what's-up* has something important to share, he/she may respond with news or information that may be unknown to the other person. The sign *what's-up* is illustrated in Figure 11.14 on the next page.

Another conversation opener that is directly related to the cultural value of keeping people informed is **hear** with yes/no questioning expression and tapping movement to communicate the question "Did you hear the news?" This conversation opener is often used when signers have something urgent to share with one another. It signals that there is important, community-related information to share. Figure 11.15 shows the use of **hear** to open a conversation.

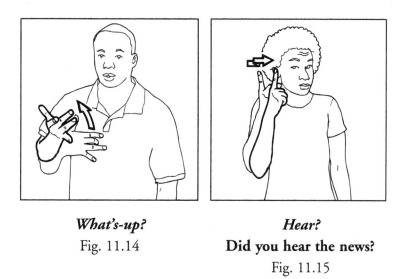

What's-up?
Fig. 11.14

Hear?
Did you hear the news?
Fig. 11.15

2. Deaf Community Networking

Deaf people value keeping others informed and networking with other members of the Deaf community. This is sometimes referred to as the "Deaf grapevine." With the Internet and pager technology, the Deaf grapevine has risen to new heights, providing the opportunity for instantaneous information sharing. Any significant incident that occurs within or affects the Deaf community in the United States (and the world) is now "old news" within a day or two.

A school for the Deaf somewhere in the United States is threatened with being closed by a state legislature. The news travels almost instantaneously throughout the Deaf community and the Deaf community rallies to support keeping the school open. Open-captioned movies will finally be shown at a local movie theatre because the local Deaf club has lobbied local theatre owners to make it happen. This "triumph" is shared nationwide through Internet listservs, national Deaf-related newspapers and magazines, and e-mail pagers.

This cultural value of keeping people informed also shows up on the local level within members of a particular Deaf community living in a particular area. Members of the Deaf community will keep each other informed about local events, including state and national events and happenings that affect the local Deaf community. Members of local Deaf communities network with one another regarding positive and negative experiences they have with businesses, doctors, lawyers, schools, programs, and agencies. When a Deaf person wants to buy a new car, he/she often consults with other Deaf people considered to have expertise and experience dealing with car purchases and particular car dealerships. Deaf people often rely on fellow members of the Deaf Community when dealing with hearing people. Some members of the local Deaf community may be viewed as more knowledgeable about hearing people or they may be considered to have better written English skills or other talents that enable them to helpful.

The Deaf community provides a cohesive network of contact with other Deaf people through which the talents of the entire Deaf community are shared. This cohesive network of contact with other Deaf people and Deaf community hearing members provides a resource to its members in negotiating with the larger hearing society. At the same time, this networking allows for comfortable social contact with other people who share many common experiences and a shared, natural language, ASL, by which Deaf community values are communicated and preserved.

3. Interpreting and Interpreters

Sign language interpreters facilitate communication between Deaf and hearing people. To interpret between ASL and English, interpreters must be fluent in both languages. Freelance interpreters work through agencies in a variety of settings that require a wide variety of skills. Other interpreters prefer to specialize and work primarily in one setting; for example, educational, medical, or legal settings.

Traditionally, interpreters have come from the ranks of hearing children with deaf parents, clergy, and teachers of the deaf. However, legislation stemming from the civil rights movement of the 1960s (federal statutes such as PL 94-142 and the ADA) required government, social, and private organizations to make communication accessible for deaf people. This created a surge in the demand for interpreters in schools and other venues.

The right to communication access led to two important developments. The first was the founding of the Registry of Interpreters for the Deaf (RID) in the mid 1960s. RID came into prominence in the late 1960s as part of a process to establish professional interpreting standards. RID is active at the national level in the certification of interpreters and has continued to evolve over the years to refine the certification process. In 1996, the RID and the NAD joined forces to revise both the certification process and the Code of Professional Conduct for interpreters by creating the NAD–RID National Council on Interpreting.

RID's efforts to professionalize interpreting and interpreters led to the second development, the implementation of interpreter training programs in colleges and universities. Over time, interpreter "training" has become interpreter education. Today, over 130 schools in the United States offer degree programs in sign language interpreting.

You can find more information about interpreters and interpreting in the RID newsletter (*RID Views*), at the RID Web site (http://www.rid.org), and in the two texts listed below:

Frishberg, N. (1990). *Interpreting: An introduction.* Alexandria, VA: RID Publications.

Stewart, D., Schein, J., & Cartwright, B. (1998). *Sign language interpreting: Exploring its art and science.* Boston, MA: Allyn & Bacon.

4. Meetings Involving Deaf and Hearing Participants

Meetings involving both deaf and hearing participants can be successful if all involved accommodate to the special communication circumstances that are involved.

If a meeting involves all participants using ASL, the rules for taking turns, gaining attention, taking the floor, and directing attention to the person who has the floor are easier to follow. The reason for this is that all participants, whether deaf or hearing, are using visual–gestural communication, thus eliminating the conflict between the conversational rules of ASL and spoken English. With spoken language, speakers and listeners can tolerate talk by two people at the same time and they can comment and ask a question immediately after someone has made a comment or asked a question. When ASL is being used, participants need time to redirect their attention from one speaker to the next.

If a meeting involves a mixture of ASL and spoken English and/or simultaneous use of signing and speaking, there is generally more violation of turn-taking protocols. This is because the rules for getting attention, directing attention, and taking turns are different between ASL and spoken English. Leaders of such meetings and all participants must make an extra effort to manage turn taking so that the meeting will run as smoothly as possible, with all participants feeling included and able to participate on an equal level.

If a meeting involves use of an interpreter, the time required for messages to be conveyed lags behind when either a signer and/or a speaker has finished. In this case, even more care must be taken to allow for the appropriate participation of all.

General principles for meetings involving both deaf and hearing participants include the following:

A. Meeting rooms should be well lit and glare from open windows and doors should be controlled. If there are movements or other distractions in the hallway, doors should be closed to reduce visual distractions.

B. It is the responsibility of the speaker and/or signer to stand or sit in a location where everyone in the meeting is able to clearly view him/her. If seating is not arranged for easy viewing of all participants, the speaker and/or signer should move to a location where all can see.

C. Allow deaf participants flexibility in choosing the seating arrangement that best suits their preferences for viewing the interpreter (if used), other participants in the meeting, and projected visuals (if any).

D. At the beginning of meetings, leaders should discuss the communication protocols to be followed with all participants.

E. If projected visuals are used, allow time for all participants to read/view information before beginning to sign and/or speak.

F. If projected visuals are used, place visual on the overhead projector, allow participants to view the entire visual, and then cover up part of the visual to direct attention to the information that will be discussed. Covering up part of the visual that is not being discussed reduces the glare from projected media and reduces eyestrain for participants.

G. Leaders of meetings should control turn taking and be aware of and repair turn taking when rules are being violated.

H. Participants should wait for persons who are signing and/or talking to finish before raising their hands to be recognized.

I. Participants should wait for meeting leaders to recognize them before commenting or asking a question.

J. Prior to speaking and/or signing comments and questions, a participant should look at all participants to ensure they have all had time to direct their attention to him/her or to the interpreter.

K. If interpreters are involved, participants should wait for interpreters to finish translating before answering or asking questions. There will be lag time between when statements or questions are made in spoken English or ASL and when the interpreters have completed their signing or voicing of messages.

1. Video Exercises

   – Sample Expressive Dialogue

   – Comprehension Practice

   – Expressive Practice Prompts

2. Grammar and Language, Culture, and Community Review Questions

3. Sign Vocabulary Illustrations

Sample Expressive Dialogue

Read the dialogue prompts below and then watch how each signer expresses these prompts on the video. Sign along with both Signer A and Signer B or with either Signer A or Signer B on the video. You may wish to practice this dialogue with a classmate outside of class time and your teacher may review this dialogue in class and ask you to sign this dialogue with a classmate.

Discussing Meetings

Signer A: Ask if Signer B has a weekly study group meeting in the room

Signer B: Respond affirmatively

Signer A: Ask Signer B for the day and time

Signer B: Respond

Signer A: Ask what the meeting is like

Signer B: Explain what the group does

Signer A: Respond positively

Signer B: Respond positively and ask if Signer A wants to go out and eat with you

Signer A: Respond

Note: Signer A wants to know what the meeting is like. He uses the sign *"looks-like."* This is similar in English to asking what the meeting is like or what students do in this meeting.

For the signing you observe, please write any helpful notes and questions that you may have for your teacher.

Comprehension Practice 11.1

Watch the dialogue all the way through and then answer as many of the questions below as you can. If necessary, view the dialogue a second time to see whether you are able to understand more and answer any additional questions.

Preparing for a Test

1. What is the concern of the woman in the grey sweater?

2. What is the other woman's suggestion?

3. How does the woman in the purple blouse establish a location in space for Pat?

4. When the woman in the purple blouse is explaining her suggestion for the evening activity, she uses a grammatical principle that indicates how many people will be involved. Name and explain what she does.

5. What is the room number and the time when this meeting will occur?

6. What does the woman in the grey sweater offer to do for this study group meeting?

7. Why does the woman in the grey sweater express frustration with herself at the end of this dialogue?

For the signing you observe, please write any helpful notes and questions that you may have for your teacher.

Comprehension Practice 11.2

Watch the dialogue all the way through and then answer as many of the questions below as you can. If necessary, view the dialogue a second time to see whether you are able to understand more and answer any additional questions.

Discussing a Workshop

1. When the man sits down what does he ask the woman? Why?

2. What is the woman so excited about?

3. Why is the man not aware of this workshop?

4. What does the woman caution the man to do and why?

5. Who does the woman advise the man to contact?

6. What confusion does the man have about where the contact person is located?

7. Where does the woman say this contact person is located? Explain specifically the directions the woman provides.

8. What conversational behavior do you see the man use after the woman explains the directions to the contact person's office?

For the signing you observe, please write any helpful notes and questions that you may have for your teacher.

Comprehension Practice 11.3

Watch the dialogue all the way through and then answer as many of the questions below as you can. If necessary, view the dialogue a second time to see whether you are able to understand more and answer any additional questions.

Finding a Time to Meet

1. What problem does the man have and what does he propose?

2. Why can't the woman meet on Friday?

3. Describe the final negotiation for a day and time for this meeting.

4. These two people need to check their schedule books and at the same time discuss a good time for their meeting. Describe what they do to maintain appropriate eye contact throughout this conversation and to take turns appropriately.

For the signing you observe, please write any helpful notes and questions that you may have for your teacher.

Comprehension Practice 11.4

Watch the dialogue all the way through and then answer as many of the questions below as you can. If necessary, view the dialogue a second time to see whether you are able to understand more and can answer any remaining questions.

Describing Convention Activities

1. How frequently and at what time of year does this activity occur?

2. What convention does the woman look forward to attending?

3. For which days of the week is this convention typically scheduled?

4. Describe how the woman signs the days of the week and then is consistent in using this grammatical principle when she tells us what occurs.

5. The woman tells us about morning lectures, afternoon workshops, and evening activities that occur at this convention. Name at least one lecture, workshop, and activity that she describes for each time period.

6. Why does the woman especially like the evening activities? What cultural value is being expressed?

For the signing you observe, please write any helpful notes and questions that you may have for your teacher.

Expressive Practice Prompts

These Expressive Practice Prompts show you the types of questions and statements you should be able to express in ASL by the end of Unit 11. Your teacher may use these Expressive Practice Prompts in class. You should practice these with your practice partner and group outside of class as well.

1. Ask a classmate if he/she does a particular activity on a regular basis. (Use signs for every morning, Monday through Friday, every Saturday, and so forth)

2. Ask a classmate what he/she does on a particular day of the week at a particular time.

3. Ask a classmate if he/she will go on a vacation this year.

4. Tell the class the workshop is cancelled because the speaker is sick.

5. Tell the class that your vacation plans have changed. Before, you were planning vacation for the third week in August, but now you will go on your vacation the fourth week in August.

6. Express that you have an ASL class from Monday through Friday morning at 8:00.

7. Tell the class that the workshop has been postponed for 2 weeks.

8. Ask a classmate if he/she can recommend a good interpreter.

9. Ask a classmate to contact you tomorrow.

10. Express that the play will start 1 hour earlier. (Please express this in two different ways.)

11. Tell the class that the speaker wants to begin but the interpreter is late. Express that everyone must wait for the interpreter to show up.

12. Tell the class that your department has meetings every Monday morning at 10:00 and every Thursday afternoon at 2:00.

13. Ask a classmate whether the workshop was interesting or boring.

14. Give a reason why you showed up late for class and apologize.

Expressive Practice Prompts (continued)

15. Tell a classmate that you have a conflict and can't attend the workshop.

16. Tell the class that the workshop scheduled for next Tuesday night from 7:00 to 9:00 is cancelled.

17. Tell the class that you have a conflict for the meeting scheduled 2 weeks from now. Ask if the meeting can be scheduled for next week instead.

18. Tell the class that you have department meetings every Wednesday afternoon at 3:00 and workshops every Thursday at 10:00 in the morning.

19. Ask a classmate if he/she agrees that the weather has been very nice lately.

20. Ask a classmate to inform you about the topic of a workshop he/she attended recently.

21. Express that you recently attended a workshop about interpreting and the information you learned was very good.

Grammar and Language, Culture, and Community Review Questions

These questions will assist you as you read the Grammar and the Language, Culture, and Community sections in this unit.

1. Explain how the singular forms of *morning, night, Monday*, and *Tuesday* may be changed to the plural forms *every-morning, every-night, every-Monday,* and *every-Tuesday.*

2. Explain how the singular forms of *week, month,* and *year* may be changed to the plural forms *every-week, every-month,* and *every-year.*

3. What grammatical principle is used to refer to a particular week in a month? Explain how this same principle is used in other contexts. (Hint: Think about when you refer to family members, names, ages, and so forth.)

4. In Units 4 and 8 and in this unit, you have learned how number handshapes can be incorporated with time adverbials (for example, *minute, hour, week,* and *month*) to show a specific number of minutes, hours, weeks, and months. This same principle of incorporating number handshapes applies to other classes of signs as well. For what other classes of signs does this principle apply? (Hint: Take a look at Units 2 and 6.)

5. Give two examples of how the value of "keeping others informed" manifests itself within the Deaf community. What purposes are served by this cultural value?

6. What led to the development of sign language interpreting as a profession?

7. What is the name of the professional organization of interpreters that was founded in the mid 1960's?

8. Why will meetings between deaf and hearing participants run more smoothly if all participants are using ASL?

9. Explain two important principles that should be followed when a meeting involves both deaf and hearing participants.

Sign Vocabulary Illustrations

advertise

agree

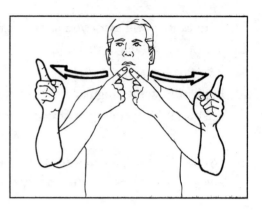

announce, *declare*

arrive

attend, *go-to*

boring

cancel

conflict

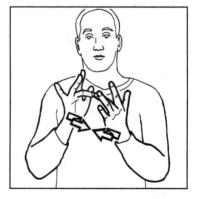

to-contact

decide

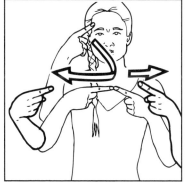

disagree

every-afternoon, *afternoons*

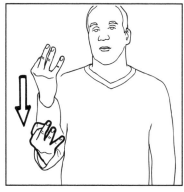

every-Friday, *Fridays*

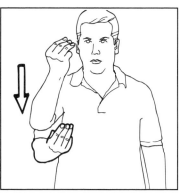

every-Monday, *Mondays*

every-month, *monthly*

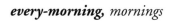

every-morning, *mornings*

every-night, *nights*

every-Saturday, *Saturdays*

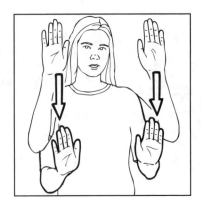

every-Sunday, *Sundays*

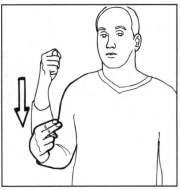

every-Thursday, *Thursdays*

every-Tuesday, *Tuesdays*

every-Wednesday, *Wednesdays*

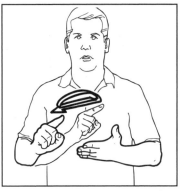

every-week, *weekly*

every-year, *yearly, annually*

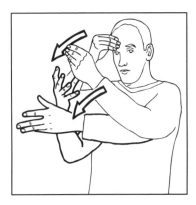

inform

information

interesting

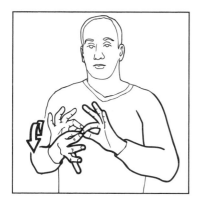

interpret

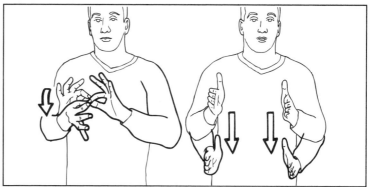

interpreter

lecture, *speech*

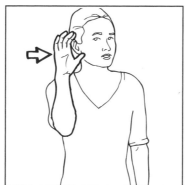

listen (1)

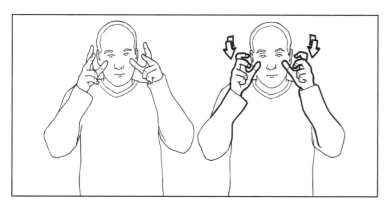

listen (2)

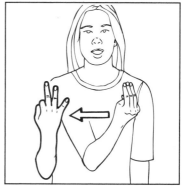

Monday-through-Friday

move-closer-to-present-time

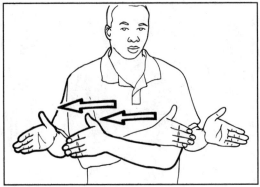

to-plan

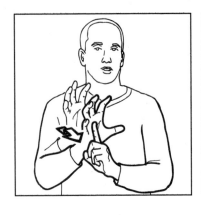

popular

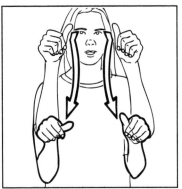

to-post

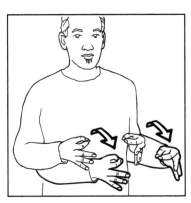

postpone, *delay*

show-up, *appear*

topic/title

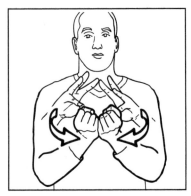

workshop, *seminar*

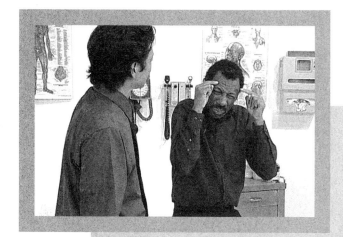

In this unit you learn to express your feelings related to common illnesses, to narrate about being sick and taking medicine to cure common illnesses, and how to express emotions related to the pain and frequency of illnesses. Also, you learn about pathological and cultural views of deafness and Deaf people.

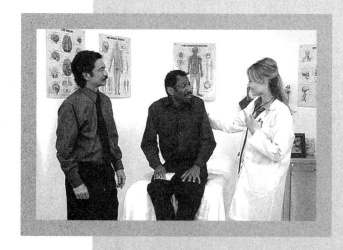

Unit 12 Overview

Learning Outcomes

1. Learn signs for common illnesses and other medical terms

2. Express degrees and frequency of pain

3. Narrate about illnesses and their remedies

4. Communicate daily routines for taking medicine

5. Learn about pathological and cultural views of deafness and Deaf people

---

Vocabulary

happy	*weak*	*physical-exam*
sad	*lousy*	*medicine,* prescription
how	*terrible*	*injection,* shot
feel	*worse*	*take-a-pill*
fine	*outside*	*improve*
headache	*head-cold*	*deteriorate*
tired	*cough*	*better*
sleepy	*allergy*	*eat/food*
worn-out	*pain/hurt*	*to-drink*
lie-down	*ambulance*	*lazy*
rest, relax	*emergency*	*habit*
sleep	*hospital*	*worry*
healthy	*insurance*	*weight*
take-temperature	*doctor*	*problem*
fever	*nurse*	*d-i-e-t*
nauseous	*patient* (person)	*increase*
dizzy	*visit*	*decrease*
f-l-u		

Grammar

1. More on Non-Manual Signals and Sign Movement Modifications for Degree

2. More on Instrumental Classifiers

Unit 12 Overview

Language, Culture, and Community

1. Opening Conversations with *"what's-wrong?"*

2. Closing Conversations with *"good idea"*

3. Pathological versus Cultural View of Deafness and Deaf People

Practice and Review Materials

1. Video Exercises

    –   Sample Expressive Dialogue

    –   Comprehension Practice

    –   Expressive Practice Prompts

2. Grammar and Language, Culture, and Community Review Questions

3. Sign Vocabulary Illustrations

1. More on Non-Manual Signals and Sign Movement Modifications for Degree

2. More on Instrumental Classifiers

1. More on Non-Manual Signals and Sign Movement Modifications for Degree

In Unit 5, Work Duties, and Unit 10, Discussing Weather, the use of non-manual signals and sign movement modifications for degree was discussed. This grammatical principle may be applied to describing conditions of health or sickness. For example, non-manual signals and sign movement modifications may be used to indicate very healthy, moderately healthy, very sick, and moderately sick. Examples of these non-manual signals and sign movement modifications are illustrated in Figures 12.1–12.4.

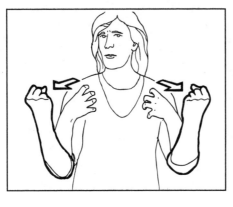

very-healthy

Fig. 12.1

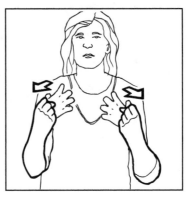

moderately-healthy

Fig. 12.2

very-sick

Fig. 12.3

moderately-sick

Fig. 12.4

2. More on Instrumental Classifiers

In Unit 9, Making Requests, instrumental classifiers were introduced. Instrumental classifiers show how something is handled, held, or used. In this unit, instrumental classifiers are used to communicate the different ways that medicine may be taken or applied. See Figures 12.5–12.11 for examples of this.

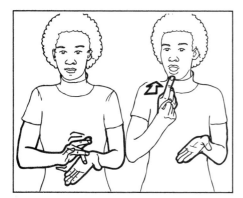

take-a-pill

Fig. 12.5

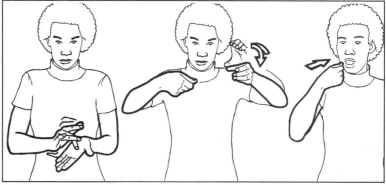

take-medicine-by-spoon

Fig. 12.6

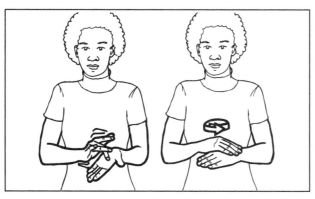

apply-an-ointment

Fig. 12.7

take-medicine-by-injection

Fig. 12.8

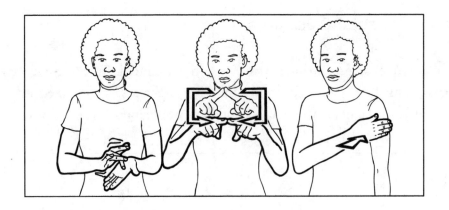

administer-medicine-by-patch
Fig. 12.9

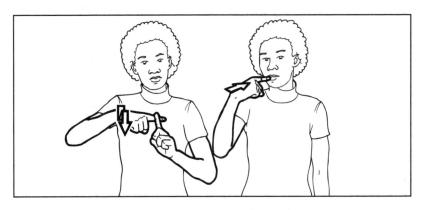

take-temperature-by-mouth
Fig. 12.10

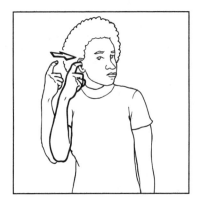

take-temperature-by-ear
Fig. 12.11

Unit 12 Language, Culture, and Community

1. Opening Conversations with *"what's-wrong?"*

2. Closing Conversations with *"good idea"*

3. Pathological versus Cultural View of Deafness and Deaf People

1. Opening Conversations with *"what's-wrong?"*

When signers recognize that another person may be experiencing a problem, they will often open a conversation with the question, "What's wrong?" or "What's the matter?" This conversation opener involves use of the sign *wrong* with wh-question expression and a tapping movement to form the question. Figure 12.12 illustrates this conversation opener.

What's wrong? or **What's the matter?**
Fig. 12.2

2. Closing Conversations with *"good idea"*

In Unit 5, Work Duties, and Unit 7, Where People Live, you learned that you may close conversations with *ok* and *see-later.* Another way that conversations may be closed is to use the sign phrase *good idea.* This sign phrase is normally used when someone has given you advice and it indicates that you appreciate and will consider the other person's advice. As you learned in Unit 11, Schedules and Events, #1 in the Language, Culture, and Community section, Deaf people often rely on the expertise and experiences of other community members. This conversation closer, which is illustrated in Figure 12.13 on the next page, reflects this cultural value.

That's very good advice.
Fig. 12.13

3. Pathological versus Cultural View of Deafness and Deaf People

Deaf people may be viewed from two perspectives: (a) as a group of handicapped or disabled people (pathological perspective), or (b) as a group of people sharing a common language and culture (cultural perspective). When we write about people who are deaf, following established conventions, we use a lowercase "d" to refer to the condition of hearing loss or hearing impairment and an uppercase "D" to refer to the cultural identity.

Within general society, deafness has traditionally been viewed as a disability. The majority of medical practitioners hold this view because there is a physical difference between individuals who have significant hearing loss and individuals who do not. And doctors are in the business of "fixing" things.

However, whether a condition is considered disabling is also determined by society or culture. In the United States in the 1800s, there was a society on Martha's Vineyard, Massachusetts, where hearing loss was quite common. This was the result of a genetic trait. Many families on Martha's Vineyard Island had deaf family members, and most islanders were able to use sign language for everyday communication (Groce, 1985). In this society being Deaf was viewed as part of normal human variation. This is an example of how a particular trait may be defined by cultural or societal norms as either abnormal and potentially disabling or as a normal variation among human beings. On Martha's Vineyard, being deaf was not considered either abnormal or disabling.

Many people with significant hearing loss view themselves as primarily belonging to Deaf culture. They understand the challenges that having a hearing loss presents and understand that they live within a larger society that views deafness as a disability. For this reason, you may see Deaf people sometimes joining forces with groups representing other disabilities to fight for equal rights and access. Human nature is complex, and defining who we are is equally complex. This applies to all of us, not just d/Deaf people. We all develop multifaceted perspectives and identities. For example, we have separate "work" identities and "home" identities. What about our gender identity? Is who we are the same in all settings and circumstances? Probably not. For the majority of Deaf people who use ASL, marry within their Deaf culture group, have significant association with other Deaf people, join organizations with other Deaf people, and socialize most comfortably within Deaf culture, being deaf means viewing themselves as a member of Deaf culture. They view themselves as complete, whole, and living a full and rewarding life as Deaf persons.

References

Groce, N. E. (1985). *Everyone here spoke sign language: Hereditary deafness on Martha's Vineyard.* Cambridge, MA: Harvard University Press.

Readings

Lane, H. (2002). Do deaf people have a disability? *Sign Language Studies, 2*(4), 356–377.

Padden, C., & Humphries, T. (1990). *Deaf in America: Voices from a culture.* Cambridge, MA, Harvard University Press. (In this book, see Introduction, pp. 1–11).

Carty, B. (1989). The development of Deaf identity. In C. J. Erting, R. C. Johnson, D. L. Smith, & B. C. Snider (Eds.), *The Deaf way: Perspectives from the International Conference on Deaf Culture* (pp. 40–43). Washington, DC: Gallaudet University Press.

Kannapell, B. (1989). Deaf identity: An American perspective. In C. J. Erting, R. C. Johnson, D. L. Smith, & B. C. Snider (Eds.), *The Deaf way: Perspectives from the International Conference on Deaf Culture* (pp. 44–48). Washington, DC: Gallaudet University Press.

Lane, H., Hoffmeister, R., & Bahan, B. (1996). *A journey into the Deaf-World.* San Diego, CA: DawnSignPress

Unit 12 Practice and Review Materials

1. Video Exercises

   – Sample Expressive Dialogue

   – Comprehension Practice

   – Expressive Practice Prompts

2. Grammar and Language, Culture, and Community Review Questions

3. Sign Vocabulary Illustrations

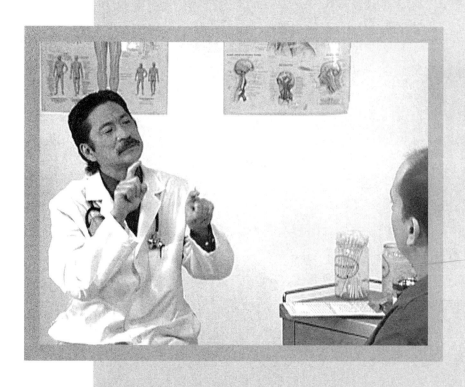

Sample Expressive Dialogue

Read the dialogue prompts below and then watch how each signer expresses these prompts on the video. Sign along with Signers A, B and C or with one of these three signers on the video. You may wish to practice this dialogue with a classmate outside of class time and your teacher may review this dialogue in class and ask you to sign this dialogue with a classmate.

Describing an Illness

Signer A: Gain attention of Signer B

Signer B: Acknowledge Signer A

Signer A: Ask Signer B if he/she is feeling okay

Signer B: Respond with symptoms

Signer A: Express concern and ask if Signer A takes medicine

Signer B: Explain that you have not taken any medicine yet

Signer A: Express that it is taking a long time for the doctor to come

Signer C: (The doctor walks into the scene) Ask how Signer B feels

Signer B: Respond with your symptoms

Signer C: Explain that these symptoms are going around now

Signer C: Perform a mock examination with stethoscope and ask patient to breathe in deeply

Signer C: Write a prescription and hand to Signer B; express that the medicine will help reduce Signer B's symptoms

Signer B: Take the prescription form and attempt to read it; express that you can't read it because your vision is blurry, hand prescription to Signer A, and politely ask Signer A to read the prescription

Signer A: Read prescription and then express that one pill is to be taken every four hours

Signer B: Confirm the directions incorrectly by stating to the doctor that the medicine is to be taken twice a day

Signer C: Correct the information expressed by Signer B stating that the medicine is to be taken three times a day, in the morning, at noon and at night

Signer C: Express that you need to leave now and ask Signer B if he/she has any questions

Signer B: Respond in the negative and express gratitude to Signer C

Signer C: Tell Signer B to take care of himself/herself and express that you will see Signer B next week

Signer A: Express to Signer B a positive comment about the doctor

For the signing you observe, please write below any helpful notes and questions that you may have for your teacher.

Comprehension Practice 12.1

Watch the dialogue all the way through and then answer as many of the questions below as you can. If necessary, view the dialogue a second time to see whether you are able to understand more and answer any additional questions.

Giving Medical Advice

1. How does the woman in the light green suit open the conversation?

2. Describe the woman's complaint, including what caused it.

3. What three types of exercise does the woman describe?

4. How does the woman who is complaining treat herself?

5. What better treatment is suggested to her?

6. Identify and describe the meaning of two classifiers that are used by the woman in the light green suit.

7. How does the woman with the complaint modify her signs to show the degree of her pain?

8. What communication behavior does the woman with the complaint use to close the conversation and what significance does it have from a cultural perspective?

For the signing you observe, please write any helpful notes and questions that you may have for your teacher.

Comprehension Practice 12.2

Watch the dialogue all the way through and then answer as many of the questions below as you can. If necessary, view the dialogue a second time to see whether you are able to understand more and answer any additional questions.

Discussing a Chronic Health Problem

1. Describe the man's symptom.

2. What did his doctor recommend?

3. When the man explains the doctor's recommendation, he uses the sign *no* in a special way. Describe how he uses this sign and what it means in this context.

4. The man does not know how to spell the name of the disease he has. Describe how he communicates this name.

5. What is the name of the disease the man has?

6. What does the man agree in the end that he needs to do about his illness?

For the signing you observe, please write any helpful notes and questions that you may have for your teacher.

Comprehension Practice 12.3

Watch the dialogue all the way through and then answer as many of the questions below as you can. If necessary, view the dialogue a second time to see whether you are able to understand more and answer any additional questions.

Giving a Medical History

1. What is the patient's name?

2. Why do you think the patient has come to see the doctor?

3. Describe the patient's family medical history.

4. How was the patient's father's heart condition treated and is he still alive?

5. Describe what the patient's mother's health condition is and what she is doing to treat it.

6. What is the patient's sister doing about her weight problem?

7. How long does the patient have to wait for the physical examination?

For the signing you observe, please write any helpful notes and questions that you may have for your teacher.

Comprehension Practice 12.4

Watch the dialogue all the way through and then answer as many of the questions below as you can. If necessary, view the dialogue a second time to see whether you are able to understand more and answer any additional questions.

Describing a Work-Related Injury

1. Describe the man's symptoms.

2. What are the man's three main work duties?

3. How do these duties affect his work-related injury?

4. What does the doctor suggest for managing these symptoms?

5. What does the man ask next?

6. When does the doctor want to see this patient again?

For the signing you observe, please write any helpful notes and questions that you may have for your teacher.

Comprehension Practice 12.5

Watch the dialogue all the way through and then answer as many of the questions below as you can. If necessary, view the dialogue a second time to see whether you are able to understand more and answer any additional questions.

Recalling an Accident

1. When and where does this incident occur?

2. What classifier handshapes does the narrator use to show the two children running into each other?

3. Right after the accident occurs, how many teachers come to her aid? How do you know this?

4. What do the teachers do to assist her?

5. Describe how the narrator uses the sign *give-injection.*

6. How does the woman show that the doctor gave her a lollipop and that she took it from the doctor?

7. When the narrator returns to school, describe what happens. What do you recognize her doing again in this short sequence?

For the signing you observe, please write any helpful notes and questions that you may have for your teacher.

Expressive Practice Prompts

These Expressive Practice Prompts show you the types of questions and statements you should be able to express in ASL by the end of Unit 12. Your teacher may use these Expressive Practice Prompts in class. You should practice these with your practice partner and group outside of class as well.

1. Ask a classmate how he/she feels.

2. Express that you were very busy at work and you are worn out. State that you want to go home and relax.

3. Ask a classmate if he/she sometimes feels lazy.

4. Express to a classmate that he/she seems to have a cold and ask what he/she will do now.

5. Ask a classmate whether his/her health has been getting worse or getting better recently.

6. Express that you became sick last Friday but you are feeling better.

7. Express that you became sick last Wednesday afternoon and that it started with a sore throat and headache. Now you have a cold and cough.

8. Express that you were using the computer keyboard all day yesterday and now your neck and back really hurt.

9. Express that you have a headache and ask a classmate if he/she has medicine for it.

10. Express that you get a flu shot every year and ask a classmate if he/she gets a flu shot annually.

11. Express that the doctor told you to take the medicine (pills) three times a day after meals.

12. Express that the doctor told you to take two aspirins, rest, and call him in the morning.

13. Express that your father recently gained weight. He needs to eat better, exercise, and take his medicine every day.

14. Express that you must visit a friend at the hospital this afternoon after work.

Expressive Practice Prompts (continued)

15. Ask a classmate when the last time was that he/she had a physical exam.

16. Ask a classmate if he/she knows the phone number to call for an ambulance.

17. Express the name of the hospital nearest to your home.

18. Ask a classmate if his/her weight has increased or decreased recently.

19. Express that you were restless last night and didn't sleep well.

Grammar and Language, Culture, and Community Review Questions

These questions will assist you as you read the Grammar and the Language, Culture, and Community sections in this unit.

1. Look at Figures 12.1–12.4. Describe how non-manual signals and movement modifications are being used to modify the meanings of the signs *healthy* and *sick.*

2. Describe how the instrumental classifier handshapes illustrated in Figures 12.5 and 12.6 show agreement between the verb *to-take* and the nouns *pill* and *spoon,* respectively.

3. Explain the significance between a capital "D" versus a lowercase "d" when referring to Deaf/deaf people.

4. Explain briefly the distinction between the "medical" and "cultural" perspectives regarding deaf people.

5. When signers want to open a conversation with another person who appears to be experiencing a problem, how may they do this?

6. When is the conversation closer *good idea* normally used?

Sign Vocabulary Illustrations

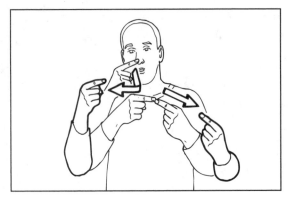

allergy

ambulance

better

cough (1)

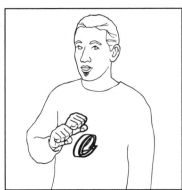

cough (2)

decrease

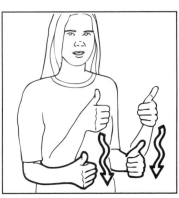

deteriorate (1)

deteriorate (2)

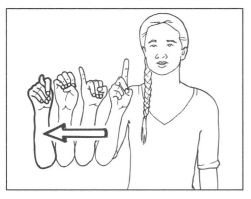

d-i-e-t

dizzy

doctor (1)

doctor (2)

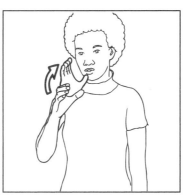

to-drink

eat/food

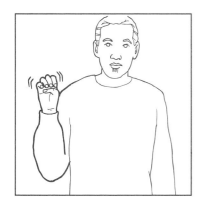

emergency

feel

fever

fine

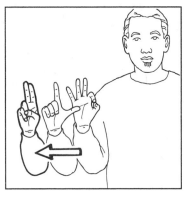

f-l-u

habit

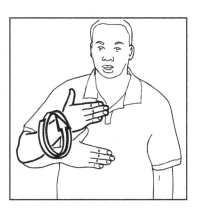

happy

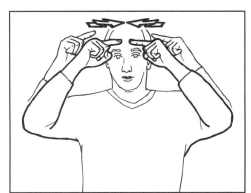

headache

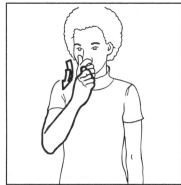

head-cold

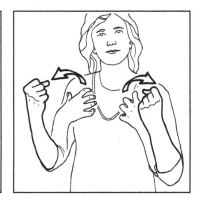

healthy

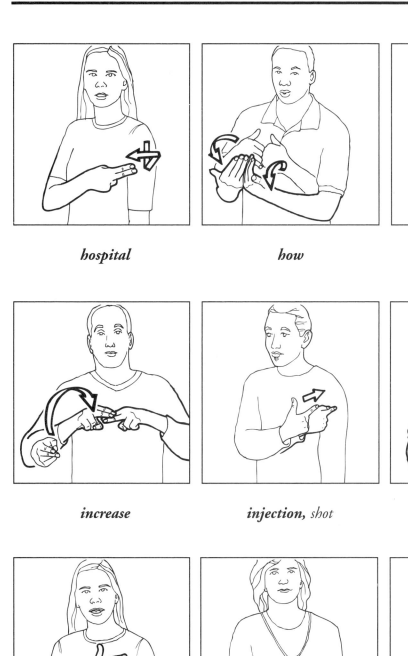

hospital

how

improve

increase

injection, shot

insurance

lazy

lie-down

lousy

medicine, *prescription*

nauseous

nurse

pain/hurt

patient (person)

physical-exam

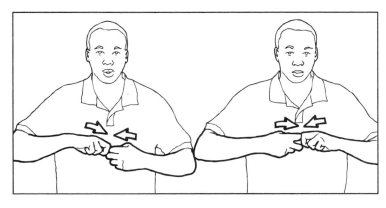

problem

rest, relax

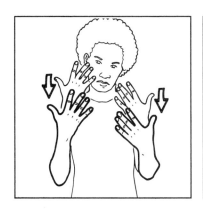

sad

sleep

sleepy

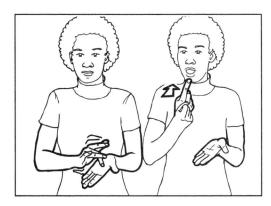

take-a-pill

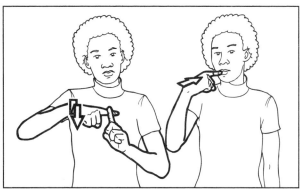

take-temperature

terrible

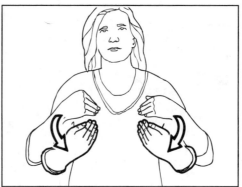

tired

visit

weak

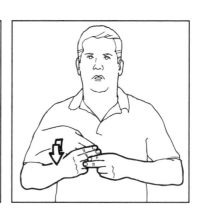

weight

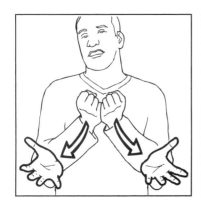

worn-out

worry

worse

Locating Objects

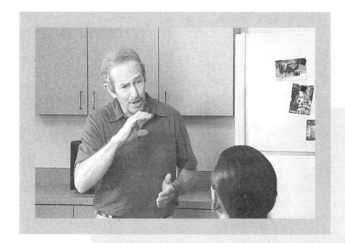

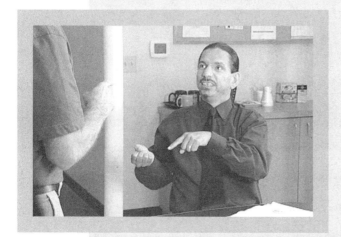

In this unit you review and learn vocabulary and grammatical structures for locating objects. You learn how to use classifiers to help make requests and to give directions for locating objects. You also learn about "Deaf-friendly" offices and appropriate ways to gain the attention of Deaf co-workers in office environments.

Unit 13 Overview

Learning Outcomes

1. Learn sign vocabulary related to locating objects

2. Express locative classifiers

3. Give directions using locative classifiers

4. Learn about "Deaf-friendly" offices and gaining the attention of Deaf co-workers in office environments

---

Vocabulary

corner	*lamp*	*plant*
shelf	*file-cabinet*	*dictionary*
cabinet	*wastebasket*	*put*
drawer	*top*	*drop-on*
wall	*bottom*	
sofa	*figurine/statue*	

Grammar

1. More Whole Entity Classifiers

2. Using Classifiers to Establish Locations of People, Places, and Things

3. Plural Classifiers

4. Using Indexing to Specify Locations

5. Using Eye Gaze to Locate People, Places, and Things

6. Non-Manual Signal "cs" for Proximity in Space

Language, Culture, and Community

1. Deaf-Friendly Office

2. Gaining Attention in an Office

Unit 13 Overview

**Practice and Review
Materials**

1. Video Exercises

   – Sample Expressive Dialogue

   – Comprehension Practice

   – Expressive Practice Prompts

2. Grammar and Language, Culture, and Community
   Review Questions

3. Sign Vocabulary Illustrations

1. More Whole Entity Classifiers

2. Using Classifiers to Establish Locations of People, Places, and Things

3. Plural Classifiers

4. Using Indexing to Specify Locations

5. Using Eye Gaze to Locate People, Places, and Things

6. Non-Manual Signal "cs" for Proximity in Space

1. More Whole Entity Classifiers

In Unit 4, Making Appointments, classifiers as a general topic and whole entity classifiers as one type of classifier, were introduced. In Unit 9, Making Requests, and Unit 12, Discussing Health, instrumental classifiers were introduced and practiced.

In this unit, additional whole entity classifiers are introduced and their use for locating objects in space is practiced. Figures 13.1–13.16 show some whole entity classifiers and provide examples for use of these classifiers.

cl:b – flat surface
Fig. 13.1

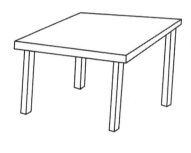

Example: a table
Fig. 13.2

cl:c – cylindrical shape
Fig. 13.3

Example: a clay pot
Fig. 13.4

cl:1 – thin stick or person standing
Fig. 13.5

Example: *a pencil*
Fig. 13.6

cl:v – person sitting/small animal/chair
Fig. 13.7

Example: *chairs in a semi-circle*
Fig. 13.8

cl:a – undifferentiated object
Fig. 13.9

Example: *a TV on the table*
Fig. 13.10

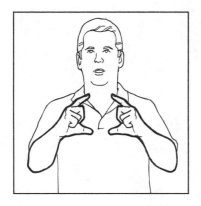

cl:ll – thin circular-shaped object
Fig. 13.11

Example: *a clock*
Fig. 13.12

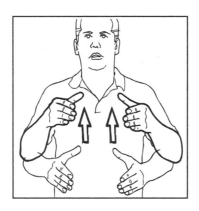

cl:cc – large cylindrical shape
Fig. 13.13

Example: *a wastebasket*
Fig. 13.14

cl:bb – a flat-surfaced object
Fig. 13.15

Example: *a wall*
Fig. 13.16

2. Using Classifiers to Establish Locations of People, Places, and Things

Classifiers may be used to establish the location of people, places, and things in space. Use of a classifier requires that the noun it refers to be identified first. A signer may wish to express that "a table is located on the right side of a room." The signer will create a predicate phrase using the whole entity classifier *cl:b.* Figure 13.17 is an example of this principle.

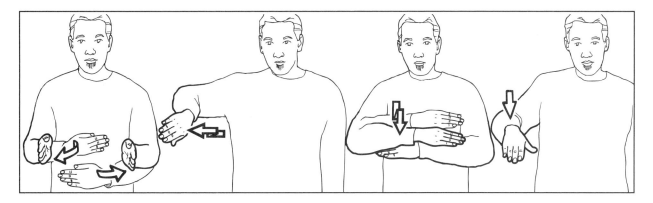

The table is on the right side of the room.
Fig. 13.17

When two objects that can be represented by classifiers are included in a predicate phrase, a complex classifier form involving the use of both is used. For example, a signer may wish to express that there is a cup on a table. Both the table and the cup may be represented by whole entity classifiers forming a complex, two-handed classifier form. Figure 13.18 is an example of this.

The cup is on the table.
Fig. 13.18

3. Plural Classifiers

Classifiers may be used to represent "more than one of something." When representing more than one, the classifier handshape is moved in space with a sweeping motion or repeated in different locations in the signing space to indicate two or more inanimate objects represented by the classifier. The exact number may or may not be specified. For example, the classifier being used in Figure 13.19 shows that there are an unspecified number of chairs in a semi-circular arrangement. In Figure 13.20, the classifier indicates that there are three pictures in locations on a wall.

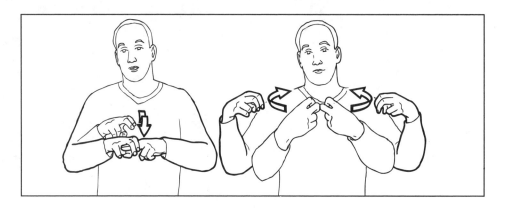

a semi-circular arrangement of chairs

Fig. 13.19

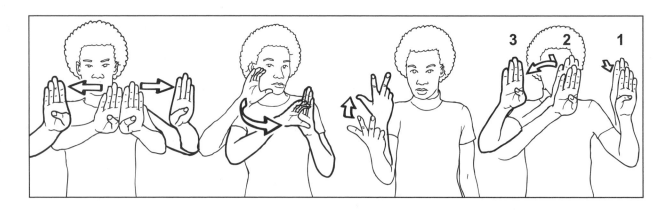

three pictures are on the wall

Fig. 13.20

4. Using Indexing to Specify Locations

Indexing, which involves pointing with the index finger, is used at the end of a sentence when describing the location of people, places and things. In Unit 3, People at Work, this principle was applied to giving directions. The description of where a room or office is located always ends with indexing, with the index finger pointing to the location of the room. This principle is also seen when classifiers are used to describe the location of an object. The final sign in a description of the location of an object will be pointing with the index finger to the location where the object has been described. Note that Figure 13.21 on the next page shows the use of indexing at the end of a sentence.

5. Using Eye Gaze to Locate People, Places, and Things

As you learned in Unit 3, People at Work, when signers need to refer to people, places, and things they will establish locations in the signing space in front of their bodies to locate things they wish to refer back to later on in their conversation. Eye gaze is an important aspect of ASL communication. Eye gaze is sometimes used alone or in combination with indexing to locate people, places, and things in space. The signer's eye gaze must be consistent with the spatial referents established. For example, Figure 13.21 on the next page shows the signer's eyes glancing toward the location being established for the bathroom on the left side of the hallway.

6. Non-manual Signal "cs" for Proximity in Space

In Unit 7, Where People Live, the non-manual signal for proximity in time or space was introduced. To review, this non-manual signal involves: (a) moving the shoulder of your dominant signing hand slightly down and (b) moving the cheek and side of your mouth toward your shoulder. An example of this for two things that are close in space is shown in Figure 13.21 on the next page.

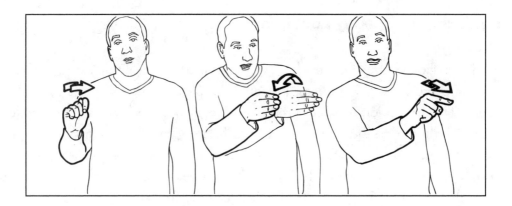

It is right next to the bathroom
Fig. 13.21

Unit 13 Language, Culture, and Community

1. Deaf-Friendly Office

Deaf and hard-of-hearing people rely on their eyes to orient themselves in their environments. In setting up an office, deaf people generally place their desks or computer stations in locations that allow them to monitor their doors for visitors. A deaf-friendly office may also have a flashing door-bell signaler to signal that there is a visitor. A deaf-friendly office will generally also have a flashing telephone ring signaler to signal an incoming telephone call and the deaf-friendly work desk will have a videophone or TTY ready to connect with an incoming call. Many deaf-friendly computer stations are equipped with videoconferencing and video interpreting technology to facilitate direct internet ASL communication with co-workers in remote locations.

2. Gaining Attention in an Office

General strategies for gaining attention to initiate a conversation were introduced in Unit 2, Learning ASL. When working with deaf co-workers, it is important to consider appropriate strategies for gaining their attention in office environments. Deaf co-workers may be focused intently on work at their workstations and may not see someone approach their doorways. If the office is equipped with a flashing light doorbell signaler, it is appropriate to use it to gain a deaf co-worker's attention. If there is no flashing light doorbell signal, it is appropriate to walk into the deaf person's office and lightly tap him/her on the shoulder to gain attention. Your main objective should be to avoid startling your co-worker. Sometimes the motion of walking through the doorway is enough to gain a deaf co-worker's attention.

It is also common for deaf persons to be engaged in telephone conversations using TTY machines or videophones. Whereas hearing co-workers talking on the telephone are readily apparent and you would know to wait until they are finished, it may not be apparent that your deaf co-workers are on the telephone. They may see you approach the doorway and gesture to you to "Wait a moment. I'm on the phone." You should not attempt to engage in conversations until your deaf co-workers signal that they are ready to do so. Sometimes during conversations there will be moments when your deaf co-workers can look away from their screens and hold a conversation with you and maintain their conversations over their TTYs or videophones. This will often depend on the seriousness and intensity of the conversations and you should respect that you may be asked to come back later when the conversation is finished. Using these strategies should help you maintain appropriate etiquette when working with deaf co-workers.

Unit 13 Practice and Review Materials

1. Video Exercises

    – Sample Expressive Dialogue

    – Comprehension Practice

    – Expressive Practice Prompts

2. Grammar and Language, Culture, and Community Review Questions

3. Sign Vocabulary Illustrations

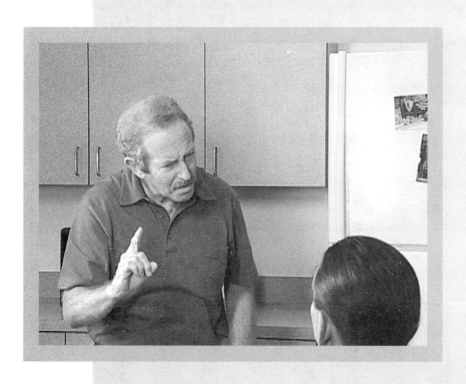

Sample Expressive Dialogue

Read the dialogue prompts below and then watch how each signer expresses these prompts on the video. Sign along with both Signer A and Signer B or with either Signer A or Signer B on the video. You may wish to practice this dialogue with a classmate outside of class time and your teacher may review this dialogue in class and ask you to sign this dialogue with a classmate.

Looking for Office Equipment

Situation: Signer B is sitting and talking to another person (Signer C) when you enter; you need to talk with Signer B

Signer A: Interrupt the conversation between Signer B and Signer C and get attention by touching Signer B on the shoulder

Signer B: Acknowledge Signer A

Signer A: Say "Excuse me" to Signer C and ask Signer B if he/she knows where the stapler is

Signer B: Respond affirmatively and explain that it is in the right-side drawer of your desk in your office upstairs

Signer A: Confirm the location

Signer B: Respond affirmatively

Signer A: Say "Thank you" to Signer C

Signer B: Express a polite close to Signer A

For the signing you observe, please write below any helpful notes and questions you may have for your teacher.

Comprehension Practice 13.1

Watch the narrative all the way through and then answer as many of the questions below as you can. If necessary, view the narrative a second time to see whether you are able to understand more and answer any additional questions.

Looking for a Book

1. Describe how the narrator sets up the location of the book at the beginning of this narrative.

2. Who enters his office first and moves the book? Where does this person place the book?

3. How do you know the narrator is describing that the book was moved?

4. Who moves the book next? What is this person's job?

5. Where does this next person put the book?

6. What type of classifier is used in this part of the narrative?

7. Who asks for the book?

8. What grammatical principle makes the conversation between this person and the narrator clear?

9. What classifier is used to show the movement of this person who is looking for the book? Describe how the narrator is consistent in his use of space.

10. How do you know that both the narrator and this other person will go into his office to look for the book?

11. Where is the book?

For the signing you observe, please write any helpful notes and questions that you may have for your teacher.

Comprehension Practice 13.2

Watch the narrative all the way through and then answer as many of the questions below as you can. If necessary, view the narrative a second time to see whether you are able to understand more and answer any additional questions.

Talking about a Burglary

1. When did the narrator discover that there was something unusual happening at work?

2. What does he see upon arriving at work?

3. What classifier does the narrator use to indicate that one police officer approached him?

4. What is the name of the police officer who approached him and what grammatical principle is being used in this part of the narrative to make the dialogue clear?

5. How does the narrator indicate that there were many questions being asked?

6. Whose office is mentioned first and what was discovered missing?

7. Whose office is mentioned next and what was discovered missing?

8. What room is mentioned next? Describe where it is located. What was missing?

9. List three questions that the police officer asked the narrator.

10. Throughout this narration, how does the narrator make it clear who is asking questions and who is answering questions?

For the signing you observe, please write any helpful notes and questions that you may have for your teacher.

Expressive Practice Prompts

These Expressive Practice Prompts show you the types of questions and statements you should be able to express in ASL by the end of Unit 13. Your teacher may use these Expressive Practice Prompts in class. You should practice these with your practice partner and group outside of class as well.

1. Ask a classmate where the dictionary is.

2. Express what your office looks like.

3. Express what office supplies are found in the drawer of your desk.

4. Ask a classmate how many bookshelves he/she has.

5. Express that the book is in the bottom drawer of the cabinet.

6. Ask a classmate on which side of his/her office desk a lamp is located.

7. Ask a classmate to drop the keys next to figurine on the right side of the table in your office.

8. Express that you put a poster on the left wall of the office.

9. Express that, on the right side of your office, there is a table and next to it, there is a small file cabinet. On the top of file cabinet, there is an ASL book; request that it be brought to the classroom.

10. Ask a classmate if he/she has an answering machine.

11. Express that you want to have a stack of books put on the chair.

12. Ask a classmate where the wastebasket is.

13. Ask a classmate if he/she has a sofa in the basement.

14. Express that the plant is on the table.

15. Express that the books are placed horizontally in a row on the bookshelf.

Grammar and Language, Culture, and Community Review Questions

These questions will assist you as you read the Grammar and the Language, Culture, and Community sections in this unit.

1. When describing the location of an object having a flat surface, which classifier handshape is used? (a) *cl:b* (b) *cl:c* (c) *cl:v* (d) *cl:a*

2. Explain a requirement for the use of classifiers to locate people, places, and things.

3. Explain how classifiers may be produced to represent "more than one of something."

4. Explain how indexing is used to specify a location.

5. The signer's eye gaze plays an important role in establishing referents. Explain how eye gaze is used when telling where an object is located.

6. How does a signer indicate that something is located "close to him/her" in space?

7. List two features of a "Deaf-friendly" office. Now, considering your experience in seeing other colleagues' offices, have you seen the features of a Deaf-friendly office? Could you make recommendations for how to make an office more "Deaf friendly"?

8. Explain two different strategies for politely gaining a Deaf person's attention in an office environment.

Sign Vocabulary Illustrations

bottom

cabinet

corner

dictionary

drawer

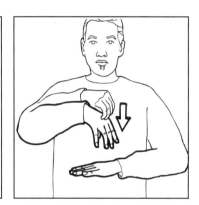

drop-on

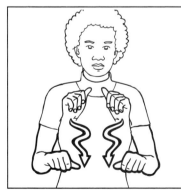

figurine/statue

file-cabinet

lamp   plant   put

shelf   sofa

top   wall

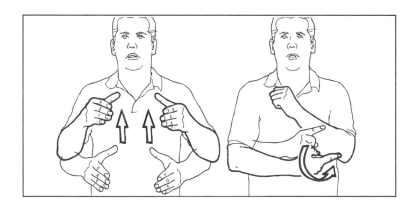

wastebasket

Hobbies and Interests

In this unit you learn to discuss what you like and do not like doing during your leisure time. You also learn about the importance of both sports and social networking in the Deaf community.

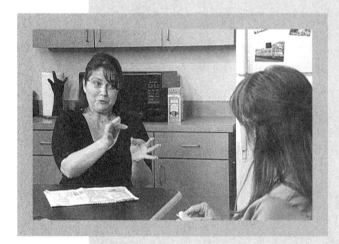

Unit 14 Overview

Learning Outcomes

1. Learn sign vocabulary related to hobbies, activities, and sports

2. Express duration of events by modifying time adverbials

3. Narrate about hobbies, activities, and sports

4. Learn about the importance of both sports and social networking in the Deaf community

Vocabulary

football	*cycling*	*beat-in-competition*
basketball	*hunting*	*win*
hockey	*traveling*	*lose* (competition)
lacrosse	*sewing*	*tied* (competition)
baseball	*cooking*	*elementary-school*
swimming	*collecting**	*high-school*
soccer	*play-cards*	*tournament*
golf	*to-watch*	*all-morning*
compete	*game*	*all-afternoon*
gardening	*team*	*all-night*
#club	*feel-like*	*all-day*
camping	*enough/sufficient*	*all-week*
fishing	*to-defeat*	*all-month*

*Note: Ask students if they collect specific items, such as coins and stamps, and introduce appropriate vocabulary.

Grammar

1. Modifying Time Adverbials for Duration

2. More on Noun/Verb Pairs

3. Narrative Structure

Unit 14 Overview

Language, Culture, and Community

1. Changing Topics in a Conversation Using *"to-set-aside"*

2. Closing Conversations with *"thumbs up"*

3. Sports and the Deaf Community

4. Getting Together as a Cultural Value

5. Playing Games

Practice and Review Materials

1. Video Exercises
    -   Sample Expressive Dialogue
    -   Comprehension Practice
    -   Expressive Practice Prompts

2. Grammar and Language, Culture, and Community Review Questions

3. Sign Vocabulary Illustrations

1. Modifying Time Adverbials for Duration

2. More on Noun/Verb Pairs

3. Narrative Structure

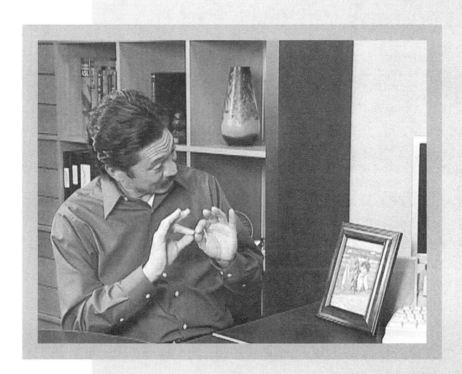

1. Modifying Time Adverbials for Duration

Time adverbial signs may be inflected to express that an activity continued over a long period. For example, the sign ***all-afternoon*** may be inflected to include information about signers' perceptions about the relative length of time. Signers make the movement of the sign slowly and use the non-manual marker "puffed cheeks" to emphasize their perceptions about the length of time.. Figure 14.1 shows a sentence with the sign ***all-afternoon*** modified to express the feeling that the activity occurred over a very long afternoon.

Yesterday I cooked all afternoon.

Fig. 14.1

2. More on Noun/Verb Pairs

Noun/verb pairs were introduced in Unit 7, Where People Live. As explained in Unit 7, noun/verb pairs share the same handshape, location, and palm orientation, but they are distinguished by their movements; that is, nouns have repeated movements and verbs having single continuous movements. A similar grammatical device occurs in English with noun and verb pairs that share a common root word, for example, "hunt" and "hunting." "Hunt" is a verb and the noun "hunting" is derived from the verb by adding "ing." Many nouns in English are derived from verbs in this manner.

In this unit, we see nouns for many activity-related concepts that are derived from their root verb. Selected examples are shown in Figures 14.2–14.5.

Verb Sign   Noun Sign

to-bowl

Fig. 14.2

bowling

Fig. 14.3

to-catch-fish

Fig. 14.4

fishing

Fig. 14.5

3. Narrative Structure

To some people it might seem that when ASL signers describe how things happened, they "begin with the end" and "end with the beginning." For example, if a signer is describing an enjoyable weekend fishing trip with friends, he/she will begin by stating how enjoyable the past weekend's fishing trip with friends was and tease the listener with one highlight of the trip such as "something very funny happened." This establishes the topic, includes the time the event occurred, hints of what is to come to grab the listener's attention, and states the signer's feelings about the event. In a sense, the signer is beginning his/her narrative with the end by telling what he/she will be talking about and how enjoyable the experience was.

The body of a well-constructed ASL narrative will then specify all the details the signer wishes to share about the experience. In the case of fishing trip example, it may include specifics about the location of the trip, preparation for the trip, what happened while fishing, details about "the big one that got away," and a funny incident that happened.

The conclusion of the narrative will restate the opening, therefore ending with the beginning; that is, signers will restate the topic, a highlight of the trip, and how much they enjoyed the trip.

This narrative structure, common to oral narratives, was first described by Labov and Waletzky (1967) as diamond shaped, with the top or beginning being the topic, widening out to include all the details (the body), and concluding at the bottom of the diamond with a restatement of the topic of the narrative (see diagram on the next page).

ASL Narrative Structure Diagram

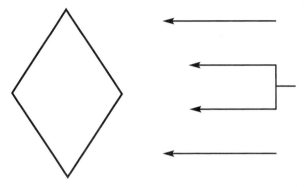

The introduction describes the overall topic and point of telling the narrative.

The body gives details and elaborates all the actions and actors of the narrative.

The conclusion restates the overall topic and reiterates the signer's main reason for telling the narrative.

Reference

Labov, W. and Waletzky, W. (1967). Narrative analysis: oral versions of personal experience, in J. Helms (ed.), *Essays on the Verbal and Visual Arts.* Seattle: University of Washington Press.

1. Changing Topics in a Conversation Using *"to-set-aside"*

Signers may indicate that they wish to change topics during conversations with the sign *to-set-aside.* This sign is used within a topic/comment sentence structure. (See Unit 5, Work Duties, Grammar section, #3, for a discussion of topic/comment sentence structure).

As shown in Figure 14.6, the signer first signs *"work"* using the non-manual signal for expressing a topic and then signs *"to-set-aside"* using the non-manual signal for expressing a comment. This indicates that he/she wishes to move to another topic of discussion. This conversational regulator is followed by a new question or statement introducing the new topic for discussion.

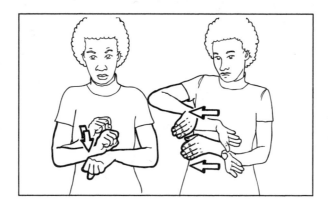

That's enough discussion of work.

Fig. 14.6

2. Closing Conversations with *"thumbs up"*

When close acquaintances part company after a conversation, they often will use the *"thumbs up"* gesture. This gesture basically means "wishing everything goes well for you." It is a friendly way of wishing someone well when parting company. Figure 14.7, on the next page, illustrates this conversation closer.

Good luck. Wishing everything goes well for you.
Fig. 14.7

3. Sports and the Deaf Community

Sports and athletic competition are important unifying activities within the Deaf community. Deaf people highly value opportunities to compete with one another in athletic events and to socialize with Deaf community members. A strong tradition of team sports has become an important part of the residential school experience for Deaf students and these positive experiences have carried over into Deaf club sports competitions and tournaments.

The first basketball tournament among Deaf clubs was sponsored by the Akron Club of the Deaf in Ohio in 1945, and this led to the establishment of the American Athletic Union of the Deaf [later named the American Athletic Association of the Deaf (AAAD)]. In 1997, the AAAD was renamed the U.S.A. Deaf Sports Federation (USADSF).

The USADSF and similar organizations of deaf and hard-of-hearing athletes from countries all over the world hold the World Games of the Deaf (WGD) every 4 years in a manner similar to the Summer and Winter Olympic Games. In 1924, 133 athletes from nine nations gathered in Paris, France, to participate in the first WGD, including track and field, cycling, football, shooting, and swimming. These games are informally referred to as the Deaflympics. The WGD is the oldest continuing international competition outside of the Olympics.

Whether it is a friendly bowling tournament sponsored by a local Deaf club, a regional basketball tournament, or the WGD, you can bet there will be enthusiastic attendance by both the athletes and their supporters, and when the competition is finished you can be assured there will be lots of chatting, catching up on news, and socializing long into the night.

Assignment: Visit and explore the USADSF Web site, http://www.usdeafsports.org/, and the Deaflympics Web site, http://www.deaflympics.com/, to gain insight into the history and value of athletics in the Deaf community.

4. Getting Together as a Cultural Value

For many Deaf people, simply "getting together" is a valued activity. This is considered a cultural value. Why? Think for a moment of how Deaf people live with hearing people every day. Often, Deaf people face many obstacles. One obstacle is communication. In educational settings that include the use of sign language, communication is accessible for deaf children. When deaf children become adults, communication with co-workers is sometimes limited. In most work environments, hearing employees do not know ASL.[a] Therefore, Deaf employees and their hearing co-workers often find other ways to communicate. Writing often is the means of communicating between Deaf and hearing employees. Writing is a challenge because it requires time to express thoughts on paper. Although acceptable for routine, work-related directives, writing is not spontaneous and is unnatural for collegial, social communication.

During weekends, evenings, and other free times, Deaf people often take advantage of opportunities to find time to get together by going to bowling leagues and other events sponsored by local Deaf clubs and other deaf-run organizations. Getting together is something Deaf people cherish because it is generally the only time they can express themselves freely by using ASL without restrictions.

---

[a]There is a fast-growing trend for many high schools and colleges to offer ASL courses to fulfill foreign language requirements. For Deaf people, encounters with hearing people who previously learned ASL are noticeably increased. This is a positive sign of increasing knowledge, appreciation, and respect for cultural diversity in America.

5. Playing Games

When playing games, Deaf people often alter the rules to accommodate a visual way of communicating. In fact, many of the hand signals used by hearing people in certain sports originated with Deaf players. For example, William E. "Dummy" Hoy, a major league baseball player from 1888 to 1902, is credited with developing the hand signals used by baseball umpires (Moore & Panara, 1996). Even in present-day basketball, when a whistle is used to stop play after a foul, the referee abruptly raises his or her arm to signal that there has been a foul. The origin of this signal has never been credited to Deaf basketball players, but it is the same signal that Deaf people use to signal that there has been a foul and play should stop. "Signing" is quite a natural part of team sports.

Another contribution of Deaf people to sports is the huddle in football. When schools for the deaf would play one another, the players would gather in a circle to hide their signing while agreeing on the next play. This idea of "huddling" to protect the play calling on the field was quickly picked up by hearing teams that played against Gallaudet College (now Gallaudet University) and continues to be used today at all levels of football. Today, football teams sometimes use a "no huddle offense" and "shouting" plays at the line of scrimmage to gain a strategic advantage. Deaf football teams can use the no huddle offense too when they play against hearing schools.

When Deaf people play board or card games, they also accommodate some rules of play to a visual–gestural mode of communication. For example, in card games when a player must signal with a spoken word, like calling out "gin" or "Uno," Deaf people have an object on the table that must be picked up quickly to signal the play of the last card. Also, when playing a game where a quick signal, usually a shout for hearing players, is needed to determine the winner, Deaf people seated at the same table will slap or pound the table with their hands or fists and quickly raise their arms as a signal.

Reference

Moore, M. S., & Panara, R. F. (1996). *Great Deaf Americans.* Rochester, NY: Deaf Life Press.

Unit 14 Practice and Review Materials

1. Video Exercises

   – Sample Expressive Dialogue

   – Comprehension Practice

   – Expressive Practice Prompts

2. Grammar and Language, Culture, and Community Review Questions

3. Sign Vocabulary Illustrations

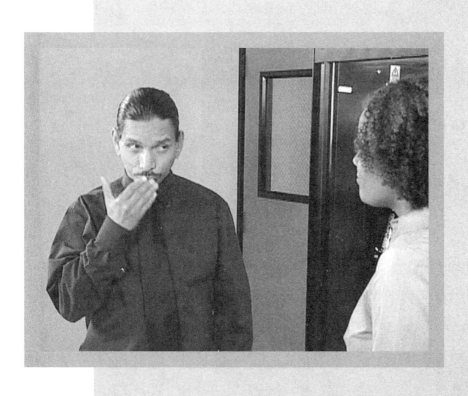

Sample Expressive Dialogue

Read the dialogue prompts below and then watch how each signer expresses these prompts on the video. Sign along with both Signer A and Signer B or with either Signer A or Signer B on the video. You may wish to practice this dialogue with a classmate outside of class time and your teacher may review this dialogue in class and ask you to sign this dialogue with a classmate.

Talking about Hobbies

Signer A: Get the attention of Signer B and ask him/her what his/her favorite hobby/activity is

Signer B: Respond with two or three of your favorite hobbies/activities

Signer A: Ask which one is most liked

Signer B: Answer appropriately

Signer A: Ask why

Signer B: Explain

For the signing you observe, please write below any helpful notes and questions you may have for your teacher.

Comprehension Practice 14.1

Watch the narrative all the way through and then answer as many of the questions below as you can. If necessary, view the narrative a second time to see whether you are able to understand more and answer any additional questions.

Describing Leisure Activities

1. What activity does the woman love?

2. Where does her family enjoy going?

3. How does the woman explain where this small town is?

4. The man asks the woman about how often her family goes to the place they are discussing. What grammatical principle does he use to indicate the frequency of the family trips to this place?

5. Why doesn't the man like the area of the country where the woman and her family go for vacation?

6. What are the man's two major hobbies?

7. With regard to the first hobby the man mentions, what does he have many of? Explain how you know this.

8. Explain the man's second hobby. What types of things does he make?

For the signing you observe, please write any helpful notes and questions that you may have for your teacher.

Comprehension Practice 14.2

Watch the dialogue all the way through and then answer as many of the questions below as you can. If necessary, view the dialogue a second time to see whether you are able to understand more and answer any additional questions.

Talking about Favorite Sports Teams

1. This video seems to start "in midstream." How does the man indicate that he is switching topics?

2. What is the woman's favorite team and what is their record this year?

3. What is the man's favorite team and what is their record this year?

4. How does the man indicate that his favorite team has a solid winning record?

5. What are the positions and the uniform numbers of each of their favorite players?

6. When the man and the woman use numbers to indicate their favorite players, what do you notice about the location where they make these numbers? What significance does this have?

For the signing you observe, please write any helpful notes and questions that you may have for your teacher.

Comprehension Practice 14.3

Watch the dialogue all the way through and then answer as many of the questions below as you can. If necessary, view the dialogue a second time to see whether you are able to understand more and answer any additional questions.

Talking about a Mechanical Breakdown

1. What do the narrator and his wife buy?

2. Where do the narrator and his wife plan to go on vacation? Be specific.

3. What type of sentence structure does the narrator use to communicate where they are going on vacation? Explain how you recognize this sentence structure.

4. Is it a short distance or a long distance that they have to drive? How do you know?

5. How long did they stay in the vacation location?

6. When they left to drive home, where did they experience a problem?

7. Describe the nature of the problem.

8. Who came to their aid?

9. Describe two different whole entity classifiers that are used in the segment when the person comes to their aid.

Comprehension Practice 14.3 (continued)

10. What does the police officer offer to do?

11. Where does the tow truck take their RV?

12. How long does the mechanic indicate they may be stuck while their RV is repaired?

13. Why can't they wait this long to have the RV repaired?

14. Describe the type of equipment the mechanic uses to diagnose the problem.

15. Describe how the mechanic fixes the RV.

16. Why are the narrator and his wife surprised when the mechanic shows them the cause of the problem? Describe what caused the problem.

17. Have the narrator and his wife experienced any additional problems with the RV?

For the signing you observe, please write any helpful notes and questions that you may have for your teacher.

Comprehension Practice 14.4

Watch the narrative all the way through and then answer as many of the questions below as you can. If necessary, view the narrative a second time to see whether you are able to understand more and answer any additional questions.

Describing Fishing Trips

1. At the beginning of this narrative, the narrator sets up the theme of the narrative by stating that she hates fishing. What type of sentence structure does she use to express that she hates fishing?

2. What relationship to the narrator is the person who was involved with her in these fishing incidents?

3. When the narrator describes the first incident at the beach, she uses classifiers to set up the scene. Describe the classifiers she uses and what they represent.

4. Describe the first incident she explains. What caused this accident? Explain in detail.

5. Describe the second incident she explains. What caused this accident? Explain in detail.

6. When the second incident occurs, describe how her brother was walking. Was he paying close attention to what he was doing? How do you know the answer to this question?

For the signing you observe, please write any helpful notes and questions that you may have for your teacher.

Expressive Practice Prompts

These Expressive Practice Prompts show you the types of questions and statements you should be able to express in ASL by the end of Unit 14. Your teacher may use these Expressive Practice Prompts in class. You should practice these with your practice partner and group outside of class as well.

1.   Express to your classmates which sports are typically played in each season of the year.

2.   Tell about your high school or college days and which sports and/or other activities you participated in.

3.   Tell about what activities you enjoy when you have free time. Explain when you do each activity, where, and with whom.

4.   Ask a classmate if he/she collects old stamps.

5.   Talk about activities that your family enjoys playing together.

6.   Tell about what you did for fun on the past Friday, Saturday, and Sunday.

7.   Tell which sport you enjoy watching the most and why.

8.   Express that you enjoyed shopping all day on Saturday.

9.   Tell a classmate that you are tired of playing cards because it is late.

10. Express that your baseball team beat another team last Friday.

11. Express that you want to travel more next year.

12. Express that you enjoy watching basketball, but you can't play because you have a bad back.

13. Express that you enjoy camping with friends. Say that you go camping once a month, the third week of each month, during June, July, and August.

14. Express that when playing cards you don't like losing.

15. Ask a classmate which games his/her family plays.

Grammar and Language, Culture, and Community Review Questions

These questions will assist you as you read the Grammar and the Language, Culture, and Community sections in this unit.

1. Explain how signs for time adverbials (for example, afternoon) are modified to indicate a time span (duration).

2. In English, "ing" is added to verbs like "read" and "fish" to mark noun forms. How is this verb–noun distinction made in ASL?

3. ASL narrative structure has been described as "diamond-shaped." Explain what this means.

4. What gesture is commonly used between friends to close a conversation?

5. Briefly explain use of the conversational regulator ***"to-set-aside."***

6. Discuss how sports and athletic activities function to create bonds among members of the Deaf community.

7. This question requires your critical thinking skills. Why are there separate Deaf Olympic Games for deaf athletes? Why are the deaf athletes not a part of the International Olympic Games?

8. Getting together is a valued activity for Deaf people. What is a basic reason why Deaf people participate in various Deaf community activities?

9. Explain the significant historical contribution made by the baseball player William E. "Dummy" Hoy.

Sign Vocabulary Illustrations

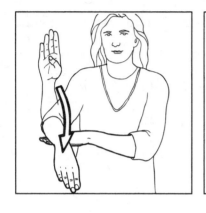

all-afternoon

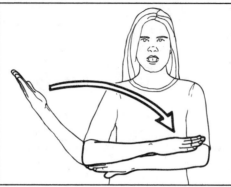

all-day

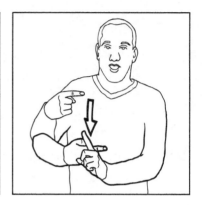

all-month

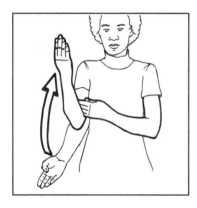

all-morning

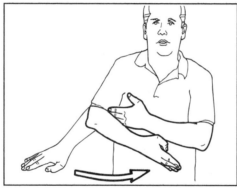

all-night

all-week

baseball

basketball

beat-in-competition

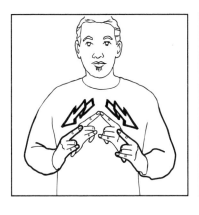

camping

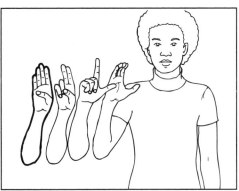

#club

collecting

compete

cooking

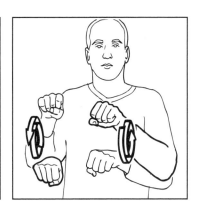

cycling

to-defeat

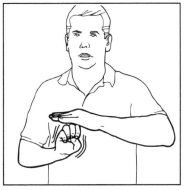

elementary-school

enough/sufficient

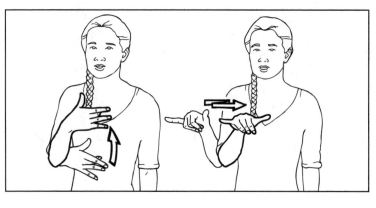

feel-like

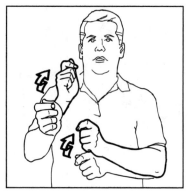

fishing

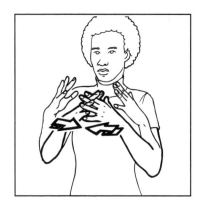

football

game

gardening

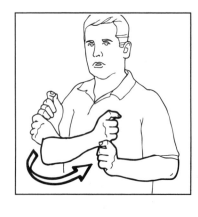

golf

high-school

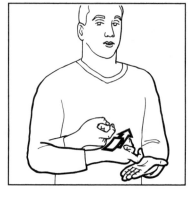

hockey

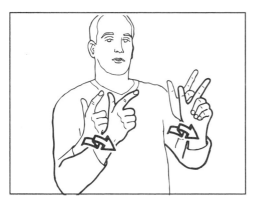

hunting

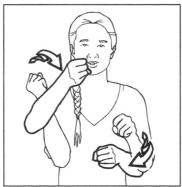

lacrosse

lose (competition)

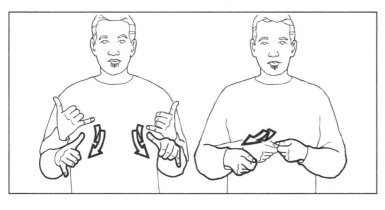

play-cards

sewing

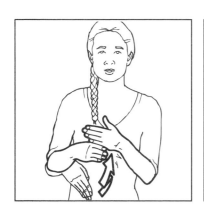

soccer

swimming

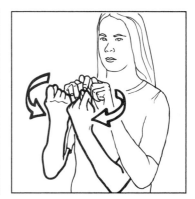

team

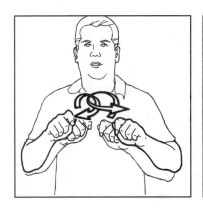

tied (competition) (1)

tied (competition) (2)

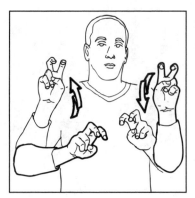

tournament

traveling

to-watch

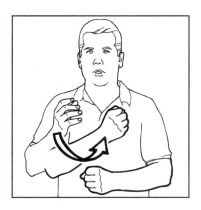

win

Spending Money

In this unit you are introduced to vocabulary and structures related to communicating about money. You learn how to list items and their costs, to discuss the total cost of a purchase, to ask for change, and to discuss banking transactions. In addition, you learn about the importance of visual communication and networking in the Deaf community, and you learn about the strong cultural value among Deaf people to create opportunities and resources within the Deaf community that will sustain its members.

Unit 15 Overview

Learning Outcomes

1. Ask how much something costs

2. Ask for change

3. Express feelings about spending money

4. Compare prices

5. Advise others about money matters

6. Express information about living expenses

7. Learn about the importance of visual communication and community networking in the Deaf community

8. Deaf entrepreneurship

Vocabulary

money	*lend*	*expensive*
thousand	*owe/afford*	*cheap*
million	*poor*	*spend*
billion	*broke* (no money)	*charge/credit card*
dollar	*rich*	*#cash*
one-dollar	*change/exchange/trade*	*to-pay*
five-dollars	*left/remaining*	*chip-in-money*
ten dollars	*buy*	*ticket*
one-cent	*sell*	*earn*
five-cents	*charge/cost*	*#bank*
ten-cents	*value/worth/price*	*deposit*
twenty-five-cents	*discount*	*put-in-bank/to-save*
total	*#sale*	*A-T-M*
count	*compare*	*withdraw-money*
borrow		

Unit 15 Overview

Grammar

1. Number Incorporation with Money Signs

2. Sign Movement Repetition for Repeated Action

3. Relative Clause Structure

4. Descriptive Classifiers

5. Horizontal and Vertical Sweep for Showing Number Arrangement

Language, Culture, and Community

1. Visual Communication

2. More about Deaf Community Networking

3. Deaf Entrepreneurship

Practice and Review Materials

1. Video Exercises
   - Sample Expressive Dialogue
   - Comprehension Practice
   - Expressive Practice Prompts

2. Grammar and Language, Culture, and Community Review Questions

3. Sign Vocabulary Illustrations

1. Number Incorporation with Money Signs

2. Sign Movement Repetition for Repeated Action

3. Relative Clause Structure

4. Descriptive Classifiers

5. Horizontal and Vertical Sweep for Showing Number Arrangement

1. Number Incorporation with Money Signs

You have learned to use number incorporation with: (a) pronouns (Unit 2), (b) time adverbials (Units 4 and 11), and (c) age (Unit 6). In ASL, this same principle applies to money. Number incorporation with money can be incorporated when communicating about both cents and dollars. Figures 15.1 through 15.4 show how numbers are incorporated with cents to communicate ***one-cent, five-cents, sixteen-cents,*** and ***twenty-five-cents.***

one-cent
Fig. 15.1

five-cents
Fig. 15.2

sixteen-cents
Fig. 15.3

twenty-five-cents
Fig. 15.4

Number incorporation is used when communicating about dollars up through **nine-dollars.** Figures 15.5 and 15.6 show **three-dollars** and **eight-dollars.** When communicating about dollars for amounts above 9, two signs are used, the number sign plus the sign **dollar.** Figures 15.7 and 15.8 illustrate **ten dollars** and **twenty-three-dollars.**

three-dollars

Fig. 15.5

eight-dollars

Fig. 15.6

ten-dollars

Fig. 15.7

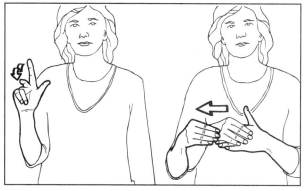

twenty-three-dollars

Fig. 15.8

2. Sign Movement Repetition for Repeated Action

Repeating the movements of verb signs indicates that actions are repeated. For example, the movement repetition for the verb sign **to-pay** in Figure 15.9 indicates that the "the signer" has many bills to pay.

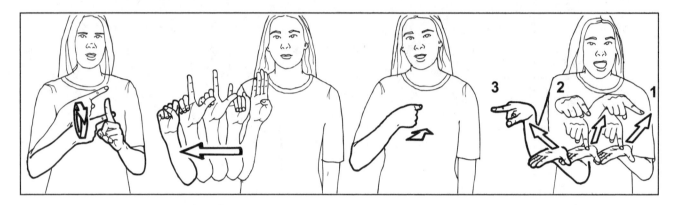

I pay many bills every month.
Fig. 15.9

3. Relative Clause Structure

Using a relative clause provides more information about the subject in a sentence. An example in English is "My brother Tom, who is a lawyer, lives in Washington, D.C." The relative clause in this sentence is "who is a lawyer" because it refers to the subject and provides more information about the subject, "Tom." In ASL, relative clause structure is similar to English. The pronoun that signals relative clauses in ASL is **himself/herself** signed against the index finger of the non-dominant hand in third person location. An example of this is shown in Figure 15.10 on the next page.

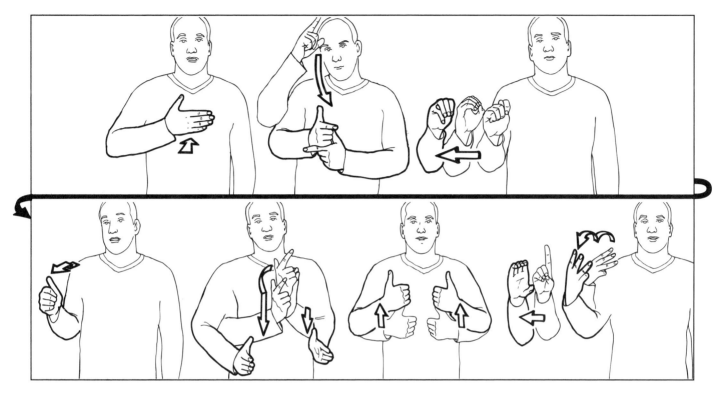

My brother, Tom, who is a lawyer, lives in Washington, D.C.
Fig. 15.10

4. Descriptive Classifiers

In Units 4, 9, 12, and 13, various classifier types were introduced. Descriptive classifiers are another type of classifier. Descriptive classifiers describe the size and shape of objects. In this unit, two descriptive classifiers are introduced: (a) the index and thumb forming a small round circle with remaining fingers extended to represent small, round, flat objects such as coins, buttons, and tokens (see Figure 15.11 on the next page), and (b) L handshapes on both hands tracing a rectangular shape to represent flat, rectangular-shaped objects such as checks, coupons, and receipts (see Figure 15.12 on the next page).

As with all classifiers, referents for the objects represented must be clear. Signers either fingerspell or sign specific referents or the contexts sometimes make referents clear. For example, suppose two people are finishing their dinner in a restaurant. One diner comments to the other, "I wish the waiter would bring the check." In this case, the classifier indicating a flat, rectangular-shaped object would be used without fingerspelling the referent "check." The context makes its clear that the classifier is being used for "check."

**Classifier representing small, round, flat objects
(buttons, coins, tokens)**

Fig. 15.11

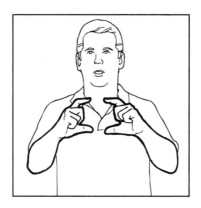

**Classifier representing flat, rectangular-shaped object
(check, receipt, coupon)**

Fig. 15.12

5. Horizontal and Vertical Sweep for Showing Number Arrangement

In Unit 2, horizontal and vertical sweep to indicate plurals was introduced. In this unit, this principle of sweeping movement is used to show the arrangement of numbers in vertical and horizontal lists to be added. See Figures 15.13 and 15.14 on the next page.

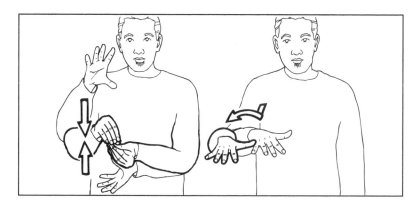

The total is 55. (vertical sweep)
Fig. 15.13

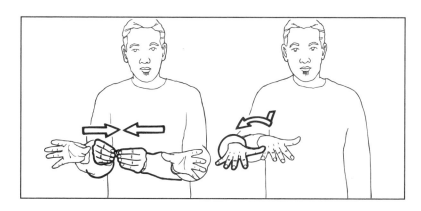

The total is 55. (horizontal sweep)
Fig. 15.14

Unit 15 Language, Culture, and Community

1. Visual Communication

Deaf people are "visual communicators" and ASL is a language entirely adapted to visual communication. Another way that visual communication manifests itself within Deaf peoples' lives is through the importance of lighting in the home. The kitchen is often the favorite room in a "Deaf-friendly" home because it is often the best lit room and communication can flow easily in this well-lit environment. Deaf homes also are equipped with flashing light signals to alert occupants to the phone ringing, someone at the door, a baby crying in another room, and fire/smoke detection.

Visual communication is becoming more noticeable in society in general. A visually friendly environment is important to communication for both deaf and hearing people. Airports are often noisy and announcements are difficult to hear. Some of the major airports are installing large message boards in passenger gate areas and throughout the airport to report gate changes, flight cancellations, and other announcements. Electronic cash registers often have a display screen showing the total charges as they are being entered and the total due to the cashier. Many banks have lighted signal signs that indicate when a teller becomes available.

These visual forms of communication help everyone, and Deaf people especially appreciate efforts to establish visually friendly environments that facilitate visual communication.

2. More about Deaf Community Networking

Sharing information in the Deaf community is critical to creating networking among Deaf people. In Unit 6, asking personal questions was introduced as a cultural value important to knowing how people are connected to the Deaf community. This value of asking personal questions is also seen in the area of personal finances. Deaf people are generally more willing than hearing people to share (with other members of the Deaf community) information about certain aspects of their personal financial dealings. This is especially true when this information may be helpful to other members of the Deaf community; for example, getting the best deal on a car or negotiating other financial transactions. If a member of the Deaf community drives to the local Deaf community event in a new car, he/she can expect to be asked how much it cost, where it was purchased, and how the deal was negotiated. In areas like salary, retirement accumulation, and inherited wealth, Deaf people follow the same taboos as their hearing peers.

3. Deaf Entrepreneurship

The notion of creating opportunities and resources within the Deaf community that will sustain its members is a strong element of Deaf culture. Historically, there are many examples of this.

When automobiles first became popular, many states attempted to ban deaf people from driving. Many states would not issue licenses to deaf people and when automobile insurance came on the scene many insurance companies would not insure deaf drivers because they considered deaf people incapable of driving safely. The NAD was instrumental in fighting for the rights of deaf drivers to be issued licenses. However, insurance rates, if they were even obtainable for deaf drivers, were exorbitantly high. The National Fraternal Society of the Deaf (NSFD) was founded in 1901 by a group of young deaf adults at the Michigan School for the Deaf in Flint, Michigan. The immediate purpose was to provide low-cost insurance protection for deaf people. The NSFD was also founded to provide social opportunities. The founding and successful operation of the NFSD for over 100 years by and for Deaf people exemplify how Deaf people themselves create their own innovative solutions to obstacles they may face.

Although obtaining affordable insurance and drivers licenses are no longer obstacles, the Deaf community, through the NAD, continues to fight for and protect the rights of deaf and hard-of-hearing citizens. More recent examples of this include fighting for access to information through closed captioning of network and cable television programs, monitoring developments in the telecommunications field, and ensuring that deaf and hard-of-hearing people have equal access in issues like 911 services, relay operator services, and other telecommunication innovations.

Creating opportunity and resources can also be seen in organizations like the National Deaf Business Institute (NDBI), whose mission is to advance entrepreneurship by the deaf through education, research, and outreach. Through its programs, NDBI aims to help empower the deaf community by increasing the number of deaf-owned businesses and deaf professionals. Read more about this initiative at http://www.ndbi.org.

The above are just a few examples that highlight the strong theme in Deaf culture of creating opportunities and resources within the Deaf community that sustain its members.

Unit 15 Practice and Review Materials

1. Video Exercises

    – Sample Expressive Dialogue

    – Comprehension Practice

    – Expressive Practice Prompts

2. Grammar and Language, Culture, and Community Review Questions

3. Sign Vocabulary Illustrations

Sample Expressive Dialogue

Read the dialogue prompts below and then watch how each signer expresses these prompts on the video. Sign along with both Signer A and Signer B or with either Signer A or Signer B on the video. You may wish to practice this dialogue with a classmate outside of class time and your teacher may review this dialogue in class and ask you to sign this dialogue with a classmate.

Talking about a Recent Purchase

Signer A: Get the attention of Signer B and share your news about buying a new house

Signer B: Acknowledge Signer A and ask where the new house is located

Signer A: Tell Signer B that you bought a new house near a golf course

Signer B: Ask a clarifying question about the location of the house

Signer A: Respond affirmatively

Signer B: Respond appropriately and ask if Signer A got a good price

Signer A: Say the house was expensive but you negotiated for a good deal and then bought it

Signer B: Respond appropriately

For the signing you observe, please write below any helpful notes and questions you may have for your teacher.

Comprehension Practice 15.1

Watch the dialogue all the way through and then answer as many of the questions below as you can. If necessary, view the dialogue a second time to see whether you are able to understand more and answer any additional questions.

Discussing a Sale

1. What does the man in the purple shirt want to buy? Why?

2. What store does the man in the blue shirt recommend first?

3. How does the man in the purple shirt respond to the first recommendation?

4. What store does the man in the blue shirt recommend next?

5. Explain the location of this second store.

6. What additional information does the man in the blue shirt give about the second store?

7. When expressing this additional information, what grammatical principle associated with fingerspelling does the man use?

8. How much of a discount at this furniture store was advertised in the newspaper?

For the signing you observe, please write any helpful notes and questions that you may have for your teacher.

Comprehension Practice 15.2

Watch the narrative all the way through and then answer as many of the questions below as you can. If necessary, view the narrative a second time to see whether you are able to understand more and answer any additional questions.

Describing Souvenirs from a Vacation

1. What reason does the narrator express for purchasing souvenirs?

2. When expressing the reason for purchasing souvenirs, what grammatical principle does the narrator use?

3. When expressing the reason for purchasing souvenirs, how do we know that he will give gifts to more than one person?

4. The narrator shows us a shirt he bought. Why does he especially like the color of this shirt?

5. The narrator explains the monetary exchange rate between the Mexican peso and the U.S. dollar. What grammatical principle does he use to make this comparison?

6. For whom does the narrator purchase a butterfly ornament?

7. The narrator is not fluent in Spanish. He purchases a Spanish/English translation device. What word does he key in to find the Spanish equivalent? What does he tell us is the Spanish translation of this English word?

8. For whom does the narrator buy a pen set? Explain his reason for buying this gift.

For the signing you observe, please write any helpful notes and questions that you may have for your teacher.

Comprehension Practice 15.3

Watch the narrative all the way through and then answer as many of the questions below as you can. If necessary, view the narrative a second time to see whether you are able to understand more and answer any additional questions.

Talking about Bills

1. How much does the narrator get paid weekly?

2. How much of her weekly pay does the narrator deposit in the bank?

3. Observe how the narrator shifts her body toward the left when signing *"go-to"* to establish the location of the bank. Describe how her signing in this segment is consistent for use of space.

4. What did the narrator do with the cash she kept from her paycheck?

5. How much did the narrator spend that evening with her friend?

6. The narrator tells us that she and her friend enjoyed their time together. What type of sentence structure does she use to tell us this?

7. What did the narrator do next?

8. How much does the narrator spend and how does she pay?

9. When the narrator is telling us about her activity on Saturday morning, she uses questions signs like *"how-much"* and *"how."* What type of grammatical principle is she using when she produces these signs?

Comprehension Practice 15.3 (continued)

10. What happens on Monday morning?

11. How much does narrator spend in the two places she visits on Monday morning?

12. What two different methods of payment does the narrator use on Monday morning?

13. What type of classifier does she use to show payment by debit card?

14. How much is the narrator's apartment rent?

15. After paying her rent, what does she tell us?

16. The narrator goes to the bank to withdraw some cash. How much does she withdraw and how does she withdraw this money?

17. What do you notice with regard to use of space when the narrator returns to the bank?

18. How many people go out to eat? How do you know this?

19. How much did the narrator pay at the restaurant? Did the narrator pay for everyone's meal?

For the signing you observe, please write any helpful notes and questions that you may have for your teacher.

Comprehension Practice 15.4

Watch the narrative all the way through and then answer as many of the questions below as you can. If necessary, view the narrative a second time to see whether you are able to understand more and answer any additional questions

---

Asking for Change

1. What U.S. currency denomination does the woman have and what form of change does she ask for?

2. When the woman asks the man for change, she uses two grammatical principles when she signs the money numbers. Identify and explain what she does.

3. Can the man satisfy the woman's request? Why not?

4. How much money does the woman ask to borrow and when does she promise to pay it back?

5. When the man asks the woman when she will pay back the money, what grammatical principle does he use to indicate who will pay and who will receive the money?

6. What does the man remind the woman about and what does he suggest she can do?

For the signing you observe, please write any helpful notes and questions that you may have for your teacher.

Expressive Practice Prompts

These Expressive Practice Prompts show you the types of questions and statements you should be able to express in ASL by the end of Unit 15. Your teacher may use these Expressive Practice Prompts in class. You should practice these with your practice partner and group outside of class as well.

1. Sign denominations of U.S. money from 1 cent to 100 dollars.

2. Express that after work you go to the bank and deposit your paycheck.

3. Ask a classmate how often he/she goes to the bank.

4. Ask a classmate if he/she has change for a dollar.

5. Ask a classmate how much he/she spends for groceries each week.

6. Ask a classmate whether he/she prefers to pay by credit card or with cash.

7. Explain that next weekend you will go out to dinner with four friends and everyone will pay for their own dinner.

8. Ask a classmate if the grocery store accepts coupons.

9. Explain that you were shopping for a small figurine to put on a shelf in your living room. State that you found a figurine in two stores, but one was more expensive and you bought the cheaper one.

10. Express that you want to take a vacation the third week of August. You looked up discount tickets for airlines on the Internet. Ask a classmate if he/she can explain how to purchase the ticket.

11. Express that you went shopping and bought two items; give the background of time and place, what you bought, how much you paid for each item, and the total cost.

12. Express that you are broke because you just paid back 150 dollars that you borrowed from your friend last month.

13. Express that you want to shop at <u>grocery store A</u> and <u>grocery store B</u> to determine which store's prices are cheaper for two items.

14. Express that your mother gave you $100 for your birthday and you decided to put it in your bank.

15. Express that every 2 weeks you deposit your $300 pay in the bank.

Grammar and Language, Culture, and Community Review Questions

These questions will assist you as you read the Grammar and the Language, Culture, and Community sections in this unit.

1. Numbers can be incorporated into the handshape of certain categories of signs. Give an example for each of the following categories and explain how numbers are incorporated into the production of the signs in each category: (a) pronoun signs, (b) time signs, (c) age signs, and (d) money signs.

2. When you notice a signer repeats a verb sign, for example, ***borrow***, what does this tell you?

3. Explain how the sign ***himself/herself*** is used in ASL to signal a relative clause structure.

4. You are in a restaurant with your friends. Everyone has completed their meals. You look up and around the restaurant for the waiter and you sign *"**wish waiter hurry bring cl:ll-rectangular-shaped-object.**"*

    A. What type of classifier have you just used?

    B. Why did you not have to fingerspell ***c-h-e-c-k*** in this situation?

5. You are asked to sign the two addition problems that follow. Explain how you would sign these two problems and what grammatical principle is being used?

$$3 + 5 = 8$$

$$\begin{array}{r} 6 \\ 3 \\ +\ 2 \\ \hline 11 \end{array}$$

6. Explain (a) two unique aspects of a Deaf-friendly home that you might not see in a home where there are no deaf people and (b) two ways that both deaf and hearing people benefit from the use of visual communication techniques in everyday life.

7. Why do Deaf people tend to share information about their personal lives and finances with community members?

8. Visit the Web site of the NDBI at http://www.ndbi.org and read Unit 15 Language, Culture, and Community section, #3. What is the mission of the NDBI and what are some of its programs?

Sign Vocabulary Illustrations

A-T-M

#bank

billion

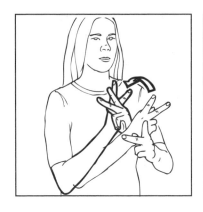

borrow

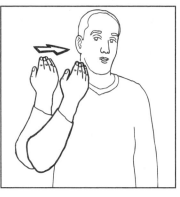

broke (no money)

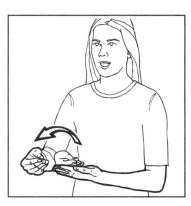

buy

#cash

change/exchange/trade

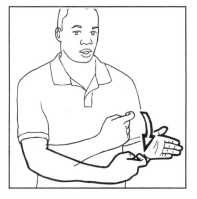

charge/cost

charge/credit-card

cheap

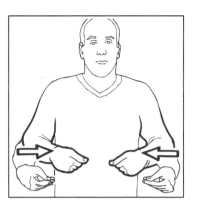

chip-in-money

compare

count

deposit

discount

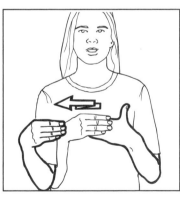

dollar

earn

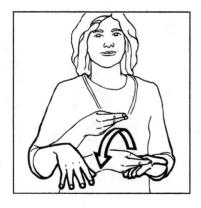

expensive

five-cents

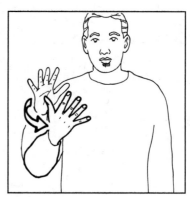

five-dollars

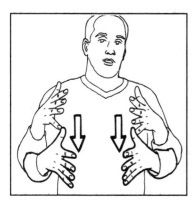

left/remaining

lend

million

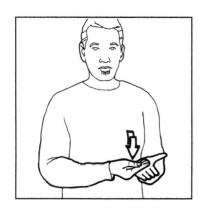

money

one-cent

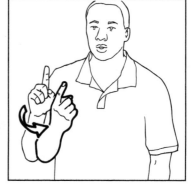

one-dollar

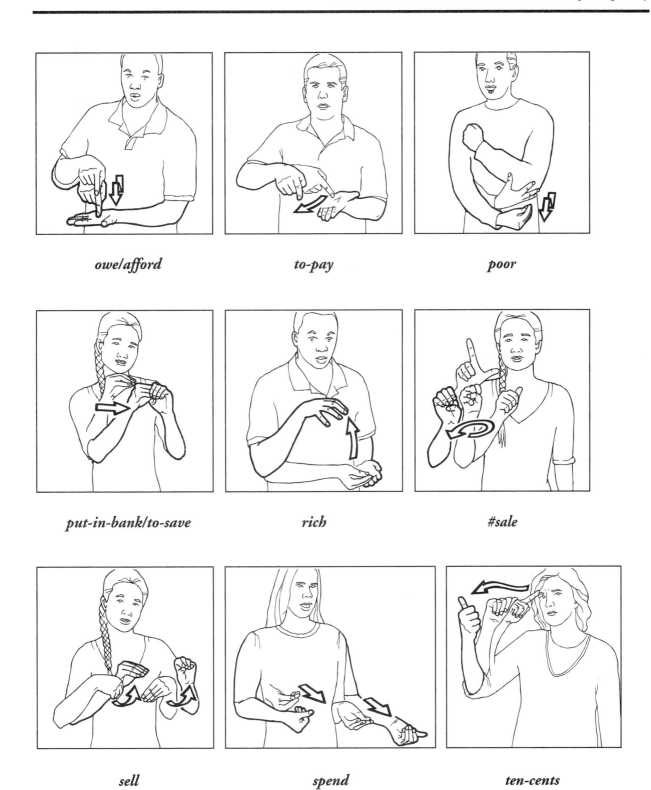

owe/afford *to-pay* *poor*

put-in-bank/to-save *rich* *#sale*

sell *spend* *ten-cents*

ten dollars

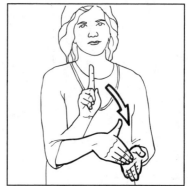

thousand

ticket

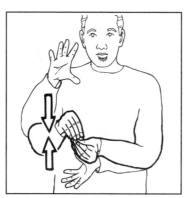

total

twenty-five-cents

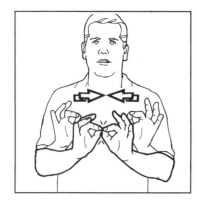

value/worth/price

withdraw-money

Explaining Procedures

In this unit you learn vocabulary and structures for explaining procedures. Fingerspelled loan signs are introduced and you learn to use ordinal numbers. Also, you learn about the Deaf cultural value of face-to-face communication and you learn about two historically significant meetings and a critical protest by Deaf people.

Unit 16 Overview

Learning Outcomes

1. Explain procedures

2. Express fingerspelled loan signs and ordinal numbers

3. Learn Deaf cultural value of face-to-face communication

4. Learn about two historically significant meetings and a critical protest by Deaf people

---

Vocabulary

next	*confused*
procedure/steps	*withdraw* (academic)
first (ordinal number)	*l-o-a/leave-of-absence*
second (ordinal number)	*#job*
third (ordinal number)	*apply*
explain, give-directions	*interview*
rank-in-order	*offer/propose*
take-up	*accept*
add-to	*hire*
drop (a class)	*decline-offer/turn-down*
fill-out	*to-lay-off*
submit	*fire-from-job*
sign-up	*grievance,* complaint
approve	*send*
must	*assign-to/apply*
require	

Grammar

1. More on Topic/Comment Structure

2. Meaning and Placement of Modal Verbs in ASL Sentences

3. Lexicalized Fingerspelling

4. Ordinal Numbers

Unit 16 Overview

Language, Culture, and Community

1. Face-to-Face Communication

2. Two Important Meetings and a Critical Protest

Practice and Review Materials

1. Video Exercises

    – Sample Expressive Dialogue

    – Comprehension Practice

    – Expressive Practice Prompts

2. Grammar and Language, Culture, and Community Review Questions

3. Sign Vocabulary Illustrations

Unit 16 Grammar

1. More on Topic/Comment Structure

2. Meaning and Placement of Modal Verbs in ASL Sentences

3. Lexicalized Fingerspelling

4. Ordinal Numbers

1. More on Topic/Comment Structure

Topic/comment sentence structure was introduced in Unit 5, Work Duties. This structure is used extensively when explaining steps in procedures. This is consistent with the prevalence of the topic/comment structure in ASL discourse. As explained in Unit 5, ASL signers signal the topic with raised eyebrows, head tilt, and pausing slightly at the end of the topic portion of the sentence. The comment is marked with the non-manual signals appropriate to the type of comment being communicated, for example, statement, question, and command.

When explaining procedures, signers use topic non-manual signals to accompany the signing of *first, second, third,* and so forth, and they use appropriate non-manual signals during the comment or explanation for each procedural step. Figure 16.1 shows the use of topic/comment structure to state the first step in a procedure.

The first step is to see your advisor.
Fig. 16.1

2. Meaning and Placement of Modal Verbs in ASL Sentences

ASL modal verbs such as *can* and *must* may be placed either prior to the main verb or at the end of the sentence. Placement at the end of the sentence communicates more emphasis.

Figures 16.2 below and 16.3 on the next page show *can* placed before the verb in a sentence and at the end position in a sentence. In these sentences, *can* is used to communicate that the person is able to or has permission to go to a job interview, with the second being more emphatic.

I can go to a job interview today.
Fig. 16.2

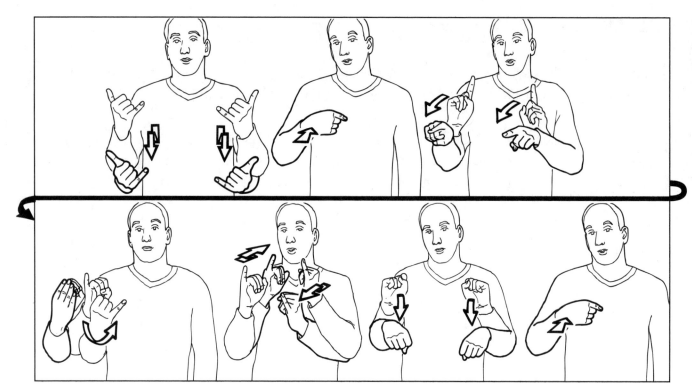

I definitely can go to a job interview today.
Fig. 16.3

The modal verb **must** is used to communicate that a speaker or a listener is required to do something or that there is some necessity. Figures 16.4 and 16.5 on the next page show the use of **must** prior to the main verb of the sentence and at the end position in a sentence. Again, the placement in the end position places greater emphasis on the modal verb **must.**

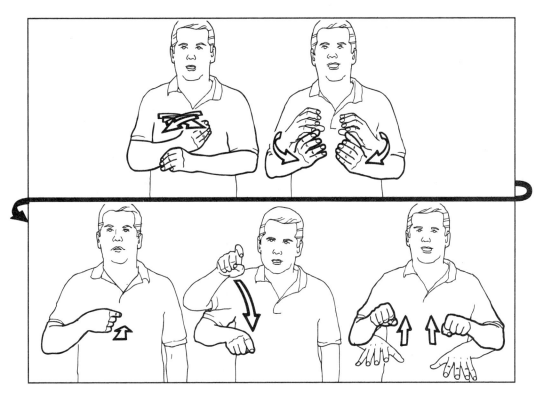

I am required to take a math course.

Fig. 16.4

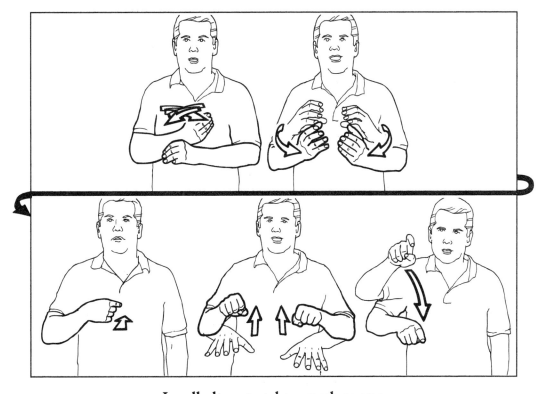

I really have to take a math course.

Fig. 16.5

471

3. Lexicalized Fingerspelling

Lexicalized fingerspelling (also called fingerspelled loan signs) is one productive mechanism for creating ASL vocabulary. Fingerspelling is a process by which English words may be spelled out using the ASL alphabet. In Unit 2, Learning ASL, fingerspelling was introduced as it is used to specify proper names of persons, places, and things. Another use of fingerspelling in ASL is the process by which short English words are spelled with movement and palm orientation changes that reflect how signs are made. This fingerspelling, therefore, takes on properties of how signs are produced, thus becoming "lexicalized fingerspelled signs." In addition to movement and palm orientation changes that are added to create lexicalized fingerspelled signs, these signs frequently assimilate medial letters of the words being spelled. For example, in the lexicalized fingerspelled sign *#job,* the middle letter "o" is assimilated into the "j" handshape as the movement occurs. Lexicalized fingerspelled words are very difficult to illustrate accurately. Please consult with your ASL teacher for further information about these unique signs. Figures 16.6 and 16.7 show two examples of lexicalized fingerspelled signs.

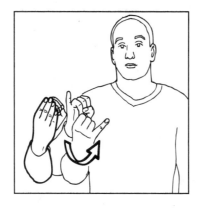

#job

Fig. 16.6

#bank

Fig. 16.7

4. Ordinal Numbers

Numbers used for counting are called the cardinal numbers. You have learned how to produce the cardinal numbers from 1 to 100 in ASL. Ordinal numbers (first, second, etc.) are another type of number. In ASL, the handshapes for both cardinal and ordinal numbers are the same; however, the movements and palm orientations for some ordinal numbers change. For the ordinal numbers from 1st to 9th, the movement of the hand twists from the palm facing forward to inward toward the body. For the remaining ordinal numbers from 10th and higher, these numbers have the same production as cardinal numbers. However, signers often will sign a specific object after the ordinal number as in *12 floor* meaning "the 12th floor." Figures 16.8–16.10 provide examples of ordinal numbers.

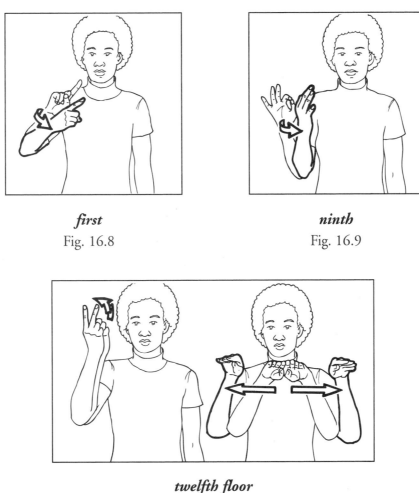

first

Fig. 16.8

ninth

Fig. 16.9

twelfth floor

Fig. 16.10

Unit 16 Language, Culture, and Community

1. Face-to-Face Communication

2. Two Important Meetings and a Critical Protest

1. Face-to-Face Communication

Deaf people highly value face-to-face communication. Before the advent of the modern telecommunications technology that allows instantaneous access to people all over the world, Deaf people relied extensively on local Deaf clubs as sources of socialization and information sharing. Even today, with instantaneous communication through e-mail and pagers, Deaf people prefer face-to-face interaction with others in the comfortable medium of ASL whenever possible. There is no substitute for face-to-face discourse when important matters need discussion and resolution.

Although attendance and reliance on local Deaf clubs are somewhat diminished in light of the advances in technology that allow instantaneous communication, many Deaf people still participate in local Deaf clubs and make a point to attend other social functions where they will have the opportunity for face-to-face communication with other Deaf community members.

2. Two Important Meetings and a Critical Protest

There are meetings and then there are meetings. Some are famous and some are infamous. For Deaf Americans, a meeting of the famous kind occurred in 1880 when a meeting of Deaf Americans was held to form an association (later to become known as the NAD). In this same year, a meeting of the infamous kind about how deaf students should be educated occurred in Milan, Italy, the International Congress on Education of the Deaf (ICED).

At the 1880 meeting of the ICED, educators of deaf students from Europe and the United States met to discuss the most appropriate methods for educating deaf students. There had been a longstanding controversy over the relative superiority of teaching deaf students via the language of signs and/or via the "combined method" (use of both signing and spoken language) versus teaching deaf students via speech and lipreading exclusively (referred to as the oral method). In Europe, except in France where signs had long been employed, the oral method was predominant. In the United States, strongly influenced by the French method, the use of ASL and the combination of ASL signs and speech (the Combined Method) were predominant. The 1880 ICED temporarily settled the matter by fiat and dramatically changed the course of education of the deaf for many decades.

Delegates at the 1880 ICED passed the following two resolutions:

> The Convention, considering the incontestable superiority of articulation over signs in restoring the deaf–mute to society and giving him a fuller knowledge of language, declares that the oral method should be preferred to that of signs in the education and instruction of deaf–mutes.

> The Convention, considering that the simultaneous use of articulation and signs has the disadvantage of injuring articulation and lip-reading and the precision of ideas, declares that the pure oral method should be preferred.

As reported by Lane (1984), of the 164 delegates, 159 were from Europe and 5 were from the United States. The U.S. delegation included the only deaf delegate, James Denison. The U.S. delegation, which represented 51 schools and over 6,000 deaf students (more than all the other delegates put together), was the only delegation to vote against these resolutions.

> In the aftermath of Milan, "pure oralism" washed over Europe (and America) like a tidal wave. Many people and schools were swept up in its advance. . . . The Milan resolutions on phasing in the replacement of sign meant that deaf professors would be fired seven years later . . . and so it came to pass at scores of schools in Europe and America.
> (Lane, 1984, p. 395)

Deaf people meeting in Cincinnati, Ohio, in the same year were founding the NAD. Robert P. McGregor was elected president of this new association of Deaf people. He addressed the convention.

> The ascendancy of the pure oral method has been attained by methods that the deaf, as honest, law-abiding citizens abhor, detest, despise, abominate. . . . Must not that be false which required for its support so much imposture, so much trickery, so much coercion; which belittles, or utterly ignores, the opinions of its own output? . . . In the war of methods the verdict of the educated deaf the whole world over is this: the oral method benefits the few; the combined system benefits all the deaf. . . . Anyone who upholds the oral method, as an exclusive method, is an enemy of deaf people.
> (Lane, 1984, p. 395)

The NAD was born out of the need Deaf people felt to protect their language, ASL, and to be heard in matters that influence them. The ICED in Milan was the catalyst that changed educational practice worldwide from 1880 until the 1970s, when the use of signing (although not ASL) began to be legitimized again.

In 1988, Deaf people won a fight that has helped bring them significantly closer to their goal to be fully heard in matters that affect them. Between March 6 and 13, 1988, following selection of the seventh hearing president of Gallaudet University, in this case a person who did not know sign language, Gallaudet University students closed and barricaded the university gates. After 7 days of protest, the "Deaf President Now" student uprising won the day. The hearing president stepped aside and a reconstituted Board of Trustees, which included a majority deaf representation, selected I. King Jordan as the first deaf president of Gallaudet University (Gannon, 1989). The "voice" that Robert P. McGregor sought, for Deaf people to govern and have influence over the institutions that affect their lives, was found. The education of deaf students would have significant influence from deaf people in all levels and in all roles and responsibilities again.

References

Lane, H. (1984). *When the mind hears.* New York, NY: Random House.

Gannon, J. (1989). *The Week the world heard Gallaudet.* Silver Spring, MD: National Association of the Deaf.

Unit 16 Practice and Review Materials

1. Video Exercises

    – Sample Expressive Dialogue

    – Comprehension Practice

    – Expressive Practice Prompts

2. Grammar and Language, Culture, and Community Review Questions

3. Sign Vocabulary Illustrations

Sample Expressive Dialogue

Read the dialogue prompts below and then watch how each signer expresses these prompts on the video. Sign along with both Signer A and Signer B or with either Signer A or Signer B on the video. You may wish to practice this dialogue with a classmate outside of class time and your teacher may review this dialogue in class and ask you to sign this dialogue with a classmate.

Assisting a Student

Signer A: Ask where the counselor is

Signer B: Inform Signer A that the counselor is not here

Signer A: Express that school is too hard and ask how to fill out the withdrawal form

Signer B: Ask for confirmation that Signer A wants to withdraw

Signer A: Confirm

Signer B: Explain the withdrawal procedure

Signer A: Restate the final step of the procedure incorrectly

Signer B: "Wave-no," correct the information

Signer A: Restate the final step of the procedure correctly

Signer B: Confirm

Signer A: Express thank you

For the signing you observe, please write any helpful notes and questions you may have for your teacher.

Comprehension Practice 16.1

Watch the dialogue all the way through and then answer as many of the questions below as you can. If necessary, view the dialogue a second time to see whether you are able to understand more and answer any additional questions.

Discussing How to Buy a House

1. How does the woman in the purple blouse gain the attention of the woman in the blue blouse?

2. What problem does the woman in the blue blouse have?

3. What reason does the woman in the blue blouse state for wanting to change her living arrangements?

4. When the woman in the blue blouse expresses that she has a problem, she uses a special form of the question sign in her sentence. Describe what she does and identify the grammatical principal she is using.

5. List the steps the woman in the purple blouse offers in her advice.

Comprehension Practice 16.1 (continued)

6. When explaining the process for buying a house, the woman in the purple blouse introduces the concept of a real estate agent who helps with the purchase process. What does she do after finger spelling this job title?

7. When explaining the process for purchasing a house, what grammatical principle does the woman in the purple blouse use to identify the steps in this process?

8. Identify three examples of subject–object incorporating verbs used in this dialogue. For each example, state who is the subject and what is the object. (Note: Remember that subject–object incorporating verbs are verbs within which the person performing the action and the location or object of the action are included in the verb movement and direction.)

9. What cultural value is displayed in this dialogue?

For the signing you observe, please write any helpful notes and questions that you may have for your teacher.

Comprehension Practice 16.2

Watch the narrative all the way through and then answer as many of the questions below as you can. If necessary, view the narrative a second time to see whether you are able to understand more and answer any additional questions.

Describing How to Register for a Class

1. Summarize each step in the registration process that the narrator explains.

2. The narrator explains three forms of payment. Explain these forms of payment.

3. When the narrator is explaining entering information into the online registration form, she controls her eye gaze and use of space. Describe what she does.

4. List three subject–object incorporating verbs that are used in this narration. Explain how these examples are used in the narrative. Who or what is the subject? Who or what is the object? Do not use *go-to* as one of your verb examples. (Note: Remember subject–object incorporating verbs are verbs where the person performing the action and the location or object of the action are included in the verb movement and direction.)

For the signing you observe, please write any helpful notes and questions that you may have for your teacher.

Comprehension Practice 16.3

Watch the narrative all the way through and then answer as many of the questions below as you can. If necessary, view the narrative a second time to see whether you are able to understand more and answer any additional questions.

Explaining a Card Game

1. Summarize the steps in the procedure for playing this card game.

2. What game is being explained?

3. When explaining the second step in the process, what classifier is used?

4. When explaining the third step in the process, what classifier is used?

5. How does the narrator's signing distinguish between the two players and their cards?

6. Explain how the narrator uses the subject–object incorporating verb ***to-gather-up*** in his explanation.

For the signing you observe, please write any helpful notes and questions that you may have for your teacher.

Comprehension Practice 16.4

Watch the narrative all the way through and then answer as many of the questions below as you can. If necessary, view the narrative a second time to see whether you are able to understand more and answer any additional questions.

Telling about Job Interview Experiences

1. The narrator explains about his job interview experiences. Is he hired after his first interview?

2. Explain the circumstances surrounding the first job interview.

3. In this first job interview description, the narrator uses a classifier. Identify the classifier he uses and explain what it means.

4. At the end of this first interview narrative segment, the narrator uses a subject–object incorporating verb. Can you identify it? Explain how he uses this verb.

5. Explain the circumstances surrounding the second interview.

Comprehension Practice 16.4 (continued)

6. In this second interview description, the narrator uses a subject–object incorporating verb when he explains that he was invited to interview again. Identify this verb and explain what it means and how it is produced.

7. Was the narrator offered a job after this second interview?

8. What is unique about the third job interview?

9. Near the end of this third job interview description, the narrator uses a subject–object incorporating verb to let us know that he got the job. Identify the subject–object incorporating verb and what it means. Notice that it is different in form from the two previous ways in which he has indicated that he either was offered a job or not offered a job.

For the signing you observe, please write any helpful notes and questions that you may have for your teacher.

Expressive Practice Prompts

These Expressive Practice Prompts show you the types of questions and statements you should be able to express in ASL by the end of Unit 16. Your teacher may use these Expressive Practice Prompts in class. You should practice these with your practice partner and group outside of class as well.

1. Express to your classmates that you signed up for a course, but now you want to drop the course because you don't like the teacher.

2. Express to your classmates that you have a schedule conflict and you need to withdraw from a course scheduled at 8:00 a.m. Mondays, Wednesdays, and Fridays.

3. Tell a classmate to fill out an Add/Drop Form and take it to the chairperson for approval.

4. Express that you read the instructions but you don't understand them and you are really confused about the steps. Say the instructions are not clear.

5. Express a three-step procedure using listing.

6. Express to a classmate who did not understand that you will explain the procedure again slowly and very clearly.

7. Express that you hired a new student assistant in your department and assigned the student to the chairperson.

8. Ask a classmate if he/she knows the procedures for filing a grievance.

9. Explain that you need your boss's signature. You just missed him/her because he/she has left for the day.

10. Express that you are upset because you have applied for many jobs but have not yet gotten a job.

11. Express that you had to lay off three staff members due to the budget cut.

Expressive Practice Prompts (continued)

12. Express that you are thinking about accepting a job offer from a college.

13. Ask a classmate if he/she has filled out the leave of absence form.

14. Express that you will have a job interview with a department chairperson tomorrow afternoon at 1:00 p.m.

Grammar and Language, Culture, and Community Review Questions

These questions will assist you as you read the Grammar and the Language, Culture, and Community sections in this unit.

1. Explain how topic/comment structure is used with ordinal numbers when explaining procedures.

2. Explain the language function accomplished by placing modal verbs like *can* and ***must*** at the end of sentences.

3. Explain the mechanism by which short, frequently spelled English words become part of the lexicon of ASL.

4. Explain the distinction in production between cardinal and ordinal numbers in ASL for the numbers 1 through 9 and for numbers 10 and higher.

5. Explain why face-to-face communication is an important cultural value for Deaf people.

6. Explain what happened at the 1880 ICED meeting and how this affected the course of education of Deaf students from 1880 through the 1970s.

7. Explain the reaction of the Deaf community to the two resolutions passed in 1880 by the ICED.

8. What is the significance of the Gallaudet University, Deaf President Now!, student protests?

Sign Vocabulary Illustrations

accept

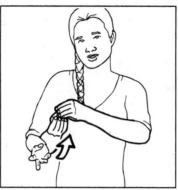

add-to

apply

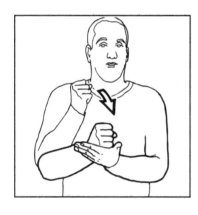

approve (1)

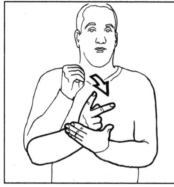

approve (2)

assign-to/apply

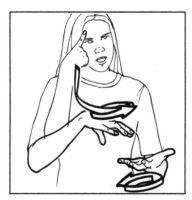

confused

decline-offer/turn-down

drop (a class)

explain, give-directions

fill-out

fire-from-job

first (ordinal number)

grievance, complaint

hire

interview

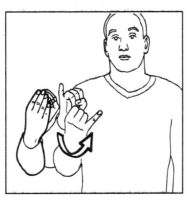

#job

to-lay-off

l-o-a/leave-of-absence

must

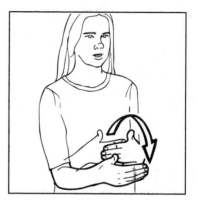

next

offer/propose

procedure/steps

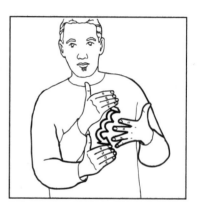

rank-in-order

require

second (ordinal number)

send (1)

send (2)

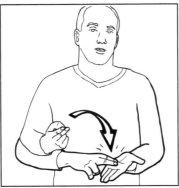

sign-up

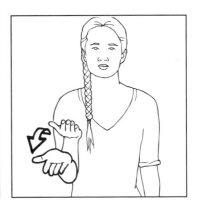

submit

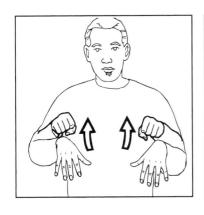

take-up

third (ordinal number)

withdraw (academic)

Index

Index of Grammar Principles

Index of Grammar Principles (continued)

Index of Grammar Principles (continued)

Index of Language, Culture, and Community Information

Index of Language, Culture, and Community Information (continued)

Index of Sign Vocabulary Illustrations

Index of Sign Vocabulary Illustrations (continued)

Index of Sign Vocabulary Illustrations (continued)

Index of Sign Vocabulary Illustrations (continued)

Index of Sign Vocabulary Illustrations (continued)

Index of Sign Vocabulary Illustrations (continued)

Index of Sign Vocabulary Illustrations (continued)

Index of Sign Vocabulary Illustrations (continued)

Index of Sign Vocabulary Illustrations (continued)